D0711585

THE BOOK OF
DIAMONDS

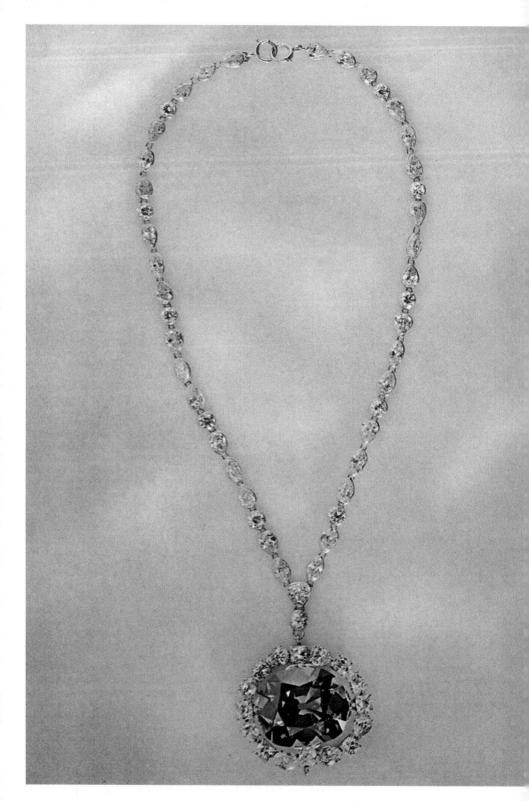

The Hope Diamond

THE BOOK OF
DIAMONDS
THEIR HISTORY AND ROMANCE FROM
ANCIENT INDIA TO MODERN TIMES

Joan Younger Dickinson

Introduction by
Harry Winston

DOVER PUBLICATIONS, INC.
Mineola, New York

Bibliographical Note

This Dover edition, first published in 2001, is an unabridged republication of the work originally published in 1965 by Crown Publishers, Inc., New York.

Library of Congress Cataloging-in-Publication Data

Dickinson, Joan Younger, 1916–
    The book of diamonds : their history and romance from ancient India to modern times / Joan Younger Dickinson ; introduction by Harry Winston.—Dover ed.
      p. cm.
    Originally published: New York : Crown Publishers, 1965.
    Includes bibliographical references and index.
    ISBN 0-486-41816-2 (pbk.)
    1. Diamonds. I. Title.

TS753 .D5 2001
736'.23—dc21

2001042398

Manufactured in the United States of America
Dover Publications, Inc., 31 East 2nd Street, Mineola, N.Y. 11501

To Bill

THIS GIRL'S BEST FRIEND

Introduction

I love diamonds. I love all jewels. My father had a small jewelry store in Los Angeles, and ever since I was quite young, jewels have fascinated me. I think I must have been born with some knowledge of them. By the time I was thirteen or fourteen, my judgment of the quality of a gem was so sure, so instinctive, that my father counted on me to advise him. He taught me dollar values but never quality. When a great gem was sent in for cleaning, I always recognized it; I could see just how extraordinary it was.

Soon jewelers became interested in my talent and were furthering my education. Each gem they showed me was like a friend to me, unique, unforgettable. When I was seventeen, a friend of my father's was sent a collection of jewels to clean, and he invited me to see them. I was thrilled. I looked at each piece, each ring, each brooch and bracelet carefully, noting the quality of the stones, the cutting, their beauty.

Fifteen years later, when I was a wholesaler in New York, my agent on the Coast called me. He said he'd been offered a "pretty nice" collection of jewels and he thought I should come out and take a look at it. He began describing the pieces. I interrupted him after he'd listed three. "Buy it," I said. He stuttered something about how I "really must see it first," that it was "a big collection," "a big purchase." "Buy it," I said. "I know every piece in it." I did, too. I began describing them to him; I could see each stone in my mind's eye. It was the same collection I had studied with such pleasure when I was a young man.

Today jewels are more than my love and my life; they are an insatiable obsession. It is not only the lure of hidden beauty that lies in a rough diamond; there is also the excitement of speculating—and the reward of having my judgment proved right.

Recently I was offered a 39-carat diamond in the rough by ten men who had pooled their money to invest in it. It was not a bargain by any means, and it had a flaw right down the middle. But when I looked at it I realized that with proper cutting that flaw would come completely out; I could see exactly what could be done and should be done to create a great pear-shaped gem.

I bought it. For weeks the cutting obsessed me, but when it was finished we had an exquisite stone, perfectly cut, and I felt the pride of an adoring father.

And gems are not the complete story of the diamond world. There are the people. Where else are tragedy and joy so closely allied? While one man is going bankrupt and selling his jewels, another is rising in the world and collecting them.

I have one client—a refugee from the Russian Revolution—who has sold me a single diamond every year for forty years. I don't know how many she has; she has never shown all of them. I have another client who gave me a blank check to carry until I found exactly the diamond he had dreamed of for his wife. When I found it in India, the price was outrageous. I cabled him saying so, and he told me to buy it anyway.

There have been times when I have felt isolated in my diamond world. Today it seems as if the whole world is going crazy about diamonds. Everyone wants them; and the bigger, the better. Recently a customer brought in a 30-carat marquise ring she had bought here not too long before, and said she'd like a 40-carat diamond instead. I was shocked. "It will cover your knuckle," I said. "Besides, it is vulgar."

"That's what I want," she replied laughingly. "A vulgar diamond."

It is nice to have so many people in love with diamonds today, but it is also important to take them seriously. I have long tried to educate the public. I gave the Hope Diamond to the Smithsonian Institution in Washington for that reason. Then I sought a perfect rough for years before I found exactly the quality I desired, and last October presented that to them too.

Of course, the best way to learn about diamonds is to own them. Their beauty seems to add individual glamour to each woman. All diamonds may seem alike, but they are not; they are, like most women, desirable and tempting. The better you know them, the more they will reward you with excitment and delight.

It is important to look at diamonds seriously, with a good idea of what you are looking for and why. There has long been a need for a book on diamonds, a book that not only relates some of their fascinating history but attempts to explain quality, that grasps both the economics and the romance of the diamond, that appreciates both the natural beauty of a diamond and the skill with which man has brought out that beauty.

I love diamonds, and I like them to be taken seriously.

HARRY WINSTON

Fifth Avenue, New York
January, 1965

The nature of diamonds and man's fascination with them form the subject matter for this book, but the true basis for the interest of Homo sapiens in these most precious of stones can only be subject to speculation. Most mammals are attracted by bright and glittering substances, as if these by their very brightness represent the concrete and material elements of the world. It would seem only natural that man finds himself similarly drawn to and fascinated by the same glitter epitomized by the cold eternal fire of the diamond. Hopefully, this rather crude relation which man shares with his animal precursors ends here, and his attraction to diamonds is developed into a more cerebral and aesthetic pursuit. I feel certain that this is exactly what has happened. Certainly the mere durability, purity, and immense value of the stone are qualities enough for merit. But beyond these, in the sheer unadulterated brilliance is distilled all of the satisfying elements of material things, and it is these that are most perfectly embodied in at once the most visible and invisible of objects—the diamond—which derives its compelling nature from its intense representation of the tangible. The diamond is a touchstone whose brightness brings the bearer closer to a hidden essence—a touchstone which perhaps reflects the effulgence of a more brilliant and steady light.

RONALD WINSTON

Contents

THE BOOK OF
DIAMONDS

1

History and Lore of the Diamond

The evil eye shall have no power to harm
Him that shall wear the Diamond as a
  charm
No monarch shall attempt to thwart his
  will
And e'en the gods his wishes shall fulfill.

Anonymous Roman poet, second
century A.D.

*I*t is recorded that the first men to know diamonds, the Dravidians of India, found them seven or eight centuries before Christ and two or three before Buddha. From them we get our unit of weight. Because apparently they thought diamonds grew in the ground like so many turnips, they balanced them on their scales against the seeds of the carob tree, the "cattie" or "carat."

Little, however, is known about these men or their methods. Indian architecture, like Indian sculpture, belonged to these prehistoric natives whose language we have not yet translated. They worked first in wood and then in stone, carving shrines out of solid rock, hollowing out cave-temples and pagodas, and decorating the openings with animal friezes and walls with the Tree of Life or dancers. Both their style and their skill was as remarkable and precise as that in the Western civilizations of Egypt and Mesopotamia, with whom they traded.

But what of their diamonds? Even as late as the fourth century before Christ when the diamond appears frequently as a well-known and precious

stone in the Buddhist stories, we find nothing factual about where the diamond was found, how it was mined or collected and how abundant it was.
Buddha, it was said, had a throne carved from a single diamond! Can it be
true? Authorities today are inclined to think it was rock crystal but the mere
idea of such a piece suggests the scope of their work and their tools.

Another legend—a favorite of mine—gives other clues. This is the
story of how Alexander the Great ventured into a diamond pit, a tale told
by a man who claimed to be Aristotle's nephew and a companion of Alexander on his great campaign through India about 350 B.C. Reportedly the
diamond pit was guarded by snakes and the snakes had a gaze of such fatal
power that when they looked upon a man he died.

But this did not deter Alexander long. He outwitted them with mirrors, held in front of his men like so many shields. And when the snakes
gazed into the mirrors their fatal gaze was turned upon themselves and *they*
died. Now Alexander himself peered into the pit and, seeing the diamonds
there, ordered his men to throw down the carcasses of freshly slain sheep.
The diamonds adhered to the fat of the flesh and the flesh lured vultures.
Soon the sky was filled with the great birds who swooping down seized the
flesh *and* the diamonds and soared skyward.

Behind them Alexander's men ran, picking up the diamonds that fell
and following the vultures to their mountain roosts to garner the rest.

Fantastic and romantic as it sounds, it is not an impossible method of
collecting diamonds. The diamond does adhere to grease; vultures do seek
meat; birds have been known to carry many objects many places and to be
tracked to their roosts for their loot. And Alexander did know diamonds; it
is a fact of history that after one of his African campaigns, the Ethiopians
presented him with a crown of diamonds. Let the scholars argue about
whether Alexander actually entered a diamond pit; what interests us here
is that this was possibly the earliest method of collecting diamonds.

A similar story is told of Sindbad the Sailor; when he was flung into
Diamond Valley to die, he observed that merchants threw flesh into it for
the vultures to gather, and, rolling himself into a diamond-studded piece,
he was picked up and carried off to the mountains and safety.

Because many of the diamonds allegedly were gathered in these vultures' nests, another legend grew up around the diamond at this period: it
was said to be a charm for women in childbirth. As these legends spread
by word of mouth, by song, by parchment and by stone pictures, it was said
that one diamond valley in Hindustan was so hot that no man dared venture
into it—"a sea of glowing, many colored fire," one early reporter put it.
Marco Polo recorded the diamond valley legends, believing them. Herodotus,

the Greek historian, tells a similar story of how cinnamon was obtained—except that the vultures in this story used the cinnamon sticks to build their nests, and great pieces of flesh were thrown by men to break down the nests and scatter the cinnamon. Some authorities suggest it is possible that the flesh was not only a diamond catcher but also part of a sacrifice to the gods for the jewels.

As well as being magical—just to gaze upon it was considered strengthening—the diamond was highly esteemed in early India for its hardness and beauty. In one very early description, probably written at the beginning of the third century, we read that the diamond ought to have five qualities: it should be large enough to bear blows, regular in shape, able to scratch metal vessels, refractive, and brilliant. Its name in India is *vajra*—the same word used to denote the thunderbolt, another form of natural power. It seems fairly obvious to me that the heavy stone carving of early Indian architecture, the marble lace, and the metal swords with their fantastic cutting points which amazed the first Aryan invaders were all due to the diamond's ability to slice through anything and to the Hindus' ability to use the diamond as both a tool and a weapon.

The Chinese, who have never found any diamonds in their vast country, knew the diamond first as a "jade-cutting knife"—not as a jewel. Jade was their most honored gem, but it astonished them, as it did the early men of India, that ordinary heat could not melt the diamond, and one noted in the third century B.C.: "Foreigners wear it in the belief that it can ward off evil influences." The Chinese thought it a stone related to gold, because it is so often found near gold.

There were also legends in this period of diamonds growing under the sea—stories which until recently, when diamonds were found in the sea, were thought to result from a confusion of diamonds with pearls. Many stories tell of fish retrieving diamonds; one tells of how Buddha himself sieved for the precious stones.

But there is disagreement as to where the earliest diamonds came from; Golconda is the city where they were traded, and it is possible that there was a mine along the Godaveri River, as it is now called. Others think the fields lay along the Kistna River, the old Parteal mines where diamonds were found in the medieval period. Around 600 A.D. they were discovered in Borneo, and these fields are still being worked today in a primitive manner: animal sacrifices are offered to the gods before the opening of a new pit; only whispering is permitted at work for fear of arousing the wrath of evil spirits; and prayers are all but continuous.

The first references in the Western world are found in the Bible. but it

An ancient diamond mine at Panna, India. Buckets carry earth to surface; armed guards control shaft entrance at right.

is believed by modern students that the Biblical authors confused magnetite and rock crystal with diamond, a confusion which extended through Pliny to Shakespeare, who seemed to think that a diamond might be magnetic— a lodestone. Pliny included diamonds in his famed thirty-four volume *Natural History,* naming five types and carrying over many myths from the Orient. He was a dedicated scientist for his period, a scientific martyr in fact, for he was smothered while examining the volcanic eruption at Pompeii (79 A.D.) at too close a range. But his science was woefully inexact when it came to the diamond: he said the true test of its strength was that it could not be smashed with a hammer—a small error which has cost the world many a large diamond. He also thought it would melt in goat's blood, would neutralize poison if eaten and, if worn, would dispel insanity and drive away worry. The part about it neutralizing poison is a strictly Plinian touch: in moorish India, it was thought that the two great purposes of the diamond were the working of stone and the poisoning of enemies.

Pliny called the diamond *adamas* from the Greek word for unconquerable, a word which gave us not only *diamond* but also *dame* and *adamant.* He said flatly that the diamond had "the greatest value among the objects of human property" and for a long time was "known only to kings and even to very few of these."

Pliny had nothing to say about diamond collecting, however. The Orient was the sole source of diamonds for twelve centuries; the stones came to Europe with ginger and cinnamon on boats manned by galley slaves, probably sailing out of Madras through the Persian Gulf to be unloaded in Arabia and packed onto the backs of camels for the long trek across the desert to the Mediterranean or to Ethiopia. We get our first dependable descriptions of the Indian operations from the great French traveler, Jean Baptiste Tavernier, who pioneered in trade with India in the mid-seventeenth century, and brought back enough jewels to win a barony from the grateful Louis XIV. His two-volume tale of his adventures in India is a fascinating document. Visiting the mines of Raolconda and Kollur along the Kistna River near Golconda in the 1660's, he found some sixty thousand men, women, and children slaving in the steaming sand, spurred on by whips. The men dug the pits to about twelve feet, and the women and children carried the gravel away in baskets to the creek and washed it, plucking out the diamonds by hand. Mining was difficult hand labor; small hoes and rake-like tools were used to gather the sand and gravel and then this debris was trundled to the wash to be picked over for diamonds.

From the mines the best gems went to the merchants at Golconda, the fabulous diamond center for centuries, and flawed ones were peddled by the

The Maharajah of Gwalior sporting pearls, emeralds and his Arabian stallion, circa 1350, when the Indians valued diamonds as cutting tools and wealth but rarely displayed them.

1. Akbar, 1556 A.D.

2. —Jehangir, 1605 A.D.

3.—Aurangzeb, 1658 A.D.

4.—Shah Jahan, 1627 A.D.

These sketches of Indian Moguls show the owners of some of the fabulously big diamonds mined in India.

small boys around the mines. The merchants demanded good gold and had fixed prices for diamonds by carat weight and quality. Tavernier's journeys—he made six of them to the Orient—began in 1631, when he was in his twenties. A single trip might take him five years; dealing was leisurely, and frequently he might spend weeks in this great house or that as a guest seeing only the slaves or the ladies of the harem until the master of the house forewent pride and admitted his eagerness to barter with the Frenchman. Only once did he sail around Africa; usually he traveled overland through Constantinople. In Europe he traveled by horse carriage; in India his wagon was drawn by oxen and he might be accompanied by as many as sixty attendants.

Tavernier began his palace deals by giving away his own strange European wares—pocket watches from Paris, emeralds from the Spanish colonies in South America, turquoises from Persia, bronze from Burgundy, boxes decorated in Florence, a brace of English pistols or an Italian telescope. Now and again he also brought ropes of pearls, beloved in India—but beloved in Europe too.

In return, he was permitted to show his pearls. Purchasers paid cash but also gave him gifts. Tavernier relates that one Indian prince bought 96,000 rupees' worth of pearls from him paying in part in rupees, in part with a horse, and in part with a robe of honor of gold and silver brocade and complete with turban. Tavernier was proud of the outfit; when he returned to France, he had his portrait painted in it. It is odd to see his round French face below the swaddling of his Oriental headgear; odd too to see how little he prized his ornaments—if he was wearing jewels that day, none are visible.

Tavernier knew his work well; his descriptions of the diamonds he bought, his weights, his understanding of flaws, cleaving, and other techniques of diamond-handling laid the basis for all Western records of diamonds. His most famous description is the collection of Aurangzeb (a detailed description of his visit to that Mogul is in the chapter on famous and infamous diamonds, Chapter 5); his most famous sale was to Louis XIV, who altogether bought thousands of carats from Tavernier and rewarded him with gold, lands and the title of Baron.

Today the Indian beds are exhausted; the source which is said to have yielded some 12 million carats of diamonds now gives forth a yearly trickle of perhaps 100 carats. But in ancient vaults, hidden in the depths of old ruins, or handed down by Hindu princes, a vast and brilliant fortune in diamonds rests in India today.

And as yet geologists have failed to trace the source of the shiny river pebbles of the Orient. The diamond is simply carbon, pure carbon, one of the commonest elements we have, found in abundance in coal, in oil, in inks, in the human body—in fact, in every living thing. The distinction the diamond has is not its purity of carbon, it is the fact that it is *crystalline* carbon —gem carbon—forged deep in the earth by the most tremendous heat and pressure, trapped in molten lava and pushed upward by explosive force, perhaps to erupt from the earth's surface in volcanic bursts, perhaps to lie embedded in escape valves. In South Africa "pipes" or escape valves of diamond-dotted rock thousands of feet long have been found going down into the molten layers of the earth. In India, where the diamonds were recorded as being found only in pits or river beds, no old pipes have been discovered although search after search has been made. Did the ancient diggers plumb these depths? Did the rock blow up and out completely in a volcanic eruption of such force that all its diamonds were flung far and wide? Or do the pipes lie somewhere under the now ruined city of Golconda or one of the fabulous ancient temples—or perhaps in the Himalayas themselves? All volcanoes are not productive of diamonds, but mineralogists believe the diamond can be produced naturally only by this phenomenon.

It has often been said by cynics that a major part of the allure of the diamond is the mystery of its Oriental origins, tricked up by legend and myth, but how can any man say that trappings are necessary to enhance the curious, uniquely grand qualities of this amazing jewel?

The diamond early India and early Rome and Ethiopia knew, however, was not the dazzling stone we know today. Cutting gave it its brilliance and cutting did not begin until the modern period. In early India the diamond was often cleaved, sometimes polished and quite frequently the stone sent to the West had the natural facets of the octahedron it is; good traders that the Indians were, they sent out at least a few samples of the kind of stone wanted. But it is a rare stone that glitters without expert faceting; roughs are dull, greasy pebbles which catch and reflect the light only by chance. For centuries they can lie around unnoticed; it takes a knowledgeable eye to spot a diamond in the rough.

The discovery of diamonds in Brazil provides an example of how deceptive they are. Let us imagine ourselves around a campfire in the forests of Brazil to get the full flavor. The time is 1726, the men around the campfire are gold prospectors who have been panning the streams all day and now are playing poker, using pebbles from the stream for chips. With them is a newcomer, a world traveler and something of an explorer. Recently he has returned from India where briefly he worked at the Portuguese port of Goa, discovered by the Portuguese Vasco da Gama about the same time Co-

Diamond washing in the Raolconda mines in Hyderabad, near the ancient Indian city of Golconda.

Eastern diamond merchants completing a bargaining deal, using hand signals.

Digging for diamonds at Raolconda, India.

Slaves, with overseers, washing for diamonds at Mandango, Brazil, about 1760.

The search for diamonds in Tejucas, Brazil, in the mid-eighteenth century.

lumbus discovered America. Since then Portugal has grown rich on diamonds; her empire includes parts of Africa, the Orient, and the vast country
of Brazil. But more and more wealth is needed to control them and Bernardo da Fonseco Lobo is a soldier of fortune seeking that wealth and the
power that goes with it, lured to Brazil by the report of gold. Was he also
looking for diamonds? History does not say. But it is recorded fact that when
he saw them he recognized them for what they were. He pocketed the shiny
pebbles as fast as he won them and bought back what he lost with nuggets
of gold. The next day he sent them home to Lisbon, to the attention of the
Crown. The day the King pronounced them diamonds was a great one for
Portugal. The whole populace was given time off to pray, to feast, to
dance, and a pronouncement renamed the small town of Tejeco in Brazil
"Diamantina."

But it took a long time to get Bernardo's find under control and his
diamonds respected. There were two problems. One was the age-old one of
working the diamond beds while guarding them from theft; the other, marketing.

To work the beds, the Portuguese Crown first threw out the gold prospectors and placed the fields in the hands of a few court favorites to control
the slave labor gangs and the diamonds themselves. Briefly the kings of
Portugal became fabulously wealthy. But the angry prospectors got even by
smuggling. The government in 1740 switched to contract tenancy; a man-
ager would lease a field for five years, say, for a share of the profits. With
independence in 1822, the Republic of Brazil took over and today anyone
may forage for diamonds there who can pay the steep land taxes and the
labor costs.

The problem of securing a steady market took almost as long. Although Brazil quickly produced some of the finest of the world's diamonds—
clear, flawless, white, and large—jealous European traders and jewelers insisted for decades the new finds were soft and of poor color. Portugal got
around this venal gossip by shipping the diamonds first to Goa and then
bringing them back as Oriental stones, but it was an expensive procedure.

The peak of the Brazilian mines production occurred in the mid-nineteenth century. Slaves—black and white, male and female—worked under
the foreman's whip. For finding a stone of 8 to 10 carats, there was a prize
of a new suit of clothes, a hat, and a knife; for a stone of more than 17.50
carats, freedom. Hundreds of thousands died of the heat, of malaria, of
dysentery, and of starvation. Food was brought inland by racketeers from
Rio de Janeiro and was incredibly expensive.

After producing an estimated 16 million carats, there trickles out today about 20,000 carats a year, most of which comes from Bahia, west of Diamantina. Here is the only place in the world where the black diamond is found, a dull spongy stone made up of tiny interlocking diamond crystals, prized for its toughness by tool makers. You or I would throw it aside like so much coal on a hot night if we found it, but finally, after almost eighteen centuries, it is the diamond Pliny dreamed of—it cannot be split by a hammer because it has no cleavage, or grain.

Brazil and India are all but played out today as sources of diamonds. South Africa is the modern source—but the most recent new discoveries have been in the U.S.S.R. In the twenties, the Western nations, led by the United States, forbade the selling of diamonds to the new communist nation; in the thirties, the Soviet Union began prospecting across a thousand mile plateau between Krasnoyarsk and Yakutsk in Siberia where geologists said the land formation resembled that of South African diamond areas. Through hot humid summers and winters of 60° below freezing they explored the land; trekking through the dense primeval forest, up the mountains, shooting the rapids—sometimes using horses, sometimes canoes, sometimes reindeer. In the fifties a young female mineralogist from Leningrad, Larisa Popugayeva, found the first blue-ground pipe near the Markha River; she called it "The Dawn." Soon afterward a second pipe was found near the river Yireleekh. Both are in the State of Yakutsk, where the natives reported old legends about a stone so bright it was called "Little Sun." Since then a great number of industrial diamonds have been produced despite incredible mining difficulties from the cold: the ground has to be heated before it can be dug, and boiling water has to be mixed with the concrete to prevent it from freezing before it is used. If the temperature goes up to 30° below freezing, it's considered a warm, pleasant day.

A trickle of gems has long come out of Russia; gem diamonds were found in the Urals in 1829; and new mine shafts have been recently sunk along the Vishera River. But Russia accounts only for a small portion of modern diamond production—less than 2 per cent. Diamonds today come from Africa: industrials from the Congo and Ghana, gems from South Africa, South-West Africa, and Tanganyika.

It was in 1866 that the first diamond was found in Africa; the scene was the African plateau, five hundred miles inland from the Cape of Good Hope near the source of the Orange River in a nothing of a place with the bittersweet name of Hopetown. Once again they first were shiny pebbles and playthings: the boy Erasmus Jacobs picked up a large one that he said later had "blinked" at him and gave it to his sister to play a game the poor Boer children liked called "Five Stones." A neighbor saw the stone on the

Early years of the South African diamond rush. At right, an "expert" has just declared the found stone a real diamond.

Dinner time at the Hebron diggings on the South African veld, circa 1870.

floor of the Jacobs' hovel and asked for it for a gift; Mrs. Jacobs gave it to him. He took it to a peddler named Jack O'Reilly who tested it in the old manner by writing his name with it on a windowpane and then took it to a mineralogist. The mineralogist tested it by flinting a file with it and asked the local bishop to look at it. He too wrote his name on a window pane with it. All agreed it was a diamond. When O'Reilly got the stone back, he sold it to the governor of the Cape colony for about $2,500 and the governor exhibited it at the Paris exhibition of 1867. Clear, blue white and about the size of a sparrow's egg, it weighed 21.50 carats and was called first the O'Reilly, and later the Eureka in the medieval tradition of giving diamonds names.

With its exhibition, the great Diamond Rush to South Africa began. The diggers—many of them experienced gold prospectors—descended on Cape Town, Durban and Port Elizabeth by the dozens and then set off across

Washing for diamonds along the Vaal River, 700 miles inland from the Cape of Good Hope in the early years of the South African diamond fields, about 1870.

Early diggings at the Colesberg Kopje, South Africa, later to be incorporated in the De Beers holdings by Cecil Rhodes.

the mountains and desert in oxcarts, on muleback, by horse and afoot to the Orange River. The stolid, hardworking Dutch farmers looked with contempt at the old men, the army officers, the beardless schoolboys eager to rent their land for digging. Land to the Boers was itself the prize—why sell the precious stuff merely for money? For two years the dreamy, hazardous, back-breaking search along the Orange went on without any remarkable result, the farmers growing more contemptuous, the adventurers more despondent; but then in March of 1869, a shepherd boy picked up an enormous pebble on the banks of the river, downstream from the Jacobs' farm, and carried it back to the same man who had first spotted the O'Reilly diamond, Schalk van Niekerk. This time Van Niekerk had to buy the stone; the 83.50 carats cost him five hundred sheep, ten oxen, and a horse, but he sold the famous Star of South Africa for $55,000. Now the Diamond Rush was on in earnest.

Next it was Barkly West on the Vaal that lured them; then at Jagers-fontein, a farmer picked up a garnet—the sign of diamonds—and digging, found a 50-carat diamond. Another tip-off came when a farmer, building his hut from the yellow clay, plucked from his wall a diamond! Now every farm of yellow clay in the region was in demand, not just the river's bed. The farmers were now surrounded, and a few sold out and moved else-where. But as the diggers left the river beds and moved south they encoun-tered even more opposition. When the dry mines were found it took years to persuade the De Beers brothers to leave; little did they dream or care that by happenchance they were also leaving their name to represent what today is the diamond world's greatest business organization—the De Beers Consoli-dated Mines, Ltd. They were simply farmers, fed up finally with the diggers' greedy ways, their clumsy, noisy wagons, their shanty towns of portable iron houses that they had brought with them from the coast, their mixtures of language and money, and their tendency to swarm like ants and erode the earth.

For by 1875 there were ten thousand diggers gathered into a town called Kimberley and working what had been the Du Toit's pond or the De Beers' farm or other patches. The Kimberley pit itself was now a patch-work of small claims thirty-one feet square, part of which was dug to a depth of twenty, fifty, or even a hundred feet, and part of which was left standing as roads for the carts. Some miners carried the dirt off to nearby streams to wash it, some didn't bother. The diamonds were thickly strewn and after a rain might even lie exposed, open to the sky, waiting to be picked up. As they had stuck to the greasy flesh of Alexander's sheep, they now stuck to the clay; as they had been carried off by vultures, they were now carried off by men, women, and children.

By 1889 the diggings were so deep that the roadbeds had caved away and the patchwork become a yawning pit, a quarter of a mile across and thirteen-hundred feet deep. Working at the bottom could swiftly be fatal when the sides caved in—and if you leapt to safety, there was still the danger of being trounced in a fight over who owned the shifting yellow soil. Today that first pit is a large, slowly filling lake surrounded by a wire fence put up after an unnamed prospector committed suicide by drowning in it. One day, according to mineralogist Emily Hahn, not too long after the diamond rush of the 1870's, Lord Randolph Churchill, father of Sir Winston, stood staring down into the pit and grew sentimental. "All for the vanity of women," he said. A sharp rejoinder came from a lady with him: "And the depravity of man."

But before this came the geological breakthrough that made the South African mines the greatest in the world's history, that brought on the Anglo-Boer War, and that made diamond engagement rings a commonplace in the western world. It was in 1876 that geologists, led by W. Graham Atherstone, reasoned that the diamond must come from an inner volcano deep in the earth and under pressure push upward in pipes toward the surface to erupt into the open air—a theory which persuaded a few diggers to go deeper below the yellow clay into the hard blue ground itself and which resulted in the discovery of diamonds not just one by one but in batches. Before this diamond gathering had been thought of as surface work; this new concept meant sinking shafts, digging tunnels—big money, big organization, big activity. Companies had to be formed; mergers had to take place between claims; financing had to be sought on a huge scale.

And so by 1880 or so the rush was over, the romantic dream of luck gone, and the big here-to-stay business was on. Just as the old mines of India had been in their heyday the property of kings, just as the Brazilian mines were taken over by the government, so now it became obvious to a farsighted few that the diamond pits and pipes of South Africa were too important to be left to chance—and rugged individualism. Visions of a great diamond trust began to dance before the eyes of financiers and the struggle began for power over what only so recently had been a neglected wasteland. But to tell this story accurately it is necessary for us to flash back to the first discoveries, put them in history, and wend through the development of the modern mining industry with all of its ramifications, in short to trace the history of De Beers Consolidated Mines, Ltd.

Kimberley, 1871. The first diggers. The huts are of corrugated iron, brought in from the Cape of Good Hope. Note the wagons, tents, and heaps of overturned dirt.

FOUR STAGES IN THE LIFE OF A FABULOUS DIAMOND MINE

Kimberley, 1872. As diamonds were found in the hard rock beneath the topsoil, the pit deepened. Claims were thirty-one by thirty-one feet and had to include a roadway for the wagons, riggings, and bucket pulleys.

Kimberley, 1875. When the roadways collapsed, the bucket pulleys became a web of rope connecting the miners with their quarry. Not until after Cecil Rhodes consolidated the companies were underground shafts built.

Kimberley, 1950. Largest man-made crater in the world: 1,520 feet across and 3,601 feet deep.

2

Mining the Modern Diamond

In Africa think big.

CECIL J. RHODES

*T*he story of how De Beers grew from a get-together of small companies in the South African Cape Colony to a huge international holding corporation which markets 80 per cent of the world's diamonds and whose profits finance gold, copper and uranium mines, governments, banks and railways is as complex as a maze and as dramatic as a rainbow. It involves thousands of adventurers, hundreds of scientists, a lot of politics and its handmaiden, war, and more money than can be readily imagined. With the discovery of diamonds along the Vaal the nearby country was transformed from a rocky wasteland which no one cared about except a few poor farmers and some roving hunters into the richest mineral cornucopia the world has ever known. And as the echoes of success flew around the world, the continent once known as "Darkest Africa" took on such glitter and allure that empire builders, financiers, and even bankers suddenly yearned to till the land which once only natives and missionaries had trod.

The first spoils, however, went to the lucky and the reckless. As soon as the news of the first "shiny pebble" reached London in 1867 a diamond merchant in Bond Street commissioned a gentleman geologist to explore the area. He spent what must have been a miserable fortnight along the Orange River never getting to the Vaal—and then declared flatly that the diamond find was accident or fake: that either it was dropped by an ostrich or, more likely, planted by someone interested in raising the price of Cape real estate.

His remarks aroused the Cape's own surveyor, Atherstone, to a closer study of the area he had hitherto viewed in terms of agriculture and he refuted the Londoner on sharp terms. Into the controversy burst the discovery of the Star of South Africa, big enough to have choked an ostrich and panicked a land speculator.

London was caught off base, and, although theory vanished instantly before fact, the first diggers crowding the banks of the Vaal were a motley assortment of wanderers with allegiance to none. An African in white helmet, a sailor in seatogs, a Fenian who marked his claims with the Black Flag, a Californian and Forty-Niner in gray top hat and frock coat—these were a few of the memorable early arrivals. Life was rough; the tents under the willow trees were lit by candles; and food was hit or miss—even a glance away from the ceaselessly rocking cradle-sieves, their "babies," might mean the loss of a diamond. But while London and the Cape were debating and the Star was being found, they had elected a president—the Forty-Niner—and were building a mud hotel and a few stores. As the second rush poured in, they were met with a hurricane: hail and wind tore through the tents, smashed the sieves, and the river of dreams swept through the valley at flood tide. Undaunted and reunited, the diggers began again. By the spring of 1871 they were well enough organized to give—of all things—a ball for their landlord, President Pretorius of the Transvaal government. The music was an accordion, a fiddle, and a bass drum; the costumes ranged from swallow-tails to overalls. Where the women came from was not recorded; ordinarily the appearance of any woman in the camp drew as big a cheer as the find of a diamond. It was a jolly occasion, but, like many similar occasions, the morning after consequences were not so jolly.

For no invitations were sent the Griquas, who claimed the territory as their hunting ground. When later they arrived in force to demand withdrawal of the newcomers, the diggers held them off with flags, bayonets, and the support of the Transvaal government. But the Griquas turned to the British for help and the diggers and the Transvaal Afrikaners were outmatched. After a lengthy inquiry, the British decided the Griquas did indeed own the land and promptly bought it from them.

Incensed though they were, there was no recourse for Transvaal Afrikaners. Their defeats and political differences with the British were of long standing; they themselves were descendants of the original settlement in 1652 by the East India Company of Dutch traders on the Cape. The first Dutch beat back the native Hottentots and Bushmen to build the Cape

Colony stockade, and when they discovered that neither group would work for them, they imported slaves from along the coast for farm labor. Slowly a language they called "Afrikaans" developed and as the Netherlands lost interest in the colony, they began calling themselves Afrikaners and the farmers among them, Boers—the Dutch word for farmers.

The British conquered the colony in 1795, fearing Napoleon might seize it. In 1820 they sent in five thousand English settlers, who in two decades anglicized the courts, set up English speaking schools, and banned slavery and maltreatment of native help.

The half-cast Griquas—a mixture of European and African—had already made a path eastward into the interior to form Griqualand; the disgusted Afrikaners, the Boers, and their slaves now trekked out of the colony and, fighting off any natives who resisted, set up a government across the Vaal River. Their constitution was anti-British and declared flatly they wanted no equality of color in either church or state; it was seventeen years old when the British ruled against their control of the diggers south of the Vaal and the diamond finds.

By then, however, much more South African land than just that of Vaal Valley was giving up its long-secret treasures. To the south-east at Jagersfontein farmers spotting garnets on their fields were renting out patches to diggers, and at Dutoitspan, where a curious natural basin filled with the wash from the ridges around it, other Boers allowed prospectors to crawl over the land on hands and knees, like so many ants, searching for diamonds. Then late in the winter of 1871, an English prospector named Richard Jackson on a combination exploring and hunting trip with a few adventurous friends discovered the first dry mines.

At the moment of his discovery, Jackson was lost. Traveling in a cart drawn by four oxen, he and his group were in good spirits from their bag of zebra and lion. When they spotted a white tent through the thorn trees, Jackson got out and approached it. Inside he found a man calmly sorting gravel. He was a shepherd working on the De Beers farm, he said, and he was paid a 25 per cent royalty on each diamond he found. As he talked, he scraped up a 2.5-carat gem from his pebbles.

Jackson called to his friends and proudly the shepherd showed off his week's finds. For two years Jackson had been digging near the Vaal but never had he or his companions seen so many diamonds in one man's hands.

During the next week they settled in, pegging claims thirty feet by thirty feet not only for themselves but for friends. They then returned to the Vaal to collect their gear. The news of the big find meanwhile swept through the camp and by the time Jackson returned to the De Beers farm a flood of miners engulfed the place. Jackson managed to save his claim; the lone prospector who had so naively displayed his gems was frightened off. Within a year the De Beers brothers had left too; they had paid $250 for the land twelve years before, now they sold it for $30,000. Later they regretted they had not asked for more. If they had held out longer they might have gotten another $10,000, they told a friend. They were simple folk. Their only book was the Bible. In the next seventy-five years almost $500,000,000 worth of diamonds was to be taken from their wretched farmland.

It took time, however, for the diggers to discover the extent of their find. The farm's topsoil was of yellow clay, and when they reached the blue-gray rock beneath it they quit claim and moved on. The realization that the yellow clay was simply crumbled blue rock and that the rock was diamondiferous came too late for many of them. Again it was chance that led the diggers directly into the pipes which were literally storehouses of diamonds.

Was it a young servingboy digging on his own who found the first diamonds in the pipes of Kimberley or the wife of a digger napping on an outcrop of the blue-gray rock? Both claim precedence, but the spot was the same: the place of encampment of the Red Cap Company, a group of miners led by the handsome Fleetwood Rawstone, the son of a local judge, a man lucky at digs and unlucky at cards. His red-capped troop consisted of other local boys, most of them sons of missionaries, who had gathered at the Vaal and then had moved south to try their luck at De Beers. Because they could not get any closer, they had pitched camp a mile away at a spot the Griquas said was haunted, a wild place of long grasses, camel-thorn trees and outcroppings of stone. Legend said it had once been the bank of a huge lake running hundreds of miles southward; certainly the ground dipped away below their ridge and after a rain mists rose from the ground.

The servingboy was Rawstone's, sent out as punishment for getting drunk to prospect a grove of thorn trees close by—a grove suspected of nothing at all but hard ground. That night Rawstone and his chums played cards as usual and at first were inclined to ignore the unexpected, excited entrance of young Damon, the servingboy. Then the boy opened his hand and showed them the diamonds he had found. In an instant the troop was outdoors, pegging the grove. Within days it was known that Rawstone had gotten two pegs—or two claims—inside the first diamondiferous pipe known to the world. It was just two months since the De Beers mine had been discovered—and now, Kimberley! The theory that diamonds originated in the rivers was abandoned; miners roared south to the new dry mines which were in reality vents of old volcanoes.

As the miners crowded the new mines, their difficulties grew: not only the physical difficulties of the mining, the living, the guarding of their treasures, but political difficulties. Many of the miners wanted to make the dry mines part of the Free State; others wanted their claims protected by the Transvaal government. The newly arrived Englishmen meanwhile were determined the area eventually must be part of the British Empire.

The strongest of these was Cecil John Rhodes—great and petty, generous and spiteful, dedicated and headstrong. When he first arrived in Kimberley in 1871 he was eighteen and had been sent out from England for his health; he had a weak heart and tuberculosis. But even as a boy his aims were mighty; a man who knew him in his teens described him as a "master schemer." He decided for himself he needed a good education and returned to England to attend Oxford University but continued to spend his vacations in Kimberley. "Diamonds are a drug . . ." he wrote a friend; then, asking himself what was the chief good in life, answered "to be useful to my country." So he committed himself to both diamonds and politics.

By the time he was twenty-eight he was an Oxford graduate, a member of the Cape Colony Legislature, the president of De Beers Company and many small diamond companies, and a millionaire with a dream of developing all Africa for his Queen, Victoria.

First, however, he intended to conquer the diamond industry. He had decided that the only solution to the marketing crises, the stealing of stones, the mine disasters, and the fights among companies and diggers was monopoly of the mines. Seeing himself as the obvious czar, he began his battle by first buying up the various companies in the De Beers mine, and then moving on to Dutoitspan and Bultfontein.

The real prize, however, was Kimberley and that was in the hands of several companies, the chief of which was the Kimberley Central Company, owned by a speculator as daring as Rhodes but not as brilliant, Barney Barnato.

Barnato at first did not realize Rhodes was out to run everything; he didn't like the price wars that sporadically wrecked the diamond market any more than Rhodes did, but he couldn't imagine an end to them by any means. He was a trader. When he first traded some shares of Kimberley Central to Rhodes in a mine deal he thought little of it; even when his friends were being tempted to sell their shares, he didn't worry too much. He fought back only when Rhodes got big money to back him—Rothschild support, among others—and then as Rhodes bid Kimberley shares up and

The vastness of his frame was matched by the breadth of his vision. While other men worried over a few handfuls of diamonds and a few miles of veld, Cecil John Rhodes recognized the dawning of Africa's greatness and foresaw the future of the stone without peer.

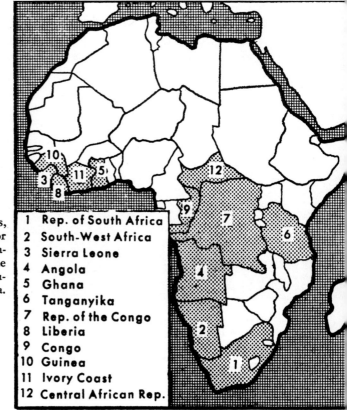

Largest check ever drawn up to that time, £5,338,650, ordered issued by Rhodes to purchase the Kimberley mine for De Beers.

Africa's diamond nations, ranked by output of gem, or jewel-quality, stones. Other major diamond sources include the Soviet Union, Brazil, Venezuela, British Guiana, and India.

1 Rep. of South Africa
2 South-West Africa
3 Sierra Leone
4 Angola
5 Ghana
6 Tanganyika
7 Rep. of the Congo
8 Liberia
9 Congo
10 Guinea
11 Ivory Coast
12 Central African Rep.

up, the price of diamonds went down and down. Rhodes inevitably won; in 1888 Barnato turned over all his Kimberley Central stock to Rhodes in return for a big block of De Beers shares. Then the two became friends. And, when a holdout group in Kimberley Central protested in court they didn't want to merge with De Beers, Barnato and Rhodes got together on a buying price for Kimberley's assets and Rhodes paid it in a single whopping check for £5,338,650.

"We had to choose between the ruin of the diamond industry and control of the Kimberley mine," Rhodes said later, putting the long struggle in a typical Rhodes nutshell. He by then had interested Barnato in gold mining in the Rand.

Speed and force were essential in diamonds and gold; patience was needed in politics. Rhodes had succeeded in becoming Prime Minister of the Cape Colony by 1890 but by 1895 his political career was wrecked. A diggers'—or outlanders'—insurrection had been brewing in the Transvaal because the Afrikaners denied the vote to new residents, and Rhodes encouraged his friends to join the rebellion. But the insurrection collapsed almost before it got underway, and his good friend L. Starr Jameson was arrested and Rhodes had to resign. He took it well, accepted silently the Afrikaner charges of treachery and only after the Anglo-Boer War broke out did he get his revenge by turning Kimberley into a British stronghold.

He is still spoken of with awe in South Africa. He did not like women or parties, spoke in a high falsetto voice and grew so large that he broke the ordinary chair sitting on it. He saw diamonds as lovers' gems and disdained them himself. His idea of a good rest was an exploring trip. Early he lived in a white bungalow in Kimberley opposite his club, where he dined, but after entering politics, he built a house called "The Great Barn" on the Cape. During the 124-day siege of Kimberley he was heroic, running food canteens, and authorizing the invention of a new gun; the shells bombarding the Boers were, under his instructions, marked scornfully, "Compliments of CJR."

Only after the siege was over and Kimberley safe from the Boers did he show strain, becoming irritable and weary. He died in 1902, at forty-nine, just before the Anglo-Boer War ended and the year a musical comedy opened in London about a man called "Piggy" who was a South African millionaire. His will asked that he be buried on a favorite hill he called "The World's View" in Rhodesia; his Cape house he left to future Prime Ministers, and a good part of his fortune went into the Rhodes Scholarships to Oxford. He knew his heart was finally failing him before he died. "So little done, so much to do." he murmured the afternoon of his death. The mighty task of controlling the diamond mines had been to him just a beginning.

Whatever history may say of him in other contexts, there is no doubt, however, that he rescued the diamond from that kind of insecure environment which is damning to a foundling. The two major reasons gem diamonds are precious is that they are beautiful and they are rare. Their beauty is internal and eternal but the supply fluctuates; in the early years price wars among the South African mining companies might have ruined not only the diamond industry but the diamond itself as the jewel without peer.

When the mines were being dug "first-come–first-served," and the claims fought over, anything could happen to the diamond's value—and did. At times the price soared; at times it could not be sold except at less than cost. The organization which Rhodes built controlled the price by controlling the mines.

But if Rhodes rescued the diamond he did not preserve it forever. His mine monopoly method was great so far as it went; it did not forsee the day when diamonds would be found elsewhere than in the mines for which he had fought so fiercely.

It took Sir Ernest Oppenheimer as chairman of De Beers to bring the new discoveries into the De Beers orbit; for almost three decades the company Rhodes founded was so set in Rhodes' mold that it could cope only with the mines he had organized.

And the next diamond discoveries were not mines at all. The first was an alluvial field, discovered by the Germans north of the Orange River, and Rhodes had said more than once that alluvial fields were not worth bothering with. The second was a very strange formation indeed: the diamonds were in oyster-shell terraces at Alexander Bay just south of where the Orange emptied into the Atlantic. Had they once poured over the great Aughrabies Falls on the Orange into the sea and been lifted back up to the land in a great underwater tremor? Or had they exploded originally in an under-sea volcano? At the mouth of the river more diamonds were found at Oranjemund under the shifting sands. Another alluvial field was found north of the Vaal at Lichtenburg.

When De Beers showed no interest in these fields, Oppenheimer collected them, organizing the Consolidated Diamond Mines of South-West Africa, Ltd. (better known as C.D.M.), to do so. He knew what he was doing; he first had come out to Kimberley as a diamond expert for a London firm, arriving there six weeks after Rhodes died, but soon found himself almost as much interested in the growth of the area as he was in diamonds. His kind of politics was not the kind Rhodes had envisioned—great empires and sweeps of power—but the handling of practical problems. He was modest, polite, quietly but dynamically capable and so persuasive that Kimberley's World War I contributions—he was mayor of the growing city by then—earned him a knighthood.

His first financial enterprises occurred in gold, however, not diamonds. He and his friend W. L. Honnold organized the Anglo-American Corporation of South Africa—with Herbert Hoover and J. P. Morgan as shareholders—for gold. Rhodes had bought gold with diamond profits; now Oppenheimer reversed the process. Slowly his success impressed itself upon De Beers' directors. In 1926 they made him a director; in 1929 he was elected chairman of the board.

His first step was to persuade De Beers to buy out Anglo-American's share in the new diamond finds and the sales organization that handled their distribution. Since mine production was slipping badly, the alluvial trading company rapidly took over the old mining, marketing syndicate, but almost as suddenly it found itself all but out of business. Supply had suddenly exceeded demand in the depression-hit market and there were simply no takers at De Beers' prices. Oppenheimer first called on South Africa, pleading with producers and traders alike not to dump their diamonds on the market at bargain prices and then went through Holland, Belgium, France, and England with the same plea to keep values up. His politicking was as educational for De Beers as it was for the traders; when his optimism was vindicated and diamond sales began to pick up, the independent diamond producers in Angola, the Belgian Congo, and Sierra Leone were eager to sell through De Beers if they could. The result was the Diamond Trading Company in London; soon it was handling all the rough diamond sales from anywhere in Africa.

Sir Ernest Oppenheimer believed in price control and so did his contemporaries. Perhaps it was the depression that convinced traders, miners, financiers, and customers alike into thinking a market and production monopoly was the only answer for the diamond industry; perhaps it was Oppenheimer's arguments that diamond production was not endless or inexhaustible, that the diamond in nature really was a rarity, and that it was just a temporary matter if it happened to be a surplus on the market. Whatever the cause, the monopoly grew into one of the world's great cartels, not to be threatened until the 1950's.

Since Sir Ernest's death in 1957, his son Harry Oppenheimer has been running De Beers, the hundred corporations allied with it and organized before his day, plus another fifty which he himself has brought in. A rubicund, jolly man he has two characteristics in common with the great men

An official portrait of Harry Frederick Oppenheimer, King of Diamonds and a man who likes to say he weighs 382,500 carats—instead of 170 pounds.

he succeeded—brains and ability. He is considered not only the King of Diamonds but the King of Gold too, and at least a Prince of Copper—but he is neither empire-minded nor monopoly-minded. De Beers today is a giant holding company very mindful of demand and supply, of local interests, and of world opinion, and it has been several years since it penalized any of its purchasers for trading in the areas outside De Beers' interests (like Brazil, say, or more recently, the Congo) or insisted that marketing control go hand in hand with loans.

One chief reason De Beers is no longer the great monolith, of course, is that today demand considerably outruns supply and prices stay up normally. Sir Ernest liked to say that annual diamond production was keyed to the number of English and American engagement rings expected yearly but Harry Oppenheimer can't today: gem demand is running way ahead of Anglo-American proposals of marriage and the demand for industrial stones is so great that De Beers has even gone into production of synthetics.

Another major reason, however, is the vast political changes which have occurred in diamond areas. The decline and fall of colonialism and the emergence of the new African nations have affected the practices of many of the diamond mines. The Belgian Congo mines for instance, once Belgian owned but De Beers marketed, now are handled completely by the Congolese Republic. Half of the Sierra Leone mines have been taken over by the government; Ghana's finds have been totally nationalized; the Williamson mine is owned jointly between De Beers and the Tanganyika government (now merged into Tanzania). Many of these governments sell at least in part through the Diamond Trading Company simply because it is good business and all regard the De Beers price as *the* diamond price; but this is cooperative action, not monolithic control of production and sales.

In 1960, after Russia discovered diamonds in the Urals, she joined the De Beers sales group. In the spring of 1964 she pulled out, reportedly for political reasons. It is impossible to say how well or how long non-participants can compete with the veteran De Beers; the worst problem at the moment is illicit diamond buying because the governments apparently can't control smuggling. Recently when the Congolese, for instance, sent in an army of soldiers to guard the fields, the soldiers rapidly discovered that a rifle was the price for a shovel and turned in their rifles and began digging. Similarly, Sierra Leone stones are smuggled across the border into Liberia; it is a not-funny joke in diamond circles that diamonds are being discovered in Liberia every day. No one should get the idea, however, that Harry Oppenheimer, an optimist like his father, is staying awake nights fretting over De Beers' future. Instead he is full steam ahead, producing and marketing all the industrials possible and, since gems are where the profit lies, concentrating on the gems. Deeper and deeper the De Beers machinery burrows into the earth—the shafts at Kimberley now reach almost a mile below the earth's surface. Wider and wider course the geologists and engineers seeking new sources: a new South African mine has been discovered in Postmasburg and De Beers is hurrying it into production. In South-West Africa the diamond fields are being worked at top speed; at the original De Beers mine, closed in 1908 because it was considered uneconomical to work, a new shaft has been sunk and modern machinery brought in for its reopening. And, although De Beers, as producers, can no longer meet the demand, as marketers they continue to encourage it. In 1963 they started a new advertising campaign to encourage more diamond engagement ring sales in Europe. It has not been traditional on the continent for any but the rich upper class to expect a diamond along with a proposal of marriage, but De Beers (spurred by the European jewelers who were in trouble because of declining watch sales) hoped to democratize diamond attitudes. The classic American advertising line "The Diamond is Forever" has been translated into several European languages, and one Belgian diamond maker has gone them one better: "The Diamond is Forever—and For Everybody," Ferstenberg's of Antwerp states pointedly on its brochures.

In the United States, meanwhile, De Beers advertisements have shifted from total concentration on engagement diamonds. One recent campaign was aimed at the married couples: "Diamonds bespeak an evergrowing love." Another suggested to the feminine customer that there are jewelry pieces which madam can get for herself in the same manner that she now gets other fashionable items—on her charge account.

As demand has increased, De Beers has raised prices and inevitably jewelers have followed suit, but these rises have scarcely slowed down sales. In fact, the results have been almost the reverse: as stones of 3 carats and upward have become harder to get, and thus more expensive, the demand has increased. A fine well-cut 4-carat or larger stone may now bring $3,000 a carat although only a few years ago it could be had for $1,000 a carat; really large stones of quality—60 carats and up—may bring as much as $8,000 to $9,000 a carat. De Beers set a new record in 1964 in gem and industrial sales: $372,921,000, but the American consumer purchasing gem diamonds alone purchased more than $500,000,000 worth of cut gems.

America's gems are bought largely for adornment; abroad—in Asia, South America and Eastern Europe—diamonds are more likely to be bought and hoarded as a hedge against inflation and a nest egg against sudden changes of government. Hong Kong, for instance, tripled its imports of cut diamonds from the United States in 1963. "Girls," said *Business Week* recently, "are De Beers' best friends." Its second best friend is the potential refugee.

The spread of democracy, of industry, of American consumer habits and of one-world communications have all played their role in increasing the demand for diamonds, but the fact remains that the world supply of natural diamonds *is* exhaustible—and the De Beers mines are nearing their hundredth birthday. How much longer they will go on being productive and what new sources will be found, are matters of speculation, but the prospects not only of a market scarcity but of a very real natural scarcity also help to push up demand. De Beers is currently selling diamonds mined the previous month and has exhausted its depression stock of reserves. Wholesale jewelers are complaining that they are running several weeks behind on deliveries as a result and large firms such as Harry Winston, Inc., are now buying from a fifth to a third of their diamonds outside of De Beers. (Winston is also involved in a search for new diamond fields in North Africa.) "We are indeed experiencing some difficulty at present in meeting the general demand," Harry Oppenheimer recently conceded.

Other problems beset De Beers.

The old fight between Dutch and British attitudes continues though in new guise and with curious effects. On the one hand, because of the South African Government's anti-black policy, sponsored by the Afrikaners group, *any* white from South Africa is unwelcome (although not banned, like South African Airways) in the new African states; on the other hand, although the De Beers group is *not* Afrikaner in either thinking or background, it can do little to change materially the South African government's policy.

For some time now indeed, Harry Oppenheimer has been a tycoon on a political tightrope. In the De Beers pattern, he has a seat in South Africa's parliament as a member of the United Party; but it is the Nationalists who run the government and who are backing apartheid—a policy of separating the non-whites from the whites by granting them a territory all their own, loans for developing it, and a vote each in that territory. Young Oppenheimer, educated at Oxford University, views such segregation in English fashion as a move which solves nothing; but he's not for giving non-whites a vote unless they are also educated. Thus neither side is totally placated, but that he is not anti-black is proven by the De Beers policy of giving *all* their workers, regardless of race, decent education, good hospital facilities, fair working conditions, and increasingly higher wages.

Who are these workers? In the underground mines the miners are usually young men from Malawi, Portuguese Angola, Basutoland or Mozambique or Rhodesia who sign up to work in the mining compounds or camps on contracts ranging up to nine months. Behind them, they often leave brides they hope to buy, pregnant wives, or farms that they covet. Sometimes they achieve their goals, sometimes they forget them. The wages by our standards are meager—perhaps one dollar to four dollars a day— but food, medicine, and education are free and the work day is only eight hours. There is no difficulty in getting workers—often indeed they must be turned away. Many like the ready-made city life the compounds (De Beers prefers to call them hostels) offer and the lump sum they receive when they get home again; in a few tribes working even briefly in the mines is considered a test of manhood, and a completed stint a status mark of important fitness and virility. On Sundays tribal dances are held in the compound yards watched by hundreds of visitors and, inevitably, police guards trained in smuggling tactics. The mixture of languages, of tribal feather work and beaded robe, of dance ritual and rhythmic beat makes these dances one of the great exotic and erotic sights of Africa. John Gunther spent a Sunday in a mine near Johannesburg and "enthralling" was his word for the performance.

The underground weekday work is duller and a lot more mechanized. Diamond mining is like all mineral mining and yet it isn't. It's not grimy like coal mining, and it's not as unsafe as lead mining. De Beers provides attractive working surroundings, good labor policies, and many fringe benefits. As Emily Hahn put it after a trip below ground in the Premier mine near Johannesburg, it can even be mining de luxe. Only in the actual area of blasting is a diamond mine moist and cave-like and lit by miners' lanterns. Shafts and passages are whitewashed and lit by electricity, and the small railway to carry off the rock, the safety gadgets, the special doors to be closed against flooding, and the air conditioning are impressively sophisticated.

Underground mining proceeds like this: First the rock is dynamited into small pieces; then the miners—the compound boys—gather up the blasted blue chunks, wheel them to the railway, dump them into the railway cars, the railway takes them to the crusher, the crusher crunches the chunks into gravel and then the gravel pours into a churning tank, where the diamonds because of their high density, sink to the bottom along with some heavy gravel. Then the bottom stuff is poured out onto conveyor belts which take it to the grease table.

All along the route workers may—but few do—spot a diamond jiggling along but the real sorter is the grease table. While water rolls off most diamonds like it does off a duck's back, grease as we've said, sticks to them—and they stick to it. The grease on this three-tiered aluminum table is

1. Diamond miners prepare to blast a section of the blue ground, the diamond-bearing ore at Premier diamond mine. The broken blue ground falls into the Big Hole, gravitates through openings and cones to underground haulages, and then is taken to the shaft to be hoisted to the surface.

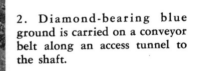

2. Diamond-bearing blue ground is carried on a conveyor belt along an access tunnel to the shaft.

3. At the surface is the crusher. Here the ore is broken up and prepared for later steps in the diamond-recovery process. Diamond-bearing gravel from the marine terraces on the South-West African coast does not have to go through this.

4. After the material is crushed it is sent through a sink-and-float process. In this cone is a chemical compound which floats off the lighter waste material while the heavier minerals, including the diamonds, sink to the bottom. The diamond-bearing concentrate is then collected from the bottom of the cone.

5. Now the diamond-bearing concentrate is sluiced with water over a vibrating table with grease-covered terraces. The diamonds stick to the grease, the rest is carried off the table as waste.

6. Here diamonds that have adhered to the grease table are being scraped from its surface. Then the diamonds with their coating of grease are taken to larger kettles of boiling water. There the grease melts and only the clean diamonds remain.

7. Sorting is the final step in the recovery section of a diamond mine. While most of the previous work was carried out by machines, this final step depends on human skill and judgment. Of the diamonds on this particular table, only twenty per cent—like the four small piles of white stones—are of gem quality, suitable for cutting and polishing into the beauty that is a diamond. The rest are useful in industry.

8. This trench on the Atlantic coast of South-West Africa is part of another type of diamond mining. In ages past, diamond-bearing gravels were carried down by the rivers and deposited in the sea. Where the old land masses have risen, the ocean has receded, millions of tons of sand are removed to expose the diamond-bearing deposits.

9. The "vacuveyor" is used in the open diamond mining along the South-West African seacoast to pick up by suction every bit of diamond-bearing gravel from the bedrock. A hundred million parts of earth by weight are removed for every one part of diamonds recovered.

about a half-inch thick and as the diamonds and gravel spread evenly over it, the diamonds are caught fast while the water flows quietly on. When a batch collects, the worker scrapes them up, grease and all, and puts them into a fine wire basket like a sieve, drops the sieve into boiling water and boils off the grease. Now finally there's a small handful of rough diamonds to show for several days of work and tons of blue rock.

The Williamson mine in Tanganyika was worked in much the same fashion but since it is newer and was found in what was a wilderness, a modern town with airport has been constructed around the mine for the workers. Here the memory of the late Canadian geologist John Thoburn Williamson is still vivid; he staked his claim out in 1933 after studying diamond mining at McGill University in Toronto and after working with De Beers. Then, aided by an Indian diamond prospector, he found a diamond pipe right where he had learned it must be, near Mwadui, its weathered crater hidden in the long grass and bush. From 1942 until 1952 he was an independent producer; then he entered into a contract with De Beers permitting him to sell 10 per cent of the world's annual diamond supply through the Diamond Trading Company. Under his management his mine became widely publicized first for the 56-carat pink diamond Williamson gave the then Princess (now Queen) Elizabeth of England, and later for the precautionary measures he took to guard against diamond smuggling. Workers sign in to live in all mining compounds for at least several months and X-raying them before they go home has long been routine; Williamson added to this an army headed by an ex-Scotland Yard detective and four Europeans and manned by two hundred Africans supported by searchlights, dogs, pony cart patrol wagons and a double twenty-foot high fence of barbed wire around the mining compound.

Field and strip diamond-gathering methods are of course considerably different from underground mining. At Orangemund the diamonds lie in ledges buried under windblown sand, which first must be stripped off and hauled away before the gravel in the terraces can be screened for diamonds. A new sorting tool in use there is based on the diamond's reflective powers: it is an optical separator—that is, when a glint of light is reflected from the gravel under inspection a gateway opens mechanically and that batch of gravel is separated from the rest. Grease tables are also used for separation here but first the gravel must be treated: alluvial diamonds do not shed water easily and thus don't stick to grease the way pipe diamonds do naturally.

In open fields, as in Sierra Leone, the modern methods are much the same as the early methods of prospecting except that now sieves and washers and sorters are likely to be mechanically run.

The newest, most fascinating development in diamond mining is sea dredging. Once thought nothing but nonsense, it is now being proved profitable by a Texan named Sam V. Collins who has invented his own underwater vacuum cleaner. Wearing a 10-carat sea-diamond ring for luck he sucks up the gravel from the Atlantic Ocean—Orange River Bay region —with his machine, processes it for diamonds and then dumps the gravel back again. According to Collins, in whom the farsighted De Beers owns stock, deep-sea diamond mining is much more efficient than either underground or field mining: 1 carat of diamond is found for each ton of sea gravel, he says, compared to the 1 carat found for each twenty tons of surface land or four tons of underground pipe. And no crusher! In the first five months of 1964 he took in almost 102,000 carats of diamonds.

Africa today produces more than 95 per cent of the world's diamonds but other continents boast a few finds: there is a pipe in Arkansas, near Murfreesboro, discovered in 1906, that has yielded one 40-carat stone and a fair number of small stones. Anyone can dig in it for a small fee since it has not been promising enough to attract big capital in recent years. Australia once claimed to produce a trickle of the hardest diamonds in the world— diamonds which could be cut only by their own dust—but little has been heard of them lately. Diamond mining continues in Borneo but in a primitive way with wages so low they make the South African miner's fifty cents a day look magnificent.

Despite the great mineral riches of South America, diamonds have been found only in Brazil, British Guiana, and Venezuela; Brazil's supplies like India's are all but exhausted. The 1962 charts of annual world production credit Brazil—which does not sell through De Beers—with some 350,-000 carats of diamonds, while India, which for twelve centuries was the sole source of diamonds, is lumped ignominiously with those nameless producers called "others."

But prospectors never give up hope. All over the world the search continues. The more promising fields swarm with geologists and mineralogists; recently, for instance, there has been some excitement in the Val d'Or (valley of gold) near Quebec. There is always a party poking and panning in Canada somewhere, for it is assumed by many that the diamonds found in the United States came via glacial drift from the North. In South America glittery-eyed men abound eager to offer the tourists a chance to find their very own diamond bed and many try, although over and over again the beds turn out to be only rock crystal.

So much for mining. Selling has its routine too. The South African sales work like this: after being mined the rough diamonds are sorted into either gem or industrial, then by size and color. All gem stones are packaged for sale to about two hundred buyers who have earned their privilege of ordering in advance from De Beers through their financial strength and dependability. They are then air-mailed to London, to the Diamond Trading Company in boxes labeled fruit, wool, or some other misleading title; there they are presented at the week-long, once a month "sights" at their offices just off Hatton Garden.

Here the top-level diamond men gather to take a look at the parcels organized for them by category and size in small cloth bags. They have two or three days to study their diamonds but there is no haggling, no exchanging—it is take all the parcel or nothing, and immediate cash.

This is the hub of the diamond merchandising world; this large, very modern building not far from St. Paul's, is the only place where uncut diamonds can be purchased regularly and in quantity. Here Harry Winston purchased the 426.50 carat Niarchos diamond plus fifty thousand other diamonds in a single parcel which cost him $8,400,000 cash.

In the main room an almost continuous table stretches under a row of tall windows letting in the north light—the only proper light in the Northern Hemisphere to sort and judge diamonds by; off it are small rooms equally well lit for the buyers to examine their gems.

Once bought, from here the roughs go out by registered mail to the cutting centers: the largest batches to Antwerp and Israel, a good number to Amsterdam, a few to London and New York. Most cities outside the lowlands buy their gem diamonds cut.

As well as the rough gems, there are also the industrials. In carat weight, these far outweigh the gems—85 per cent of production is sold for industrial use.

Indeed, the diamond is vital to modern industry. It is the only edge that will cut other tough stones like marble—the only knife that will go through sandstone as if it were so much butter. It tips the edges of giant circular saws which whirr through great building blocks for the skyscrapers of New York, the edifices of London, the marble halls of Italy. But its chief use is for cutting, grinding and polishing metals—from watch cases to automobiles: as the use of metal has increased throughout the world so has the use of diamonds. In 1939, 5,000 carats of industrials were sold; in 1964, more than 30 million.

The diamond is also invaluable in drawing wire; those yards of wire thread in the back of a wristwatch, a radio, a TV set are made by being drawn through infinitesimal holes in diamonds, holes which keep their precise size for months, despite the friction created by the steel. Diamonds also help grind cavities out of your teeth, play the records on your phonograph, cut the bumps out of concrete roads and, in pasta factories, slice spaghetti.

Even if the diamond dropped suddenly out of fashion tomorrow, the diamond itself would retain its preciousness to modern builders, tool-makers, eyeglass-makers, dentists, jewel-cutters—and so much of our world today is dependent on the diamond that without it the wheels of industry would slow to a snail's pace.

The fine natural diamond has no equal. Over and over again men have sought to duplicate it artificially and failed. But industrial diamond grit— hard and tough and powdery—is another matter: both the General Electric Company and De Beers produce a steady, large supply of industrial diamond grit out of sugar or charcoal; they are as hard as the natural stones and better for some grinding wheels.

Industrials are usually purchased in London wholesale from the Central Selling Organization of De Beers and then resold to the users: like gems they may go through many brokers' hands before they reach the customer. And so there are, throughout the world, thirteen societies of brokers with their special exchanges, clubrooms and bourses for the selling and trading of diamonds. None are as beautiful as the new modern De Beers sales office in London but all share the same characteristics: the high windows north above the equator, south below; the work tables; and the men bent in concentration or gathered in discussion about their glittering baubles.

The day I visited the major New York bourse or Diamond Dealers Club on West Forty-seventh Street just off Sixth Avenue, it was a dull day— literally. It had been raining earlier that morning and since the daylight was not considered too good for diamond viewing, the overhead special lights were lit. But the place was thronged. Most of the men carried their diamond paper packets in large black wallets of many pockets but some were hawking single diamonds wrapped only in waxy paper envelopes. On some tables the diamonds were heaped in piles about as large as an overturned tea cup. On others were large individual diamonds.

It was a mixture of men as well as diamonds. Many were the familiar gray flannel types of New York, but others wore the beard and cap of the Orthodox Jew, for while today the majority of the cutters are Catholic and Protestant, the majority of the merchants remain Jewish. English, Yiddish, and Hebrew filled the air, but there was no aggressive selling. A man presented his diamonds to another man's view, and named the price per carat. The buyer studied the gems or perhaps took them to the official to be weighed or moved around the room with them or showed them to a friend. When he decided on the ones he wanted he told the salesman—who at any moment might turn buyer of other diamonds himself. The salesman then sealed the bargain with the words: "Mazel un b'rachah." It is an old Yiddish phrase which, freely translated, means "good luck and prosperity." Thus the diamond.has changed hands for centuries; no check or cash seals the deal, only these words. The next day, a bill will be presented, but not at the moment of purchase.

Those who betray this traditional diamondman's agreement either by welshing on the bill or by passing off diamonds of less worth than declared are dealt with by the clubs themselves. Off the salesrooms are the executive offices and here disagreements are settled by an arbiter; flagrant violations are published by posting the name of the offender and denying him entrance to the club. No cases involving diamond sales at the clubs go to court; so strong is the hold of these bourses that their law *is* the diamond law.

From the clubs the diamonds go to the cutters or the stores, either by way of the wholesalers who purchased them there or through buyers who never see the uncut stones themselves. A few big merchants in need of big stones may go direct to London or Antwerp; but most American retail merchants rely on a wholesale house in New York to find them the diamonds they need. The clubs are the hub of a small world which no man enters without introductions and references, preferably from relatives in the business. Now and again a woman belongs briefly; she is not one of the few women jewelers but a widow of a diamond merchant, granted the purchasing and selling privileges that her husband once held, privileges she never had as a wife. For while it's women who wear the diamonds, women who command the number mined and sold, it's men who mine them, finance them, buy them, sell them, set them, sell them again, and finally buy them for an individual woman: a chain of diamonds carried by a chain of men, linked together by the giant hands of De Beers—the small hands of beloved, betrothed girls.

3

Perfecting the Diamond's Beauty

The diamond is the crystalline Revelator
of the achromatic white light of Heaven.

THOMAS H. CHIVERS (1807–1858)

*M*edieval historians, preoccupied with kings and wars, popes and dogma, paid very little heed to diamonds except when they turned up as royal wealth or church symbols, and then mentioned them only in passing. It is not enough to explain, as did Pliny earlier, that after all diamonds were only owned by kings; no king went out and mined them himself, someone shipped them to him from India, someone polished them, someone set them in gold or sewed them into cloth, and someone brought them to court so the kings could sport them in battle or their ladies could display them in court.

We get some knowledge of such affairs from diaries, wills, and the reports of such traveling diamond merchants as Jean Baptiste Tavernier but in the great period of Church conformity that lasted from the fall of Rome in the eighth century to the Reformation at the end of the fifteenth, men who kept personal records were rare. The wind of change that swept through Europe in the fifteenth century at the beginning of the modern scientific period increased the importance of individual learning and decreased the strength of religious dogma. Only in its wake did modern man, the individual, emerge in any numbers; only then did men think well enough of their personal experiences to record them in journals and notebooks. Many reports were laconic: Pepys' repeated "and so to bed" is typical.

The commonplace was usually ignored, the unusual emphasized, and the to us fascinating details of a way of life usually taken for granted.

And so we can discover through his will that in 1368 the Duke of Anjou owned eight dazzling polished diamonds, set in gold, with foil backings to make them glitter, but where and how he got them we don't know. We know that there was some facet cutting as well as polishing of diamonds because there was a law against imitating diamonds in rock crystal and three of Anjou's diamonds were said to have had four-cornered facets. But there is extant no description of how the difficulties of obtaining or working with diamonds were overcome.

Certainly diamonds were coming in from India, and there were by now enough of them to circulate among the powerful of Europe. In 1407 it was recorded that John the Fearless, the Duke of Burgundy, at a great dinner for the King of France, gave away eleven diamonds to the King and his guests. Like Anjou's, these were prized for their beauty but who polished them, how they were polished, or where, remains still unknown. Only a diamond can cut a diamond; only mathematical precision and long tedious work can cut a diamond beautifully.

Writing of his father's work as a goldsmith of that period, Albrecht Dürer described it as "great toil and stern hard labor"—how much worse must have it been for the jewelworkers who "kept their noses to the grindstone" in the historic phrase. Even today when grindstones are run by electricity instead of elbow grease, diamond work remains a nerve-racking, back-breaking, invalid-making task with little of the clean sparkle of the gem itself and even less of the profits. It is not only the hours of patient, precise mathematical thinking, the hard handiwork of the actual cutting, that wears a man out; there is also the nervous tension of working with something vastly precious that may be either ruined or enhanced by what is done to it.

When Edward VII of England, for instance, decided the great Cullinan Diamond—3,024.75 carats—should be changed from one massive chunk of stone into a collection of smaller ones, his cutter, Joseph Asscher of Amsterdam, took two months to study the stone before touching it with his cleaver. Then on the day of the cleaving, after Asscher measured, deliberated and planned his work, he struck the first determined blow with a nurse and doctor standing in attendance. The blow was sure; the stone split cleanly into three stones, later to be cleaved again into nine. But Asscher himself, as he had feared, fell to the floor in a faint.

That was in 1907. Had Asscher failed he would have lost his reputation but not his life. The jeweler who wrecked a diamond experimenting in the Middle Ages risked all: his reputation, his fortune, and his life.

Some believe, however, that the Indians not the Europeans did the experimental work on diamonds, and that as early as the eighth century A.D., diamonds were cut and polished in the Orient. There is the suggestion that the skill became known to the Levantine trade and entered Europe through the great Christian capital of the Eastern Roman Empire, Constantinople. The treasures of Constantinople (in the Topkapi), however, reveal no cut diamonds until Suleiman the Magnificent—the Sultan of the Ottaman Empire from 1520 to 1566. Suleiman wore a large but lumpy diamond in the feathers of his turban and collected countless silver cups studded with cut diamonds; it was believed that it was impossible to obtain an audience from him without a presentation of one of these cups. Who cut these diamonds? Probably Venetians, possibly Egyptians, working along plans drawn in Paris.

But there is no history of stones coming in from ancient India already cut, although many had been cleaved. The first thing Louis XIV did with the stones Tavernier brought him from India in the seventeenth century was to send them to the royal jeweler. Tavernier declares flatly that the Moguls themselves liked a stone merely rounded off, or if flawed, the pits polished

Frederick Wells beside the four-inch-long rough diamond he found.

The Cullinan in its rough state.

After the first cleaving, the Cullinan in two major parts: left, 1,977.50 carats; right, 1,040 carats; and four fragments.

With specially made tools in his hand, a year's study of the stone in his head, a police guard around the factory and a nurse in attendance, Joseph Asscher prepares to cleave the 3,124.75-carat Cullinan.

CUTTING THE CULLINAN

After girdling and cutting, nine diamonds were made. The center stone, top, is Cullinan I; top left is Cullinan II. Both are now in the British royal regalia.

out—and that the one-faceted stone they had was cut by a visiting Venetian.

The thought that the Hindus and Persians began cutting diamonds before they were cut in Paris in the late Middle Ages is based on the supposition that the diamond would not have been as highly prized in ancient India as it was had it been known only in its natural state. But this is to misunderstand early Hindu culture. It was practical and plain, solid and sensible, and without the fantasies of display and adornment that the Roman emperors, the European courts and the early medieval churches exhibited.

Early Indian history of the diamond—recorded in stone and sung in legend—indicates that the Hindus as well as the Dravidians valued the diamond chiefly for its utilitarian hardness and strength, its ability to serve as tool or weapon, rather than as a jewel, although slices were sometime set as idols' eyes.

Before Buddha decreed that there must be no killing of any living thing, there was a legendary sword of such tremendous slicing power that it terrorized the invading Aryans who had to hack back at the Hindus with clumsy iron swords. Such was their fright that the Aryans recorded that the Hindus' swords were made entirely of diamonds, foot-long weapons of murderous glitter. This is preposterous; never has a diamond been discovered even approaching that size. Without doubt these ancient swords were diamond tipped.

Early India's use of the diamond as a cutting edge was far in advance of European use and the Hindu method of making diamond-pointed tools has been improved upon only slightly today. Doubtless the method was discovered by trial, error, and some reason.

First, apparently, the Hindus noticed that a diamond when struck on an anvil did not smash but imbedded itself in the anvil. Pliny recorded this in Rome in the first century A.D. But while Pliny then stated flatly that a diamond was stronger than iron under all conditions, the Hindus subsequently went on to discover that under some conditions, an anvil blow could break a diamond.

Did they know why? A blow must hit the diamond precisely on one of its cleavages to split it, a fact not utilized by European cutters until the eighteenth century. The Indians found it out by accident but at least they did not make the European mistake of thinking that because a diamond split it was not a diamond; instead they began wrapping diamonds in sheets of lead or wax and hitting them sharply. Then they opened the sheets, lined up the splinters in a straight line, and struck them with the edge of an heated iron sword or the tip of a hot tool. In this manner they made diamond-edged knives and diamond-tipped tools; it is, indeed, a method improved on only mechanically today. The diamond splinters enter the iron precisely and the cutting edge is deliberately created.

The great wheels used by industry today to cut marble are tipped in this manner; nothing else will cut marble with precision. The cutting edge the Hindus produced was equally superb; it could slice jade like butter, create marble lace, cut glass, carve out stone and, in the earliest years before Buddha, sever the heads of enemies from their bodies. The early stone cave architecture of the Dravidians suggests they used diamond-pointed tools before Christ; the marble tracery of the early palaces of the Moguls, the inscribed diamonds, the delicately etched jewels of Chinese jade—indeed, the pictograph for diamond in Chinese is directly related to the pictograph of a jade-slicing knife—came later, but still earlier than Europe's use of diamond point for anything but glass working. In the twelfth century the Bishop of Rennes, Marbod, an educated man for his time, summed up Western mineralogy with the report that a sapphire held in the hand during prayer brought a more favorable answer from God, an opal folded in a bay leaf rendered a man invisible, an amethyst provided immunity to intoxication, and a diamond in the hilt of a sword or in an amulet promised invincibility.

India was also ahead of Europe in mathematics. While the Hindus used zero and the decimal system, European mathematicians—that is, astronomers, builders, and accountants—measured time and space in the clumsy Roman numerals—I, II, III—like children counting on their fingers. But strangely enough the study of optics raced ahead in Europe—why, no one knows.

In the twelfth century Euclid's work on optics was translated into Latin when a Frenchman disguised himself as a Moor, learned Arabic, and stole a copy. It took a year for a monk to copy it and about a century for it to make any real impression on scholastic thought but by the mid-thirteenth century essays on the rainbow, on the structure of the eye, and on reflection and refraction were being circulated. (The invention of eyeglasses followed.)

The study of optics, of course, relates directly to the faceting of the diamond and the use of it as ornament. Brilliance and beauty in the diamond are the action of light upon and within the stone and cutting is making the best possible use of this play of light through faceting.

If lack of mathematical understanding and interest hindered the development of cutting in previous centuries, however, progress in the early Renaissance was delayed by a lack of diamonds themselves. In 1322 it was reported that a Jean Boule was working in Paris with diamond faceting; in

1400 someone called only Hermann was considered a master. But the stones of that period show little change from earlier ones; not until a steady flow of diamonds began coming into France do we see any real change in the diamond's beauty.

The turning point came in the mid-fifteenth century when Jacques Coeur, one of the world's great international traders, adorned the beautiful Agnès Sorel with the first diamond necklace in history in a deliberate effort to make the diamond esteemed as an ornament. Together they launched the modern diamond—and modern Paris, today still the world capital of luxury goods.

For while Jacques Coeur was the first diamond merchant to make history, he did not limit himself to diamonds. His position in France was that of chief financial adviser to the melancholy Charles VII, the man who followed Jeanne d'Arc's revelations to become King and then allowed her to be burned at the stake as a witch. Born humbly, the son of a furrier in the outskirts of Paris, Jacques Coeur became known as a coin-maker of facility; when quite young he was exiled for competing with the royal mint. To regain favor he joined the Pope's military forces and fought the anti-Pope with such ferocity and success that he was granted permission to trade with the infidels and travel among the heathen. When he came to the attention of Agnès Sorel he had a fleet of fourteen ships in Barcelona and fame throughout the Mediterranean.

She was by then the mistress of King Charles, a girl of eighteen with chestnut hair, pale-white skin and tranquil, smiling blue eyes. Historians have not granted her much in the way of brains, but they agree on her beneficent influence and credit her with compelling the erratic Charles (who preferred hunting deer) to throw the British out of Normandy and regain Paris. The story of his courtship is pertinent. It was in 1437 that the King first glimpsed her, the daughter of a poor but noble family; immediately he asked her to return with him to the palace at Bourges, a house so poverty-stricken that it was said that the King himself went barefoot there to save his shoes for public appearances.

She at first demurred. Looking at his portraits one might sympathize with her; he appears long-nosed and watery-eyed. But chroniclers of the period declare neither his face nor his poverty deterred her, that it was his burning of the Maid. In the language of today, she had identified with Jeanne d'Arc. Thinking his proposal over, she realized that here might be her chance to fulfill the Maid's mission and she went with the King to his astrologer. The astrologer, doubtless with one eye on the King, told her what might be expected—that it was her fate to be the love of a strong and

Agnès Sorel in a modest costume. Known as the Dame de Beauté of fifteenth-century France she was the first commoner to wear diamonds.

powerful king. She turned the prophecy to her advantage. She responded that in that case she must join the British, there was no such king in France. Charles got the point. He vowed to throw the British out of Paris if she joined him and so she agreed. After he finally succeeded in reconquering Normandy, she rode into Paris beside him trailing a train second only to the Queen herself, and trains were a major status symbol in those days.

A few moralists sneered at Agnès Sorel but most historians praised her, and the Queen's own mother, Yolande of Aragon, was said to be the brain which aided her in the exceptionally sound advice she gave the King. Probably it was through Yolande that she met Jacques Coeur; she sought him out for loans for the King's armies and he was said personally to have contributed a fifth of the amount needed to drive out the British and to have borrowed the rest, probably from the Pope.

When the battle was over, Agnès Sorel pursuaded him to become the King's financial adviser and in due course director of the mint. His ships, meanwhile, sailed continuously between Occident and Orient—pilgrims, missionaries and adventurers on the way out, laden with goods on their return. And what goods! For the first time the ladies of France had linen to wear next to their skins, sables to trim their silken gowns, pearls to drape over their lowcut bodices. The artists got cochineal and indigo, litmus and henna; for the cooks there was sugar, licorice, nutmeg from Egypt, candied fruits from Damascus, tea from China, and lemons from the Near East. Men as well as women purchased coral rosaries, ostrich feathers, pearls from Japan, and ivory from Africa. There was incense and musk for the churches, "all the perfumes of Arabia" for those who could afford them—rubies for the scabbards of nobles and coats of mail for the knights. And diamonds!

Kings had worn diamonds before, and so had a few queens. But now Jacques Coeur directed the perfecting of the diamond's beauty to change it from a royal symbol of power and wealth to a feminine ornament without equal. He imported diamond-workers from Venice and Constantinople; he sent traders into India in search not only of the big stones of status but smaller ones for necklaces and brooches as well.

And he made Agnès Sorel his mannequin. Upon her lovely neck, he placed the first diamond necklace ever made; upon her bodice were pinned gold brooches set with diamonds; and the sash of her gown was held with a diamond belt buckle. She did not like the necklace; it was heavy, she said, and the points of the stone rasped her neck. Was it because of these complaints that he set his workmen to faceting more precisely? Or did he desire more glitter for glitter's sake?

Certainly nothing but the best was good enough for Agnès Sorel to wear. And for good reason. Her silken robes lined with sable, her fur-lined shoes, her stitched-leather gloves, her bodice so decorated with rubies, emeralds and diamonds that it was said to be a "showcase of jewels"—all these brought fashion and its profitable business to the needy capital. What a pair they were, she and Jacques Coeur. She was known as the Lady of Beauty—Dame de Beauté—both because of her charms and because the castle granted her by the King was known as the Château de Beauté. Coeur was so successful a trader, importer, and banker that to be "as rich as Jacques Coeur" became slang for being as rich as the richest. Agnès gave the King three daughters who were brought up in court, playmates to his children by wedlock and then she died giving birth to a fourth who lived a scant six months after her. Her tranquil face can still be seen in the face of Fouquet's *Madonna at Antwerp;* her jewels became part of the royal jewels of France; after her death, the King bestowed them briefly on the favorite who succeeded her, her niece.

Jacques Coeur's handsome mansion still stands just south of Paris at Bourges, a fairy-tale house decorated with proverbs and adorned with witty stained-glass caricatures. Soon after the death of Agnès Sorel, a trumped-up charge that Coeur had poisoned her was made by his debtors and King Charles had him thrown into prison. His ships, his mines, his markets, and his worldly goods were confiscated and the mansions—altogether some forty —on which he held mortgages were returned debt-free to their noble owners. His wife died while he was incarcerated. Eventually he was acquitted of the poisoning charge on the insistence of the Renaissance Pope, Nicholas V, but the two years of dungeon-living had wrecked him. He died soon afterwards.

What would Paris be like today if he and Agnès Sorel had never lived? It is hard to imagine for they bent it as a twig into the tree of luxury it has continued to be ever since despite revolution, war and occupation. As for the diamond, it is more than a coincidence that in 1456 shortly after Jacques Coeur's downfall the discovery in Belgium of a "perfect" method for faceting diamonds was proclaimed.

The cutter was Louis de Berquem. He had perfected his work after studying mathematics and diamond polishing in Paris. Obviously with his protector and patron Jacques Coeur gone he needed new markets, and he was advertising for them. He developed a mathematical plan for cutting facets symmetrically plus a sauce for the jewel grindstone: diamond dust mixed with olive oil. What turned the polishing wheel? A horse? A man? A boy? Berquem's nephew, Robert, grew up in the jeweler's trade; it may be that his was the hand that first turned his famous uncle's wheel. In India

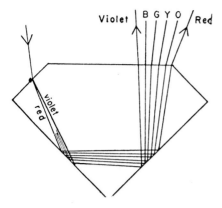

When a ray of light strikes a top facet of a diamond, part is reflected and part refracted, or bent into the stone. The part entering is then dispersed or refracted in color rays. The result, greatly exaggerated in this picture, is the diamond's fire, or blaze of color.

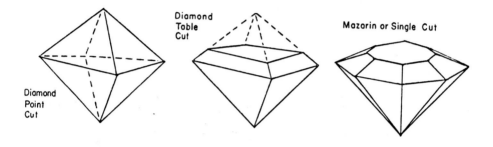

Diamond Point Cut

Diamond Table Cut

Mazarin or Single Cut

STANDARD BRILLIANT CUTS FOR DIAMOND

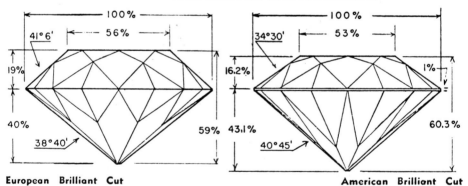

European Brilliant Cut

American Brilliant Cut

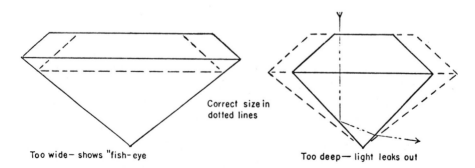

Correct size in dotted lines

Too wide— shows "fish-eye"

Too deep— light leaks out

This is refraction and every known gem has its own index of refraction which when measured accurately serves to identify it as precisely as a thumbprint identifies each individual human.

The diamond has a high refractive index. Refraction is the bending of light when it moves from one kind of transparent structure to another. The diamond—far more than glass, and even more than the prismatic rock crystal—pulls in light and bends it into its center as if it were a magnet catching a hairpin.

This is, of course, the "shining" quality of the diamond, and it was this which was enhanced by the next style of cutting: the Mazarin cut. The first diamonds which came to Europe from India were largely octahedrons, that is, they had eight sides and were shaped like two pyramids stuck together base to base—although many were missing a point or two. By the sixteenth century, however, many cleavage diamonds were coming in: four-sided pyramid chunks splintered off larger diamonds. It was natural that the cleavage side should be polished on these and obvious too that a few facets were needed on this side, but not until the seventeenth century with Cardinal Mazarin, a luxury lover like Jacques Coeur, were cutters encouraged to cut these splinters with the facets carefully placed to reveal the diamond's inner play of light.

In terms of the machinery of their time they did a handsome job; the Mazarins were the forerunners of the old mine cut and in turn today's brilliant. But they made one major mistake; they cut only 17 facets, making a sleepy stone, for light dropped through the bottom or went out the sides in great amounts. Who realized this could be stopped and how, we don't know. Slowly cutters experimented with base or pavillion facets and in 1700 a Venetian named Vincent Peruzzi cut the full 58 facets top and bottom and this was credited with making the first standard brilliant.

It was still a far cry from today's dazzling gem, however great an achievement. For while Berquem lacked an appreciation of the diamond's brilliance, or inner light action, Peruzzi lacked an appreciation for the diamond's handling of color.

This is, of course, technically known as dispersion—the separation of light into its six major colors: red, orange, yellow, green, blue, and violet. Put these together in pigments and you get black. But darkness so far as we can see it has no color, while light—although the naked eye cannot separate them—has all the colors, each color being a distinct ray vibrating at a different speed and bending (or refracting) at a different angle when it enters an object.

The diamond's reflective ability and its prismatic construction plus its dispersion make even mathematicians grow lyrical. As Marcel Tolkowsky put it: "When a ray of light passes through a well-cut diamond it is refracted through a large angle and consequently the colors of the spectrum becoming widely separated strike a spectator's eye separately so that at one moment he sees a ray of vivid blue, at another, one of flaming scarlet or one of shining green while perhaps at the next instant a beam of purest white may be reflected in his direction."

Once we understand these great optical properties other events in the diamond's romantic history become clear—why it was not considered much of an ornament until its facets were cut, why it achieved really great popularity, finally surpassing the ruby and the emerald, only with the bright light of electricity—and why a diamond-cutter is encouraged to sit and stare at the rough stones for days on end studying them and turning them over in his mind before being expected to make his faceting plans. We see too how important the mathematicians were to the diamond—why slowly weight became secondary to cut and why flaws, obstacles to the passage of light, lowered the diamond's beauty—and value.

We see too how it was that Louis de Berquem who began it all gained such renown that his statue still stands today in the harbor at Antwerp, once the greatest port in the world and still the world's greatest center of diamond cutting.

Louis de Berquem's best known assignment was to cut three big diamonds given him by Charles the Bold, then Duke of Burgundy. The most famous of the three was the presently named Florentine, an irregularly shaped diamond now weighing 137 carats. Under Berquem's steady, skilled hands and eyes, it was faceted symmetrically all over its front and back with triangular facets—an extraordinary task on a handdriven wheel.

The second stone Berquem cut was given by the Duke to Pope Sixtus IV, and according to the memoirs of that great goldsmith and lover, Benvenuto Cellini, it weighed 14 carats, was thin and long, and Berquem faceted it and set it in a gold ring to be used by the Popes at grand sacred functions.

The third was reportedly misshapen, but was cut by the clever Berquem in triangular form and set for the Duke in a friendship ring, the center of two clasped hands, and given to King Louis XI of France, the melancholy Charles VII's son, as a loyalty pledge.

For this work, Berquem got 5,000 ducats and a measure of fame; he may deserve more or less. I would think more, and that it was he who cut the belt buckle of Agnès Sorel and polished the necklace with its painful points. Certainly Benvenuto Cellini thought him the great cutter—certainly

Mr. Coster at work on the recutting of the Koh-i-Noor in a shop set up in Buckingham palace in London. His watchers are British royalty; they claimed to have helped him.

Mid-nineteenth-century cutting wheel and its parts: A, wheel shaft; B, solder dop; C, dop holder; D, hot coals for dop solder.

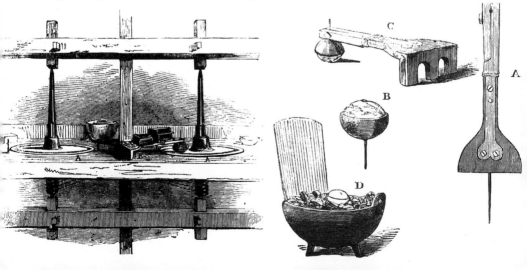

A sketch of the statue of Louis de Berquem now standing in Antwerp, Belgium.

A glimpse of the Coster diamond-cutting shop in Amsterdam in 1867. The power wheels at the left were turned by an unseen worker, probably female. Then as now tourists crowded the factory.

the great Duke of Burgundy would not trust his valuables to an unknown. Berquem must have been one of Jacques Coeur's trusted diamond workers, perhaps imported from Venice—some say his name was Luigi—perhaps entrusted with a few pages of Euclid. And undoubtedly he was protected by Jacques Coeur for like most diamond cutters of that era Berquem was a Jew and needed protection in those years of Christian violence towards non-believers. Diamond cutting until recently followed the peregrinations of the Jews; it was not so much that the medieval Jews were *allowed* to cut diamonds, but rather that they were *not* allowed to do so many other things that they had to find things no one else wanted to do and then pass these skills on to their sons and nephews, cherishing their hard-won secrets of weaving and dyeing and jewel-polishing from generation to generation, despite their homelessness, their risks of massacre and pillage.

As well as attracting customers, Berquem attracted pupils among these wanderers and just as the persecuted Huguenots brought their knowledge of silk weaving to England, the Jews of Europe took their diamond skills to the Lowlands and made Antwerp the diamond-cutting center of the world.

Not until two centuries after Jacques Coeur were they encouraged to come back into Paris by the great Cardinal Mazarin. The Cardinal loved diamonds and had twelve stones in the French crown recut in the so-called Mazarin or single cut. He also encouraged the rose cut—which later became a favorite of the Victorians. It was flatter than the Mazarin on the base, but on the top side its facets were cut like the opening petals of an old-fashioned cabbage rose. Because it was not designed to bend light up from the bottom it had little glitter by today's standards; it is a cut rarely used now.

Who or what stimulated Peruzzi to cut a full 58-facet diamond in Venice we don't know; Venice was then more of a glass bead center than a diamond center. In any event the new cut moved quickly through Europe and by the middle of the century it was being slightly redesigned to make the marquise—a pointed oval cut named after Louis XV's mistress, the fabled Marquise de Pompadour. The only distressing thing about a really big stone cut round-brilliant style (admittedly the finest cut) is that it is clumsy to wear as a ring. The marquise and oval cuts are elongated to fit the finger better.

The standard round brilliant of today with its incredible dazzle developed along with the South African discoveries and the American boom of the 1890's. The cutters claim they hit upon the precise angles by trial and error earlier. Henry Morse of Boston maintained he cut the Dewey Diamond, found in 1865 in Virginia, by "ideal standards." It was round, unlike the squarish British cuts, and dazzling. But not until 1919 when Marcel

5.   6.

These are the popular cuts for the solitaire diamond and the arrangements of the top facets:

1. Emerald cut, so called because it was first a favorite for colored stones, especially emeralds.

2. Round brilliant. Many fancy cuts are variations of the brilliant.

3. Oval cut, a fashion based on the brilliant.

4. Pear or pendeloque. Also used as a drop diamond on a neck chain.

5. Marquise diamond, a pointed oval.

6. Heart-shaped diamond, basically a brilliant cut.

Tolkowsky published *Diamond Design* were any precise angles set forth. The chief difference between the new brilliant and the old mine besides accuracy and roundness was the depth of the pavillion or base: a too-shallow diamond "leaks" light and therefore lacks brilliance.

Properly done with precise accurate angles as close to Tolkowsky's "ideal" angles as is practical, the modern round American brilliant is so alive with light and color that it appears more like a blaze of hot fire than the piece of cold stone it is. It has become the "flame of love" jewel, and is no longer a symbol of invincibility.

The pendant, pear, or lavaliere diamond is drop-of-water shaped but is also cut along brilliant lines. It is the favorite for pendant necklaces, earrings, and is seen up-ended in tiaras or flower pieces where it plays a petal or leaf role. Sometimes it is not cut but merely polished—a style called cabochon.

The heart-shaped cut is another modified brilliant cut; here the girdling makes all the difference, the faceting is standard.

It is hard to believe that a diamond in the rough will ever look like one of these beauties. It is coated with a sort of skin which dulls its luster, and it is just plain greasy. Beautifying is the long tedious exacting job of the cutters, a job which although now highly mechanized still takes hours, days and months, depending on the size and difficulties each particular diamond presents.

To make the brilliant, there are five procedural stages, each one a skilled task in itself: planning, sawing or cleaving, girdling, blocking, and brillianteering.

The planner is the man who takes the risk of deciding where a rough should be cleaved or sawed and what sort of shaping it should get afterward. If it is a big stone the planner is likely to be the owner himself; Harry Winston studies a big rough almost as long as his chief cutter does and more than once has personally put the India ink lines on the stone which indicate the sawing line. Joseph Asscher, Jr., also does his own planning on big stones, despite his skilled staff; it is said that it was he, when he first began, who showed that modern flaw-detecting machines were necessities. He studied a large stone briefly with the newly developd polariscope and marked it for cutting along one line. One of the firm's veteran sawyers cleaved it along another and the stone splintered as it hit a flaw invisible to the naked eye.

Not all stones need cleaving or sawing. Some stones come out of the mine ready to be cut. Cleaving is better for misshapen stones; sawing for octahedrons. Cleaving was not frequently done in this hemisphere until

Wollaston in 1790 began buying up unattractive, flawed stones cheaply and cleaving off the good sections for a nice profit. To cleave a stone properly the natural grain must be ascertained and the diamond grooved precisely on the plane with a diamond-pointed tool called a "sharp." Into this groove goes the cleaving knife, which the cleaver strikes with a sudden blow. Done properly, the diamond splits cleanly and the fragments fall into the box below. (It was at this point that the Cullinan's cutter fainted.)

Sawing is less dangerous, more economical on a rough and used much more widely. The saw is a paper-thin disc of phospher bronze iced with diamond dust and spun against the diamond at high speed. But it is still exacting. If the sawyer is not on a proper sawing line, the saw simply wears down; even when the line is picked precisely, it takes a full day's work to saw through a 1-carat rough.

Sawing developed in Antwerp in 1900 shortly after the first girdling machine was invented in Boston. Before this mechanical girdler, a diamond was shaped by whittling away at it by hand with another diamond. A modern girdling machine holds one revolving diamond while the cutter presses another against it; each diamond must be angled correctly and worked just long enough—or one or the other will be ruined. The old mine cut was squarish with rounded corners; the girdling machines have made possible the precise, symmetrical rounding off of the modern brilliant.

After girdling, the brilliant goes to the blocker—the man who will open up the first facets. When he receives it, the diamond is still dull; he presses it against his whirling scaif and "opens a window" into its fiery heart.

But before the wheel is started, the diamond must be carefully, accurately set either in a dop (a hot solder mass) or a clamp at the correct angle for cutting. Sometimes the blocker does this for himself; sometimes a specially trained man called a "setter" does it. The major task of the blocker is to put on the 8 main or bezel facets around the large, top table facet, the table facet itself, and the 8 facets on the base, or pavilion. When the blocker finishes he has a single cut of 17 facets but his angles are different from those of Mazarin's time.

Once the blocking is done, the diamond goes to the polisher or brillianteerer who finishes "making" it by putting on the smaller facets—24 more on the top and 16 more on the bottom. If he works in New York or Amsterdam he also makes a tiny protective facet (the culet) at the bottom point of the diamond; in Antwerp, he doesn't. Different ways still prevail in different centers; different secrets in different families. It is a clannish world, this world of the cutters, the kind of society which sociologists call primitive because of its reliance upon traditions, rituals, and relationships rather than books, laws, and officials. It has many inside secrets: one family will have its own private recipe for diamond dust sauce, another its special solder mixture for setting diamonds. It also has its own trade terms, constructed through the centuries out of French, Dutch, Belgian, and Hebrew. In Antwerp a majority of the cutters are now Catholics; in Amsterdam they are Protestants. The medieval Jewish families who began as cutters have now become merchants.

It is also curious that although successful faceting requires precise mathematical angles, the cutters themselves perform their exacting work with no study of theory at all. Instead they practice for "instinctive" knowledge. For at least three years they work under teachers learning the ways of the stone itself by looking at it and the ways of their major mechanical tools by handling them: the lathe, the wheel, the holder, the magnifying glass, and the anglers. The lathe is the cutting machine used in girdling: only the most skilled cutters become girdlers. The wheel, steeped in diamond dust, is so powerful that one slip of a finger means the loss of flesh; it moves at such speed—2,500 r.p.m.—that each facet of the diamond can be ground in a matter of minutes—unless a knot in the grain is struck. The holder may be a modern clamp or the traditional dop. The magnifying glass may be an eyepiece or a handpiece and is referred to by the cutters as a "loop" or "loup." The anglers or gauges are small steel matracers which, placed against a facet, check the mathematical angle.

It is a rare experience to watch a diamond in the process of being cut. I saw my first cutting in Philadelphia, on Sansom Street, the heart of Philadelphia's diamond district, in the shop of Jules Schwartz. Only three cutters are left in this city; in the Gay Nineties, when new money was pouring in from the coal, steel, and oil boom in western Pennsylvania, there were probably more diamonds in Philadelphia than in any other American city. Today Los Angeles, New York, and Dallas are way ahead. Many diamonds

MODERN DIAMOND CUTTING

1. MARKING. After the planner examines the stone through a magnifying glass or "loupe" (shown above) to decide how the stone should be cut, he then marks it with India ink to indicate cleaving or sawing line.

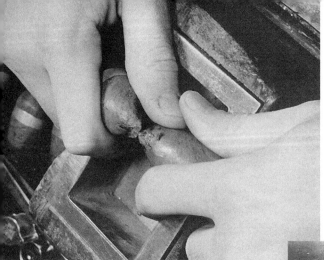

2. CLEAVING. If the diamond is to be divided with the grain, it is cleaved. It is set in a shellac mixture at the end of a "dop" (which means "little cup"). A groove is then cut into it to guide the knife along the cleavage plane. Since only a diamond can cut a diamond, the groove is made by a pointed diamond set in another dop (the lower one in the picture). Diamond dust ground out is caught in the container below for use in other steps of the cutting process.

3. CLEAVING. When the groove has been finished, the diamond and dop is set upright in another rigid holder. The cleaving knife, a specially prepared steel blade, is held in the groove. A wooden mallet or steel rod is poised above the knife, ready to strike. This is the crucial moment. If the stone has been properly marked and grooved, just a light tap of the mallet splits the diamond cleanly in two along the cleavage plane. But if the marking and grooving are off, the mallet's tap can shatter the diamond into bits.

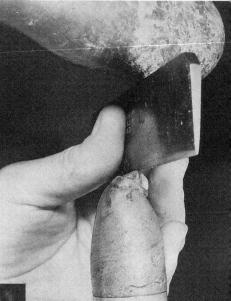

4. SAWING. A diamond is sawed when it is to be divided across its grain. It is set in solder in a metal dop which is then clamped into an arm above the saw so that the blade will cut along the line marked on the diamond. The phospherbronze blade, 35/10,000ths of an inch thick, has an edge impregnated with diamond dust. As it revolves against the diamond, it continually impregnates itself from the stone it is sawing. Although the saw runs at high speed, it takes hours to cut through even a small diamond.

5. SAWING. This picture shows three steps in the sawing operation. The four rough diamonds in the center are marked for sawing. The three holders around them have marked diamonds ready for the saw. At the bottom is a holder with one part of a diamond which has been sawed in two, while the part that was sawed off lies beside it. Each part will be finished as a gem diamond.

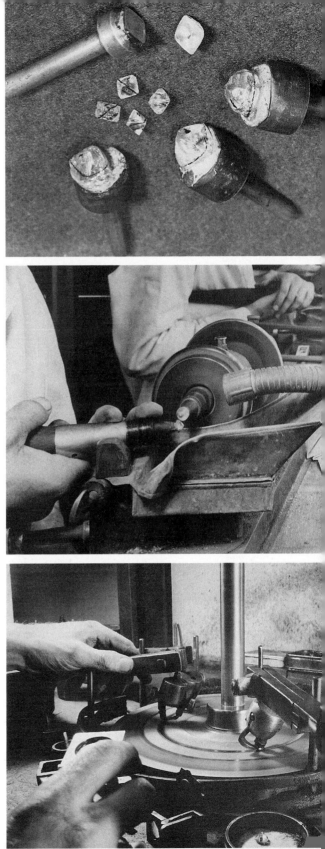

6. ROUNDING. When the diamond is to be made into the standard round or "brilliant" cut, it must be rounded after it has been sawed. The sawed part is set in a holder shaped like a spindle and mounted on a lathe that revolves at high speed. Another diamond, set into the end of a long stick, is held against it as it spins. When this operation is completed, the diamond is perfectly round at its diameter or "girdle." (Sometimes the operation is called "girdling.") The girdles of pear-shaped, marquise and oval diamonds are made in a different type of operation.

7. BRILLIANTEERING OR POLISHING. This is the final step in cutting a diamond. The stone is set into a dop and held against a revolving iron disk coated with a mixture of oils and diamond dust to produce the diamond's flat surfaces or facets. Most diamonds have 58 facets, and the angle between adjacent facets must be formed with minute accuracy; variations of even a fraction of a degree can reduce the brilliance of the finished diamond. Therefore, the cutter must check the diamond continually throughout the time it is being polished on the disk.

remain in Philadelphia's jewel cases and safe deposit boxes, but thousands were sold during the depression, partly because the heirs of the old wealth needed ready cash more than they did jewels, but partly because the Victorian diamonds looked so dowdy and few realized what new cutting could do.

This workshop was typical of a one-man workshop of the past; more and more, cutters work in companies. It was one flight up a grubby staircase; as I opened the outer door a bell rang automatically. Behind this door was another. To get inside it I had to push my credentials through the top grill. Diamond cutters don't run to posh offices of wall-to-wall carpeting; their workshops—even at Harry Winston's palatial mansion on Fifth Avenue— resemble the factories they are, but for obvious reasons all are as well guarded as a rajah's treasure house.

Most of the time, Jules Schwartz said, he worked on old mine cuts, turning them into modern brilliants; it was rather like a reducing program that ladies went on, the diamond would be a lot more beautiful when it had a better shape. Perhaps a third of the stone would be lost in the cutting, perhaps as much as a half, and only a part of the dust would be recaptured for the cutting of another diamond. He would be paid about $35 for the job: the diamond belonged to a customer of a retail store. He stopped the wheel and showed me the diamond he was working on, a tiny shining face in its lump of gray solder, then he placed it against the turning wheel again. Most modern cutters prefer a clamp to a dop, but he still used the old holder he'd gotten from his Dutch father, who had gotten it from his father.

Sometimes, he said, he cuts his own diamonds which he gets through the Diamond Dealers Club in New York. "Here," he said, "I'll show you what I got recently."

He tossed me casually what appeared to be nothing but a folded bit of white waxy paper. I fumbled with it fearing I might lose the diamond he said was in it. He took it from me and opened it expertly, popping the diamond from its inner pocket with a tapping of his little finger. The diamond sprang into view, blinked at me and dropped back into its pocket.

A few months later I was taken through Harry Winston's diamond factory and salon on Fifth Avenue and I watched a whole roomful of cutters at work on big stones and little ones. Each has his own wheel and worktable, each his own specialty. Their workshop was not rickety but it too was diamond-dusty and well-guarded. The door of the salon on the first floor can be opened only from the inside; the workshop doors can be opened only with a series of keys. On the top floor there are locks within locks—a large walk-in safe protects millions of carats of diamonds, all in waxed paper packets within brown envelopes, filed by size, shape and color.

Visitors properly accredited are welcome at Winston's Fifth Avenue salon-cum-workshop but few who are not customers or friends venture up the stairs from the handsome first floor into the designers' rooms and the cutters' area. In Holland the pattern is different. All visitors to Amsterdam are encouraged by advertisements, street signs and hotel posters to see the diamond plants in operation. While there I chose to go as a tourist through Asscher's. I entered first into a lecture room where glass models of rough and finished diamonds were shown and a description of cutting given. Pretty girl guides with multilingual abilities took us upstairs; no locks were obvious, except upon the elevator, which opened only with a key. At the end of a visit to the cutting floor we were shown examples of the various diamond cuts, all of which we were casually told, were for sale.

In Antwerp, still the world center of diamond cutting, there were no signs and no advertisements but I went to see Ferstenberg's great workshop and found a newly installed showroom on the first floor with seven diamond cutters at work but eager to discuss their methods and their stones, and a helpful guide to show tourists around. They used no old-fashioned dops, only clamps; the dust vanished swiftly in the air conditioner; though they were Belgians they used the same traditional mixture of French and Dutch words for the tools I had heard in Philadelphia, New York and Amsterdam. After the delivery of my credentials, Mr. Ferstenberg himself received me in his palatial upstairs office and showed me his collection of 360 colored diamonds or "fancies." Each was uniquely beautiful whether pale green, mauve, or bronze in tint—each cut to show off most perfectly its individual character.

Mr. Ferstenberg gets most of his cutters today from professional schools run jointly by the trade and the city of Antwerp. The workers are tightly organized. They study for three years before they are apprenticed to expert diamond-workers, and then they work another three years before they achieve status as cutters. Only in recent decades have these schools of dia- mond working been necessary; the system of family apprenticeship lasted much longer in the diamond business than in other trades. There are other schools in Puerto Rico, Ireland, Israel, and South Africa but the old myth prevails that there is only one way to learn to cut a diamond, and that is by doing it.

But more than one man has learned through mathematics—the most notable being Mr. Briefel, now of the cutting firm of Briefel and Lemer in London. Briefel was the man who cut the Elizabeth Pink when it was known as the Williamson because of the mine it came from rather than the queen who received it. He is a man with a degree in mathematics from the Uni- versity of Vienna and would probably be a math professor today had not

The diamond-cutting showroom of Ferstenberg's, Antwerp, Belgium.

An industrial diamond blade cutting through a block of Brazilian agate, a very hard stone. Made by MK Diamond Products, Hawthorne, California.

the Nazi purge of Jews in Austria sent him to Belgium as a refugee. There was no work there for a mathematician but there was for a diamond-cutter, so, working out his angles with pencil and paper he became one. "They said I couldn't do it that way; that they had done it their way for generations," he told Emily Hahn in 1956, "but I did it my way and succeeded."

There is more to cutting than angles, of course, but the angles are the secret not only to the play of light but also the elimination of flaws. In order to remove pits or black spots, for instance, it is necessary to cut the angles so that the black spots will find themselves near the surface of a facet and thus be in a position to be ground away as the facet is finished. An experienced cutter sees such spots and gauges their position immediately; beginners are confused by the angled light within the diamond as to where the spots actually are. Another difficulty for the beginner is what color the diamond is: even experienced diamond cutters can be surprised by a diamond that has several shades of color—usually yellows—in it. The goal here is to cut the diamond down to its purest white, except when the color is of such strength that the finished stone may be valued as a fancy.

Louis de Berquem is honored in Antwerp as Lodewyck van Berken, the name he was known by when he first lived in Bruges, the medieval port of Paris, and copies of his statue are sold as souvenirs in the Pelikanstrat, Antwerp's diamond way. When he came back from Paris after Jacques Coeur's death he went to work in Antwerp. His statue shows him wearing his working clothes: a short dress or jerkin, with a holster on its sash which presumably carries the tools of his trade; he is holding a diamond the size of a marble in his right hand. In this diamond center of the world—the place where fourteen thousand diamond-cutters work and where four thousand traders, manufacturers, and brokers make diamonds their way of life—the inventor of modern cutting is the legendary hero—one of the few of history's workmen ever to have been so honored.

A diamond cutter of the Renaissance and his hand-driven wheel. The small pan is for the diamond dust sauce.

4

Famous and Infamous Diamonds

The diamond is beyond contradiction the most beautiful creation in the hands of God in the order of inanimate things. This precious stone, as durable as the sun, and far more accessible than that, shines with the same fire, ties all its rays and colors in a single facet and lavishes its charms, by night and day, in every clime, at all seasons.

MARQUISE DE MONTESPAN, mistress of Louis XIV, in her *Memoirs*.

*I*t is a curious experience for anyone who knows anything of diamond history to stand before one of the great old diamonds now boxed in museums. There like a tamed giant it rests in its velvet-lined case, boxed in by bulletproof glass, locked in by careful hands, guarded by hired trustees, its beauty exposed to any passing tourist but the secret of its power hidden in its still and silent crystals.

Standing there, looking into it, I find in myself both triumph and frustration. My heart pounds out exultantly: "There it is—the great whatsis!" It is as if somehow, by a miracle, I have come face to face with a great immortal hero of the past. But at the same time I am annoyed. I want to cry out to it: "Speak up! Tell me what really happened to you—what made you happen."

And then I look hard at it, seeking in it some hint of the first slave to see it, the first shah to turn it in his hand, the spot where it lay when the robbers were searching for it. But there is only its glittering brilliance; none of the violence and passion of its life shows in its face, none of the power and the glory it has reflected, and created, and wrecked is visible.

It is not difficult today to see one of these great old diamonds. The Koh-i-Noor is permanently in the Tower of London; the Hope in the Smithsonian Institution, the Regent in the Louvre and the Orloff in the Kremlin. From time to time historic diamonds tour the not-so-great museums; some, indeed, are to be seen on display at charity shows and fund-raising fairs. Anyone can look at them now; anyone can study the small cards beside them coolly relating high points in their history. The small boys whistle and cry "Howja like that rock?" the girls giggle to each other and a man says to his wife: "A bit larger than yours, isn't it?" There is excitement in just looking, but there is an even greater excitement waiting for those who know what they see.

The Koh-i-Noor presents us with the greatest stuff of dreams because the Victorians claimed it was an ancient important diamond. It was alleged to have been found by the Godaveri River and held as a sacred treasure by the rajahs of the huge territory in India then called Malwa—now divided into Indore, Ghopal and Gwalier—since "time out of mind," as a rajah reported in 1304.

When the Moguls invaded Malwa, reportedly they either seized it from the rajahs or exacted it in tribute. It then came into the hands of the famed Sultan Baber, founder of the Mogul Empire in India. He was a direct descendant of Tamerlane and a diary keeper. In his diary of May, 1526, he mentions a "famous diamond," a jewel so valuable that it would pay "half the expenses of the world." It weighed, he said, around 200 carats.

For almost two centuries the Moguls ruled Malwa, building the famous city of Delhi, trying to subdue the Hindus, trying to convert the non-believers into Moslems. In the early eighteenth century, the Mogul kingdom and all its jewels were seized by the Persians, who boasted particularly of having found "the famous diamond of history."

But what was the most famous diamond in history to them? The largest or the oldest? For there was a great diamond newly found.

It was in the seventeenth century that that adventurous French diamond merchant Jean Baptiste Tavernier traveled to India and recorded a number of Indian diamonds, many of which he saw when he visited the last of the great Moguls, Aurangzeb. Aurangzeb was a mighty man with as great an inheritance as any man who ever lived, the son of Shah Jehan, the descendant of Baber. Although he never achieved his ambition to rule the whole of

The intrepid Jean Baptiste Tavernier, French diamond merchant who traveled the Orient for jewels for Louis XIV. Note the fur-lined cape and turban—presents from the Shah of Persia in 1670.

India, but only held the northern half, he tried. He imprisoned his father, fought off his brothers and invented an iron claw which he wore like a glove but used as a disemboweling weapon. He called himself with reason Alamgir, or Grasper of the Universe; he had a taste for extravagant show and a weak son, but neither killed him; he died in his bed at eighty-nine before his enslaved and suffering subjects could revolt. Behind him he left a poor, rioting, vulnerable citizenry.

When Tavernier saw him in 1665 he was at the height of his power. A scholar who spoke not only Hindustan but Turkish, and a lover of jewels, Aurangzeb welcomed the Frenchman and after entertaining him several times offered to show him his diamonds, most of which he had seized from his father, along with the court jeweler, Mir Jemla, who dealt with Golconda, the fabulous diamond market.

Despite his many travels Tavernier never had seen such magnificence. Aurangzeb sat on one of seven jewel-encrusted thrones and watched while four eunuchs brought in two large trays lacquered with gold leaf and covered with small cloths, one of gold-embroidered red velvet and one of green, and all but the great Aurangzeb stood at attention while two keepers of the jewels counted each stone three times and wrote out an inventory. This clearly took a maddeningly long time; Tavernier injects into his description at this point the nervous remark that "the Indians do everything with great care and composure, and when they see anyone acting in a hurry or irritated they stare at him in silence and laugh at him for being a fool."

Finally, however, the head keeper placed the jewels in Tavernier's hand. The first was a giant diamond, a rose-cut piece later called The Great Mogul which had been cleaved and faceted by the Venetian cutter Hortensio Borgia who had visited India sometime earlier. Tavernier called this diamond "the great diamond"; he said it weighed 280 carats but was only part of a greater jewel recently found near Golconda, which had once weighed 900 carats. In form, he said, it was like an egg cut in half. He was not shown any historic diamond.

In 1739, some thirty years after Aurangzeb's death and almost seventy-five after Tavernier's visit with him, Nadir Shah of Persia invaded India and captured Delhi and the fabulous Mogul palace. For fifty-eight days he systematically looted the city seeking among other things a famous diamond known throughout the world to be among the Mogul jewels. At last a woman from the conquered Mogul's harem betrayed the secret; the jewel, she said, was hidden in the folds of the emperor's turban. It was not customary at that time and place to attack enemy leaders personally so Nadir Shah took advantage of an old Oriental tradition and invited the emperor

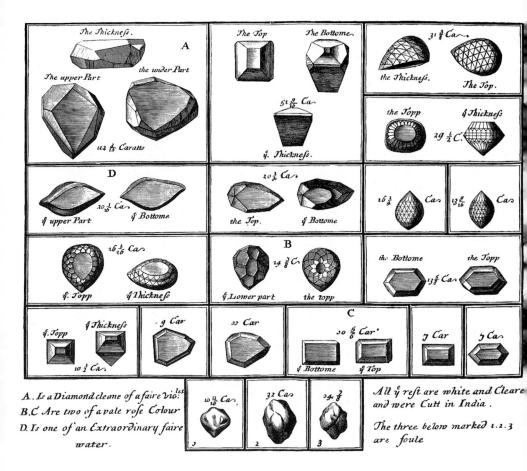

A. Is a Diamond cleane of a faire Viollet
B.C Are two of a pale rose Colour
D. Is one of an Extraordinary faire
water.

All ÿ rest are white and Cleare
and were Cutt in India.

The three below marked 1.2.3
are foule

Copy of an illustration as it appeared in the first English translation of Tavernier's book on his travels to India. The King referred to in the heading is Louis XIV. Tavernier picked these stones as "the fairest" out of thousands of diamonds he sold him. Louis' own favorite, Diamond A, is the violet-blue diamond from which the Hope Diamond was cut. Many of Tavernier's customers liked presents: he gave pistols, watches, bronze objects and pearls to them and paid in gold for diamonds, rubies and harem veils of silk embroidered with gold thread.

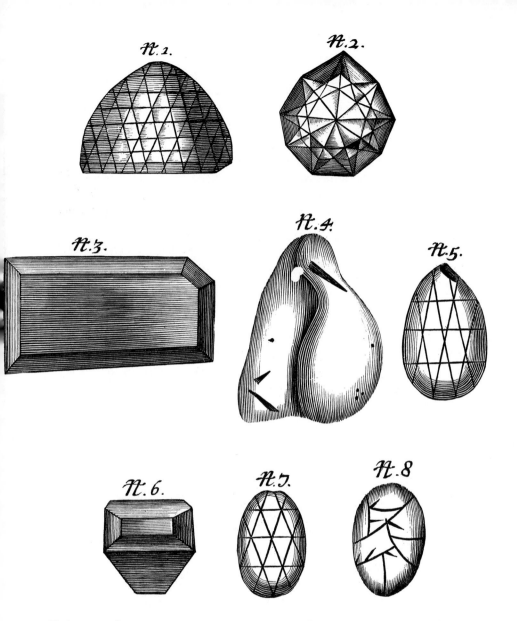

Eight gems known to Tavernier and portrayed by him in his seventeenth-century book. No. 1 is the almost 280-carat stone which belonged to Aurangzeb—known as the Great Mogul, from which the Koh-i-Noor was cut. No. 2 is probably the Florentine; Tavernier calls it a citron-colored diamond and said it belonged to the Grand Duke of Tuscany. No. 3 is a 242-carat stone from Golconda which Tavernier refused to buy as too costly: Streeter later named it the Great Table; some think today it was a ruby. No. 4 was an Indian cut diamond Tavernier bought for "a friend." No. 5 is the same stone after being recut in Europe. No. 6 is a diamond from the Tollur mine in India as it was cut at the mine. Nos. 7 and 8 are the cleavages from a single stone Tavernier bought in India and had cut in Europe. The certain whereabouts of none of these diamonds are known today.

to a banquet celebrating the Persian victory. At dinner, he suggested politely that the two rulers, the victorious and the vanquished, exchange turbans. Even while speaking he effected the change, removing first his own sheepskin turban adorned with gems then removing the other's and shifting the latter swiftly to his own head. The emperor showed neither chagrin nor concern; indeed, so unperturbed was he that the Nadir Shah feared he had been duped. Hastily he withdrew to his tent and unrolled the silk to find a single great diamond. "Koh-i-Noor!" he murmured. "Mountain-of-light!" and so he named the stone.

Was it the Great Mogul? Or was it the stone Baber knew? If Nadir was disappointed he gave no sign of it then or later. The Koh-i-Noor became his prized possession, the most renowned of his many jewels and upon his assassination the most fought over of his treasures. Upon his death it went to his son, who died by torture rather than give it up; it went then to a friend, who went through a few more tortures—including boiling oil on the head—to keep it in the kingdom. It was lost eventually with the kingdom and went first to the Afghans and then to the Sikhs; it was in the treasury of Lahore when that state was annexed to British India in 1849. The British seized it then as reparations—by now the empire term for booty—from the Sikhs. Two officers were then ordered to take it to London and in 1850 it was presented to Queen Victoria at a great levee at St. James's Palace.

But although it had been no disappointment to the Nadir Shah, it was to the British who were expecting something the size, shape, and glitter of the Great Mogul. Instead of 280 carats it now weighed 187; it looked mutilated rather than faceted. It was placed on public exhibition and people said it was dull, without fire. It was said the British were duped. And so, despite the beliefs that it carried an ancient curse, the Queen decided to have it recut in the hopes of gaining greater brilliance.

A Mr. Voorsanger of the great Coster firm in Amsterdam was imported to cut it and was paid $40,000 for the job. A steam engine of 4 h.p. to drive the cutting wheel was set up in the workshop of the crown jewelers. It took thirty-eight days of twelve hours each to complete the task. Prince Albert set the stone in the dop, or holder, and the Duke of Wellington started up the wheel. The job was not much good. During the process the Koh-i-Noor lost 78 carats in weight—from 187 to 108.93—and gained almost nothing in brilliance. Prince Albert said openly he was dissatisfied; diamond collectors of the period said that now only the legends surrounding the stone gave it value. There was no desire then to put it in the crown, or the sceptre or any other important place; for a long time it was kept

The Koh-i-Noor as it was set by the Persians.

The Koh-i-Noor on public view at the Crystal Palace Exposition in 1851.
Most people were disappointed in it.

The present Queen Mother's Crown containing the Koh-i-Noor.

in a box in Windsor Castle with a replica sitting in the Tower for tourists to look at. Once in a while Queen Victoria wore it as a brooch and when she did, her subjects in India were relieved to notice that it did not bring the troubles to an empress that it had to emperors. Victoria left it to her daughter-in-law Queen Alexandra who wore it to her coronation, but it was not until 1911 that it was used as a power symbol, and placed as the central ornament in the crown of Queen Mary.

Meanwhile, in 1883, Victoria's royal jeweler, Edwin Streeter, in a book entitled *The Great Diamonds of the World*, declared flatly the Koh-i-Noor was Baber's ancient diamond, not the Great Mogul that Tavernier saw. The Great Mogul, he said, was lost. Other diamond buffs jumped into the controversy and suggested that maybe, on the other hand, Tavernier described the Great Mogul inaccurately, that it was Baber's stone. In 1889 a geologist specializing in India, Dr. Valentine Ball, edited an edition of Tavernier replete with footnotes and appendices. In it he proved that the Koh-i-Noor was clearly the same diamond as the Great Mogul and that it was Baber's stone which had vanished. Unfortunately, jewelers rarely read scholars in those days, and Ball was ignored for some time. In 1929, however, Oxford University republished his work with footnotes of their own, and credited both Tavernier and Ball generously. Although the story continues to be related that the Koh-i-Noor is the oldest diamond known to man, all the facts suggest it isn't—it's just one of the oldest: the Great Mogul, mutilated and badly cut.

In 1937 the Elizabeth who was the wife of George VI, and who is now Queen Mother, had it transferred to her crown where it still is, except for the few occasions when she removes it to wear as a brooch. Most of the time it is on view in the Tower. The present Queen Elizabeth II has never worn it though it is highly doubtful that she fears it. As Streeter put it in his 1883 account of the diamond, "a strange fatality presided over its early vicissitudes but its alleged 'uncannie' powers have now ceased to be a subject of apprehension."

Looking at it today in the Tower, one can see how it might have disappointed the Victorians, and how, purely as a diamond, it is outshone by far by the modern Cullinans near it. But the questions of its origins, of who first held it, when and where and whether it was once the most esteemed diamond of the Moguls gives it an attraction no "new" diamond can match—even for those who suspect that Streeter, a devoted admirer of the great queen, meddled with diamond history to add to Victoria's glory.

But do not think for one moment that Aurangzeb or his father, the Shah Jehan, the man who built the Taj Mahal, thought of the *present* Koh-i-Noor diamond as their finest diamond. For they knew diamonds of all sizes and shapes, as indeed did all the men of South India, and the diamonds they cherished most were big, bold and beautiful, even when poorly cut.

There was the diamond that today we call the Orloff, for instance, an almost 200-carat gem, shaped like half an egg, and once one of a pair of diamonds set in the eyes of an idol of the god Sri-Ranga in a small village temple about two hundred miles above the southern tip of India. When they were placed there and by whom, we do not know; the temple in which the god sat was magnificent, with seven distinct enclosures, lofty towers and a gilded cupola, all of which was surrounded by an outer wall some four miles in circumference. According to a French traveler named Dutens writing about precious stones in 1783, this magnificence attracted another Frenchman, a grenadier who had deserted India's foreign legion and found some sort of a job near the temple in order to steal the renowned diamond eyes. Since no Christians were allowed near the area, he disguised himself as a native Brahmin and went constantly to the temple to pray. In due course he was trusted with the job of guardian to the inner shrine and one stormy night managed to wrest one of the eyes from its socket, and making his way to the coast, sold it in Madras to a British sea captain for £2,000. The captain returned it to England where he sold it for £12,000. It wound up in the hands of a Persian jeweler named Khojeh. The Persian took it to Amsterdam and in 1774 met Prince Orloff there and persuaded him to buy it as a gift for his Queen, Catherine the Great of Russia.

Prince Orloff was delighted with the chance. He was in Amsterdam because he had displeased Catherine with his handling of a Turkish-Russian crisis—or perhaps she was just bored with him. They were not exactly a charming couple; she had been a German princess and she married Peter of Russia—whom most historians considered a foolish sort of fellow—solely to get the Russian throne. She got it, too, declaring herself Empress the first time Peter went out of town, and then kept it with the help of not only Gregory Orloff but also his three brothers all of them reputedly her lovers. At the feast of her name day in 1776, Gregory presented her with the jewel instead of the traditional bouquet of flowers. Graciously she accepted it but unluckily for the by now out of power and impoverished Orloff boys, she did not reinstate Prince Gregory or his family in her favor.

For a final touch of irony, she had the diamond mounted on top of the double eagle in her imperial sceptre—the sceptre she would have neither won nor held without the Prince's early devotion, and his diplomatic skills. She preferred collecting jewels to men, however; she established her own cutting mills near the gem mines in the Ural Mountains and was said to wear 2,536 diamonds in her crown alone.

Now for another question from history: Is the Orloff perhaps in truth

the Great Mogul diamond? Since it was shaped like half an egg many diamond scholars state quite flatly that there is no doubt at all that it is indeed the selfsame half-egg diamond that Tavernier held in his hand while
Aurangzeb watched. It also is cut like a rosette with a large number of
small facets, just as Aurangzeb's father was said to have had the Great
Mogul cut. And it has never been recut since it was cut in India; Catherine
was content merely to mount it in her sceptre, not change it. Of course,

Two brooches, a jabot pin and necklace worn by Catherine the Great of Russia in the late eighteenth century. She demanded perfect gems and perfect
workmanship and got it. Note the unusual pear-shaped pearl and diamond
leaf on the jabot pin.

the Great Mogul diamond reportedly weighed almost 100 more carats than does the Orloff and no one can explain how, if it did once belong to the Moguls, it wound up in a Brahmin temple—but such details do not unduly perturb those who wish to take sides in the bloodless but intense present-day diamond battles and who pay no heed to Dr. Ball's scholarly investigations.

A third major diamond in public view today is the Hope Diamond, famous for its violet-blue color and its fascinating history of bringing bad luck to its private owners. There is no doubt that it was one of the diamonds Tavernier brought back from India but just how he got it is something of a mystery; an English cutter charges he stole it from the eyes of a god named Rama-Sita and the bad luck that followed it is part of Rama-Sita's revenge. This same cutter, however, states that Tavernier himself suffered from his theft: that he was devoured by wolves on the steppes of Russia. It is quite true that Tavernier died during a trip to Russia and quite possible he was chased by wolves (although wolves are not in truth the man-hungry beasts legend would have them) but it is also true that it was winter and Tavernier was eighty-four at the time of his death and could have died of a bad cold.

In any event, Tavernier first showed a magnificent blue among other diamonds to Louis XIV in 1668 after returning from his sixth trip to India. Le Roi Soleil or Sun King, as he liked to be known, liked practically all of the diamonds and he bought 45 large ones and 1,122 smaller ones, paying what amounted to about a third of a million dollars for the lot, and granting Tavernier a barony in the bargain.

The blue was the largest. It was 112.50 carats and Louis XIV admired it so much he designated it "The Blue Diamond of the Crown." According to one of his mistresses, the Marquise de Montespan, he kept his prize jewels in a special closet of rosewood divided within "like cabinets of coins into several layers," and he was ever greedy for more diamonds, paying any price to get them. The Marquise shared his passion but feared the blue because of its legend of ill-fortune.

It was first cut Indian style but about five years after Louis bought it he had the royal goldsmith cut it in the form of a heart. In 1774 Louis XVI inherited it and Marie Antoinette wore it. When the revolution broke out, the tribunal placed the blue, with the other crown jewels, in a glass case in the Garde Meuble, listed it on the inventory and then guarded it so carelessly that robbers—if indeed the robbers and the guards were not the same people —had little trouble carrying it off. Unlike some of the other jewels, however, the Blue Heart was never seen again.

It is probable it was sold in Spain and cut there into three smaller stones.

Louis XIV (in black wig) of France loved diamonds. It was he who first wore the unlucky blue which later was cut to the Hope. He bought it from Tavernier, the great seventeenth-century diamond merchant, along with more than one thousand other diamonds.

The Goya portrait of Queen Maria Louisa shows her wearing a deep blue diamond cut much like the one that was offered for sale in London in 1830 —now 44.50 carats of rounded oval. Henry Philip Hope, a rich banker, bought the diamond for $90,000; it was exhibited in the same Crystal Palace exhibit that showed up the Koh-i-Noor. Soon after it was recognized (by Streeter) as a piece of the French Blue; but it stayed in the Hope family until the turn of the century and the legend of its sinister influence began again.

It was recalled that Montespan had lost her place in court soon after wearing it, that Louis XIV had died a miserable death of smallpox, and that Louis XVI and Marie Antoinette had been executed. The Hopes themselves added to the stories: the original Henry Hope died without marrying, the nephew he left the stone to willed it to a grandson who changed his name to

A Goya portrait of Queen Maria Luisa of Spain proudly wearing her share of the French Blue, presently known as the Hope Diamond. Painted in 1799, the portrait is now in the Taft Mueseum in Cincinnati.

Top stone is the French Royal Blue Diamond brought .to Louis XIV by Tavernier before it was cut to a heart shape. The small bit known as the Brunswick Blue was proven part of the original blue. The second from bottom stone was cut from the French Royal Blue, probably in Spain after the diamond was "stolen" from the Garde Meuble, the French treasure house, during the Revolution. It is the same stone as seen in the Goya portrait. At bottom is the stone as set when Evelyn Walsh McLean first saw it in Cartier's in Paris. By then it was known as the Hope Diamond. These sketches were published originally in color by Streeter in 1882.

get it, but whose wife ran off with another man. The last of the Hopes went bankrupt and the stone was sold to a jeweler.

It changed hands frequently in the next few years. A Folies' star who wore it was killed by her lover; a Greek broker who bought it fell off a cliff with his wife and children; the Sultan of Turkey was forced to sell it when faced with revolution. And then Pierre Cartier the French jeweler bought it.

It was at Cartier's that Mr. and Mrs. Edward B. McLean found it. He was the son of the millionaire publisher, John R. McLean; she was Evelyn Walsh, the daughter of a miner who, in her words, "struck it rich," and they each had $100,000 from their respective fathers for "something nice in a wedding present." Two hundred thousand was exactly the price Cartier wanted for the Hope, but Mr. McLean didn't want it enough to give up any part of his cash for it. Mrs. McLean settled for another diamond but she still yearned for the Hope and when, a year later, Cartier arrived in Washington with it reset in a necklace she raised $154,000 to buy it from him.

She loved it. There was no doubt of that. Their son was killed in an automobile accident, their daughter died of an overdose of sleeping pills, and Mr. McLean himself suffered a nervous breakdown and died in a mental hospital; but while gossip said the Hope was their undoing Mrs. McLean placed no stock in the legends about her diamond. She wore it almost constantly, stuffed it in a cushion when she didn't, and hired a detective to stand by on all occasions so that she wouldn't be robbed of it. At one point she pawned it to raise money to help find the Lindbergh baby, but the man she aided was the impostor Gaston Means. Many were the friends who handled her necklace; countless were the World War II servicemen hospitalized at Walter Reed Hospital in Washington, D.C., whom she entertained with a look at it.

Mrs. McLean died in 1947, a legend in her own time, and the Hope Diamond was bought by Harry Winston along with other jewels in her estate for more than $1,000,000. He first displayed it in his Fifth Avenue salon, then sent it on display about the country in charity shows, and in November, 1958, mailed it to the Smithsonian Institution. The stamps cost him $145—$2.44 for postage and the rest for insurance of $1,000,000. It hangs in a case there now along with another diamond Winston once owned—the Portuguese, a 127-carat emerald-cut diamond that in the twenties belonged to the much-married Peggy Hopkins Joyce, and which later belonged to Marjorie Post May. Along with the Washington Monument and the White House the Hope is one of the tourists' favorite sights. Rarely is the spot in front of the case empty and most who look at it, young and old, fall silent briefly before its colorful splendor. Is it indeed unlucky to own it?—to fall in love with it? Many are those who think so; many are those who find something sinister in its sea-blue depths. Others call its legend nonsense and suggest that the First Lady should be allowed to wear it or that it should be used for science because of its amazing power to conduct electricity.

There are four other blue diamonds which gemologists have thought at various times to have been cut from the rest of Louis XIV's Blue Heart. One is a small stone of 6 or 7 carats put on sale in 1874 by the heirs to Karl II, Duke of Brunswick. Another is a larger stone, of the same blue, of 13.75 carats, which came from the same collection but after close examination, it was decided that this was too large to have been cut from the Blue Heart when the Hope Diamond was, although it may have been part of the original blue Tavernier brought home. A third is a blue diamond tip of about 1 carat that Streeter himself acquired soon after he determined the Hope was part of the French blue. The whereabouts of these diamonds is unknown today— nor is there any knowledge of whether they too are considered harbingers of bad luck.

The Regent, although its tale also begins in skulduggery, brought at least one owner good fortune, although it all but ruined his reputation doing it. Its story begins with a sharp-eyed slave working in the famous Parteal mines on the Kistna River in India in 1701. In the rough, the diamond was enormous—410 carats—and when the slave spotted it he was willing to risk his life smuggling it out rather than simply turn it in for a prize. Cutting a hole in his leg, he stuffed the stone into the wound, secured it by bandages and took off for the seacoast where he found a British skipper he thought he could trust. His mistake was fatal. The captain offered him an escape to freedom for half the value of the stone but once at sea, stole the stone and flung the slave overboard. Returning to shore, the captain then looked up a man named Jamchaud, the largest diamond merchant in the Orient at that time, sold the stone to him for a £1,000, squandered the money, and eventually hanged himself.

Jamchaud now had a hard time selling the diamond, partly because of its size, partly because it was stolen property. It is possible Thomas Pitt, who eventually bought it, knew this, for he drove a hard bargain with the merchant. Pitt was the British-appointed governor of Fort St. George, near Madras, a young man on his way up and not rich. Having heard about "large diamonds to be sold," as he put it in a report later, he invited Jamchaud to come down to Madras as his guest. Jamchaud brought the huge rough diamond with him but while Pitt bought some small ones, he balked at the £85,000 price (almost $500,000) which Jamchaud asked for the big one.

The Regent Diamond. Once the worrisome possession of the Pitt family of eighteenth-century England, it now belongs to the Louvre Museum in Paris.

The Tiffany Diamond, the largest canary diamond in the world, now set in a diamond, platinum and yellow-gold ribbon clip by Jean Schulberger.

The Stewart Diamond, one of the early lucky finds in South Africa.

Over a period of months Jamchaud came to and fro, trying to make a deal. He finally came down to £20,400 and the diamond was Pitt's. News of the stone got around slowly but it *did* get around and by the time Thomas Pitt returned to England some eight years later, he was being referred to as "Diamond" Pitt and the stone was named the Pitt. Few believed he had come by it honestly, however, and repeatedly he had to answer slanderous attacks with an account of his purchase. He sent the stone to cutters and it took them two years working by hand to cut it to the brilliant of 140.50 carats it is today: it cost him £25,000 to get the job done but he retrieved the dust, sold it for £7,000 or £8,000 and had the extra bits turned into some rose cuts Peter the Great of Russia bought. All together Pitt made a profit out of the cutting but the job of selling the big diamond itself was difficult.

This was particularly so since Pitt suffered from a morbid fear of theft and murder. While carrying the diamond he disguised himself, never slept in the same house more than two nights and if recognized refused to show the diamond or admit he carried it. Finally in 1717 he sold it for £135,000 to the Duke of Orleans, then the Regent of France because Louis XV was too young to rule. The negotiations cost him £5,000, but he turned a tidy profit on the deal and with this he restored the fortunes of the ancient House of Pitt, a family which was soon to give us William Pitt, the member of Parliament who favored fair treatment for the American colonies and for whom Pittsburgh was named. Thomas Pitt himself, however, was not able to clear his name; seventeen years after his death his account of the original transaction was published for the second time by his son, to whom he had left the account in his will.

After its sale in France, the Pitt was called the Regent but its adventures were far from finished. In the royal inventory of the French court it ranked as the crown's most valuable stone—appraised at £480,000—or almost $2,500,000.

In 1792 when Louis XVI and Marie Antoinette were imprisoned, it was, like the other jewels, placed in the Garde Meuble and, like the others, stolen by the robbers who scaled the colonnades and shattered the glass case. Unlike the Hope, however, the Regent was immediately recovered from a ditch near the Champs Elysées in Paris. It was then sent to the Ministry of France who put it in the cellar but used it for collateral on loans. When Napoleon came to power it was free of debt, and he had it set in the hilt of the sword he carried when crowned emperor. It stayed there until he went into exile to Elba, when Marie Louise, his wife, pried it out and took it home to Austria with her. Her father, however, made her send it back to

Napoleon divorced Josephine when she bore him no children. When Marie Louise, his second wife, bore him a son, Napoleon gratefully showered her with diamonds. Portrait is at Versailles.

Paris and Charles X of France wore it on his crown. When Napoleon III came to power he loaned it to Empress Eugénie. French queens are not crowned and cannot wear royal jewels, but she had it set in a Greek diadem for her hair, which she dutifully left behind her when she escaped from Paris in the carriage of her American dentist, Dr. Evans of Philadelphia. When the crown jewels were put up for auction in 1887 the diadem was kept back and placed in a case in the Louvre where it has remained since—except for that period during World War II when the Germans occupied Paris; then it went into hiding in a stone-covered safety box at Chambord. It is not the draw the *Mona Lisa* is, nor the familiar friend the *Venus de Milo* becomes; like a horse put out to pasture it rests quietly, attracting little of the attention it drew in the days of the Pitts, the Bourbons, and the Bonapartes, when it was said to be worth about $5,000,000 not only because of its flawless brilliance but because of its then unique size; it was the largest cut diamond known in the Western world until the African diamonds were discovered.

The Regent Diamond went from the British to the French; the Grand Sancy Diamond reversed this route. It went from the French to the British.

The Sancy's story begins in Constantinople in 1570 when Nicholas Harlai, the Seigneur de Sancy and the French Ambassador to Turkey bought the stone in Constantinople. It was an almond-shaped beauty faceted Indian-fashion on both sides. Although a jewel fancier with quite a collection, Sancy used this one to advance himself by loaning it out to the pleasure-loving King Henry III of France. Henry had become totally bald at twenty-six and liked to cover up the fact; the diamond went immediately into a brooch for his turban and was worn continuously. He was not an attractive man and was a hated king; he spent his time cuddling lap dogs and entertaining himself with a group of dwarfs, ignoring the fact that the country he allegedly ruled—Catherine de Medici, his mother, did the real ruling—was rent with wars and counter-wars, for this was the period of religious revolution. Finally Henry was stabbed to death by a fanatic monk, the throne passed out of the House of Valois, and the diamond was returned to Sancy—now the French Ambassador to London.

Henry IV of Navarre, the new king, however, attempted to borrow it back because he wanted it for fund raising purposes. Sancy agreed but the messenger he sent with the stone vanished on his way to the king and for some time it was thought that either the boy had run off with it, or he had been murdered for it. Going over the route the messenger took, Sancy found the lad dead, but, believing in his loyalty and his wit, explored the matter—and found he had swallowed the diamond. This time Sancy took the diamond back to London with him and sold it to the British Crown. In 1605 James I listed it with a group of other precious gems as part of a large brooch called "The Mirror of Great Britain." Then, in 1644 when England was in a decline Queen Henrietta Maria, the wife of Charles I, took some jewels to Paris and sold the Sancy Diamond separately to Cardinal Mazarin, the French diplomat. Before his death Mazarin willed it and seventeen other diamonds to the French crown with a request that they be known as the Mazarin diamonds. The next time we know of it being worn is when it was set with hundreds of other diamonds in the fabulous crown Louis XV wore at his coronation. At the famous inventory of 1791, it was valued at a million francs—about $250,000.

It was stolen from the Garde Meuble like the others, but it is thought it turned up in Russia—although no one really knows. The next documented fact is almost a century later. In 1906 William Waldorf Astor gave it as a wedding present to his son's fiancée, Nancy Langhorne of Virginia. As Lady Astor she had the 55 carat pear-shaped beauty set in a tiara and wore it at coronations, balls, and now and again at the famed parties she gave at the Astor country house, Cliveden, during World War II. Heralded in her youth for her beauty and in her middle years for her acid wit, Lady Astor retired from public life in the 1950's—she had sat in the House of Lords—but she kept her famed Grand Sancy and in 1961 allowed the Louvre to exhibit it. In 1964 she died at eighty-four. The English government decreed the stone a national treasure and her heirs paid no inheritance tax on the ancient, priceless stone.

As well as unconfirmed reports of another large Sancy, there is also a "Small" Sancy. This is 34 carats, but it is a splendid brilliant and was called by the French Beau Sancy, and by the English, Little Sancy. It went to Germany; it was bought by Prince Frederick Henry of Orange in 1647 and passed down to his grandson King Frederick I of Prussia. It was identified at a Hohenzollern wedding in Berlin and listed in the Austrian jewel inventory of 1913. No one knows where it is now; it has not been put up for public sale despite the fallen and impoverished state of the Hohenzollern family since the 1918 German defeat.

Another diamond that may well have been purchased by Nicholas de Sancy since it turned up in the French court about the same time as the other Sancies is the pear-shaped, pale pink diamond of 50 carats now known as the Chantilly Pink.

This diamond, like sweet Chantilly crème and Chantilly lace, got its name from the beautiful and famous Château de Chantilly in northern France, the home in the seventeenth century of the princes of Condé, and today owned and run by the Institute of France as a combination museum and park. The first Louis, Prince of Condé and Duke of Bourbon, was a great fighter; when only twenty-one he was placed in charge of the armies of France and in the first five years of the Thirty Years War became a national hero. The pink diamond—then known as the Grand Condé—and the estate of Chantilly were given him as reward by Louis XIII. The châtelet, or small house, he lived in and where in his later years he and his son entertained Molière, Racine and La Fontaine is still standing; the immense palace built in the nineteenth century burned down but fortunately the Condé treasures were safe in the old châtelet.

The Grand Condé Diamond remained in the family until 1892 when it was bequeathed to the French government in return for a promise that it never leave the family chatelet and the other family treasures.

To those who come fresh to the study of diamond history the fluctuating adventures of the old diamonds swarm with confusion. The threads of their individual lives influence not only their own histories but history in general —for they were not merely beloved jewels, but wealth as well. It is the theory of the British historian C. Veronica Wedgwood that the sixteenth-century purchases of diamonds by the Tudors contributed greatly to the Tudor

Queen Henrietta Maria of England, wife of Charles I. It was her task to sell the Crown Jewels in Paris in 1644. This portrait was painted by Van Dyck.

bankruptcy, since the Tudors were inclined to give diamonds away as gifts, bribes, and rewards for loyalty oaths. Miss Wedgwood points out that if Henry VIII had stuck with gold posey rings, or even land as presents, he would have left a far greater inheritance to Elizabeth the Great, and she in turn might not have died in debt if she had sold off her diamonds or at least not gone on buying new ones.

Although the French were finally wrecked in a too-brilliant display of extravagance, their interest in diamonds began with more caution, viewing them at first as merchandise—as encouraged by Jacques Coeur in the fifteenth century—and later as good things to be borrowed or presented rather than purchased and given away.

Charles V had forty-three diamonds in his crown. Francis I was a great diamond collector but with Louis XIV of the seventeenth century the downfall of the Bourbons began. He was the great royal purchaser of French diamonds. His purchases, his bankruptcy, the robbery and subsequent sale of the crown jewels from the Garde Meuble in 1792 can easily be paralleled with the Tudor's purchases, their eventual bankruptcy, and the sale of the British crown jewels in 1644 during the Puritan revolution. It is curious to note that among the major diamonds only the Sancy was involved in both these debacles—and that the man Sancy himself, like Tavernier, was more interested in *using* his diamonds to advance himself than he was in sporting them as displays of power or giving them away as bribes.

In a sense, of course, it can be said that the English were the customers of the French until the modern period. Certainly there is no great English merchant of luxuries to match either Jacques Coeur or Tavernier, or even Sancy—Pitt bought only one diamond of note. The English crown family revived, however, about the time the French crown was giving out; by the nineteenth century England had India and South Africa to give them diamonds both as booty and tribute.

Over and over again in the histories of different diamonds we come upon the same handful of names and these can be easily divided into diamond lovers, diamond users, and more recently diamond students. The merchants like Coeur and Tavernier and, generally speaking, Sancy and Cardinal Mazarin, who used diamonds for their own advancement, were French; the lovers are of all nations—the Tudors, the Bourbons, Napoleons, the kings of Portugal and Spain, the czars of Russia. The students begin with Edwin Streeter and Valentine Ball of the nineteenth century and include such modern gemologists as Robert Shipley, G. Robert Crowningshield and Richard Liddicoat. With the American-born diamond lovers like Mrs. McLean and Lady Astor the beginnings of the Western democratic period appeared wherein private citizens competed and cooperated with government museums so that the range of diamond merchandising, study, and adoration was spread among millions.

The most influential *piece* of diamond jewelry in Western history is rarely mentioned in lists of historic gems today but the role it played was greater by far than that of many another famous jewel. I am talking, of course, about the diamond necklace which Marie Antoinette of France vowed in vain that she did not buy, the necklace which in historians' eyes set off the French Revolution, the necklace which involved the whole court of Versailles in scandal, which . . . but it is necessary to begin at the beginning of the story.

In the first place the necklace was not made for Marie Antoinette at all but for Madame Du Barry, mistress to the old King Louis XV. But he died of smallpox before it was purchased and the royal jewelers, Boehmer and Bassange, who had spent two years in collecting the flawless stones for it, were in desperation when they found they had no customer. For this was no ordinary necklace; it was, in the gaudy language of Thomas Carlyle "a glorious ornament . . . fit only for the Sultana of the world . . . indeed, only attainable by such."

And what diamonds! Five hundred of them . . . "A row of seventeen glorious diamonds, as large almost as filberts, encircle, not too tightly, the neck a first time. Looser, gracefully fastened thrice to these, a three-wreathed festoon, and pendants enough (simple pear-shaped, multiple star-shaped, or clustering amorphous) encircle it, enwreath it a second time. Loosest of all, softly flowing from behind in priceless catenary, rush down two broad three-fold rows; seem to knot themselves around a very Queen of Diamonds, on the bosom; then rush on again separated, as if there were lengths in plenty; the very tassels of them were a fortune for some men. And now lastly, two other inexpressible threefold rows, also with their tassels, will when the Necklace is on and clasped, unite themselves behind into a doubly inexpressible *six*fold row; and so stream down, together or asunder over the hind neck—we may fancy like lambent Zodiacal or Aurora-Borealis fire."

The mere description leaves one gasping. The jewelers, however, began weeping at Louis XV's death. For three years they traveled Europe talking to kings and queens, but there were no buyers. They returned to France, to the teenage Louis XVI. He was taken with the necklace, but Marie Antoinette— who admittedly had "a passion for diamonds"—rejected it. "We have more need of a ship of war than of necklaces," she said. The American Revolution raged around France. She had already spent a fortune on jewels. Once more the jewelers came back, now literally in tears. "Take your necklace to

An exact replica of the famous Diamond Necklace which brought scandal to Marie Antoinette. If duplicated in fine diamonds today it would be worth something like $4,000,000. This paste piece was made in Paris.

pieces," she said scornfully. "Even if you drown yourself in weeping, you will get no help from me."

But this was not the end of it. There lived near Versailles "a bright-eyed tatterdemalion," a young woman named Jeanne de St. Remy de Valois, the descendant of an illegitimate son of the Royal House of Valois who received a pittance from the court for her heritage and married an equally poor count, La Motte. But she was ambitious. And so was born "The Affair of the Diamond Necklace."

Let us begin by tersely stating the original plot: as hatched in the greedy minds of the Countess La Motte (sometimes called La Valois) and her husband it was simple enough. By pretending that Marie Antoinette had changed her mind and wanted to buy the necklace secretly, the La Mottes hoped to get the necklace for their own uses. Unable to pull off the swindle alone, they gathered in accomplices: (1) the foolish Cardinal de Rohan, who was only too eager to believe the Queen—who disliked him and showed it—needed his help; (2) a young prostitute who pretended for a few francs one moonlit night to pose as the Queen; (3) a friend-forger who would sign the Queen's name; and (4) for extra courage a magician-soothsayer named Cagliostro.

How nearly they all pulled it off! How carefully they plotted! They succeeded in hoodwinking the jewelers, arranged excellent terms (payable in five installments), and received the necklace; then they hacked it to pieces with a kitchen knife and the forger and the Count went off and sold it in London. But they were hoist on their own petard. As the money rolled in from the sale of the diamonds, the La Mottes' extravagance knew no bounds: he soon wore two or even three emerald and ruby rings on each finger; she traveled in a satin-lined carriage with six horses, their harnesses glittering with diamonds and topazes. Indeed, the La Mottes spent their booty so furiously that they could pay only the interest on the first installment of the necklace's cost—not the principal—and when time for the second installment came around, they had no money left for it—and dared not offer one of the diamonds! So inevitably, but unwittingly, the jewelers again came pleading to Versailles and suddenly, the whole swindle came apart like a flimsily made toy.

If Louis XVI and Marie Antoinette had had either wit or money at that moment perhaps even then they could have been spared the scandal that rocked France, shocked the world—"it filled me with dread like the head of Medusa might have done" wrote Goethe—and which finally brought them both to the guillotine. But the Bourbons' bankruptcy foreclosed bribery, and pride shut out perception. The Cardinal, astounded that he had been duped, offered to pay for the necklace, but the King would have none of it. Crime and lese majesty must be punished; the conspiracy must be made public. And so he called upon Parliament to arrest and try the bumbling Cardinal, the sinister La Mottes, the pretty young prostitute, the eloquent Cagliostro.

Now the whole wayward, extravagant, playful life of Versailles rumored about so long became public knowledge; now the anti-royalists and the courtiers confronted each other openly. The judges dealt swiftly with the obvious; the Countess La Motte was sentenced to be beaten twelve stripes, branded with a V—for *voleuse* or thief—on her shoulder, and imprisoned. The prostitute was exiled, Cagliostro censured. But the Cardinal? For sixteen hours they deliberated the Cardinal's guilt. Had he been criminally disrespectful toward the Queen when he believed she came to him by moonlight in a secret conspiracy of frivolous greed? Or had it been understandable that he would believe her capable of such a thing? The crown begged the Queen be upheld and he be found guilty; the people cried that even his arrest was camouflaged to protect the extravagances of the Queen.

He was acquitted. The Queen, once so beloved, had lost her last vestige of respect. Lists of her alleged lovers (male and female) circulated through the crowds cheering the Cardinal; horrid ditties of court debauchery mingled with lewd laughter. The rumors about Versailles, of the masked balls, the set of intimates at the Petit Trianon, the reports of elaborate gowns, dazzling jewels, and favors easily granted—all had readied the hungry, dowdy people of Paris to believe the worst. "Though in all the preposterous intricacies of the necklace affair Marie Antoinette was, in a sense, blameless, she remains blameworthy that so gross a swindle could have been attempted and victoriously achieved under cover of her name," the historian Zweig summed it up; Carlyle had said it before him even more picturesquely: "Beautiful Highborn that were so fouly hurled low! *Thy* fault in the French Revolution was that thou wert the Symbol of the Sin and Misery of a thousand years."

And the necklace? There is a single strand of twenty-two diamonds belonging to the Duke of Sutherland. Who knows where the rest are? No jeweler has ever boasted of handling them—no woman ever knowingly gazed at them fondly. Wherever they went, into rings, stomachers, tiaras, to be recut, reset, they are lost to history. The glorious ornament fit only for a Sultana perished with shame; the five hundred diamonds gathered painstakingly from the ends of the earth to enhance the beauty of one youthful neck succeeded only in extending another's to the axe.

But nothing can stop great diamonds from gathering in great hands. In the Near and Far East some historic ones are still held by rulers, others have disappeared—but may appear again—and at least one was purpose-fully pulverized.

Of the diamonds now in the East, the best known is the Akbar Shah, heralded largely because it was one of the stones believed to have been in the famous Peacock Throne of Aurangzeb. Tavernier saw it there at a fabulous ceremony of the Great Mogul in 1665. The traditional weighing in was an annual festival rather like a birthday party; the shah was weighed on a balance scale, the other weight being precious metals and jewels. The point of the act was to see whether the shah was "worth his weight in gold" as the saying became. Aurangzeb did not; he refused even to have himself weighed. The nobles of his court presented him with precious baubles as presents and the shah was expected to give away his weight in gold to the people. During the preparations for the event, Tavernier was permitted to come to the palace and look about.

The sights he saw were dazzling; even Versailles in all its glory was not so splendid as Aurangzeb's palace built by Shah Jehan. Try to imagine it: the courtyards are covered for the event in red velvet embroidered so heavily with gold that "the poles which are erected to support them are of the size of a ship's mast" and those near the great hall are "covered with plates of gold of the thickness of a ducat." Inside the Palace are seven mag-nificent thrones. One is wholly covered with diamonds, the rest with rubies, emeralds or pearls. (The Moguls by religious decree could not *wear* jewels.)

On what Tavernier calls the Great Throne, soon to be called the Peacock Throne, he counts 108 huge rubies and about 116 emeralds. Above it hangs a canopy the underside of which "is covered with diamonds and pearls with a fringe of pearls all around, and about the canopy, which is a quadrangular-shaped dome, there is a peacock with elevated tail made of blue sapphires and other colored stones, the body of gold inlaid with precious stones, having a large ruby in front of the breast, whence hangs a pear-shaped pearl of 50 carats and of a somewhat yellow water. On both sides of the peacock is a large bouquet of the same height as the bird, con-sisting of many kinds of flowers inlaid with precious stones. On the side of the throne opposite the court there is a jewel consisting of a diamond of from 80 to 90 carats in weight, with rubies and emeralds round it, and when the Emperor is seated he has this jewel in full view. At four feet distant from the throne two umbrellas are fixed, on either side, the sticks of which for 7 or 8 feet in height are covered with diamonds, rubies and pearls . . ."

Many other Europeans saw the Peacock Throne but Nadir Shah of Persia, the conqueror who got the Koh-i-Noor and/or the Great Mogul diamond, destroyed it, keeping some of its jewels and selling or trading others. The Akbar Shah reputedly was one of the peacock's eyes; it was 116 carats in weight and eye-shaped. It was further enhanced by three inscriptions, one of which gives it its name: "Shah Akbar, the Shah of the World, 1028 A.H." It is unhappily inaccurate: Shah Akbar ruled NOT in 1028 A.H. (for *after hegira,* meaning the flight of Mohammed out of Mecca) but a century earlier.

The mistake reveals that Akbar did not do the inscription—that Shah Jehan, Aurangzeb's father did. The second inscription reads proudly: "To the Lord of Two Worlds, 1039 A.H. Shah Jehan," (1630 A.D.), and it is well known that Shah Jehan kept his own jeweler and knew as much about diamonds as any man. Engraving a diamond is a fantastically difficult art.

Undoubtedly the Akbar Shah Diamond was taken to Persia when the Nadir Shah went in 1739, but after that it disappeared until 1866 when an Englishman with the unromantic name of George Blogg bought it in Constantinople and took it home with him to London. There, alas, he followed the fashion of his time and had it recut, losing 46 carats in the process and changing it from eye-shaped to tear-drop-shaped and losing the old inscriptions. But it was still desirable in Oriental eyes, fortunately for Mr. Blogg, who promptly sold it to the Gaekwar of Baroda, for £35,000 or about $175,000. Presumably it is still among the Baroda treasures.

Another stone from the famed Peacock Throne is simply called the Shah. It too is inscribed but in this case the inscriptions appear to be more accurate. The first places the stone in our year 1591: "Bourhan Nizan Shah II in the year 1000," it says. The second is "Son of Jehangir Shah, Jehan Shah 1051"—or 1641. So we are back again to Shah Jehan, the creator of the palace at Delhi as well as its fabulous Peacock throne, the builder of the Taj Mahal in Agra—indeed the Pericles of India. To me it is eminently fitting that Shah Jehan should be known both for his great collections of diamonds and for the delicate marble beauty of the Taj Mahal. If it is true as I have theorized that it was a diamond-pointed tool that made this type of building possible it would indeed take a diamond lover-cum-user to carry it out. What did the Shah Jehan use to make his diamond inscriptions? Obviously, a diamond—for nothing else will work on a diamond. Shah Jehan may not have been a good diamond faceteer—but this work requires both higher mathematics and the use of diamond dust. Obviously what Shah Jehan knew was diamond knives or diamond-pointed tools.

But back to the famed Shah Diamond itself. The Persians who captured Delhi had a third inscription put on it: "Kadjar Fatkh Ali Shah," a shah who reigned in our year 1824.

Mumtaz Mahal, wife of Shah Jehan. The Taj (or tomb) Mahal was built to honor her memory. Jehan planned another Taj of equal beauty facing it for himself but their son Aurangzeb imprisoned him before he could build it.

Shah Jehan, builder of the Taj Mahal, owner of great diamonds and fifth Mogul of India: 1628–1658.

The stone stayed in Persia sixty-five years. Then when the Russian ambassador to Persia, Griboyedoff, was assassinated in Teheran in 1829 the Persians gave the Shah Diamond to Czar Alexander III, partly in reparation, partly as "a token of grief." It is now believed to be in the Kremlin, a part of the Russian Treasury of Diamonds and other precious stones.

By tradition the Darya-i-Noor was said to be the other eye of the peacock on the great Peacock Throne of Shah Jehan and Aurangzeb but it seems unlikely that it and the Akbar Shah were ever a pair. The Akbar Shah was only 116 carats before it was cut; the Darya-i-Noor was—and still is—186 carats. Streeter thought it might have been one eye and the Koh-i-Noor the other, but remember, if we agree to that we must then disagree with Professor Ball, who said the Koh-i-Noor was the badly cut version of the Great Mogul, which Tavernier held in his hand while the peacock still had both its eyes. It is Ball's theory instead that the Darya-i-Noor was Baber's diamond. It was certainly the same weight.

In any event, the Darya-i-Noor, or "Sea of Light," formed part of Shah Jehan's collection and was studded about somewhere on the Peacock Throne or some other throne. Certainly it was one of the stones Nadir Shah brought home to Persia with him in his wagon-loads and camel-packs of loot. His successor possessed the stone along with another great diamond, the Taj-e-Mah—"Crown of the Moon"—which was about the same size, and Aga Mohammed had to use torture to get them plus the throne of Persia. When he won, however, he put both diamonds in two great bracelets which he wore one on each arm on court occasions to impress British visitors who came away exclaiming over their fire and beauty. We get the first rapturous accounts after the British treaty with Persia in 1739. More recently, in 1961, Queen Elizabeth and Prince Philip of England were impressed by the Darya-i-Noor (no one knows what happened to the Taj-e-Mah) on their state visit to Iran.

So much for the stones of the Peacock Throne. It is a great yellow diamond, the Florentine, we will call into focus next, and no one knows its origins or its present whereabouts.

The Florentine's history begins in 1475 when Berquem cut it. In 1477 Charles the Bold, one of the dukes of Burgundy, was said to be wearing it when he fell in the battle of Nancy. Where he got it no one knows; it is reported that it was among the diamonds Jacques Coeur imported into Paris. A foot soldier filched it from the dead Duke's body—"a large lump of yellow glass" he thought it—and sold it as a death souvenir for a florin.

For about two hundred years it changed hands many times, reportedly

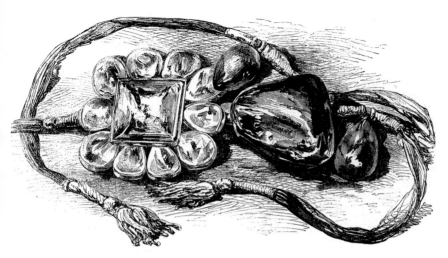

The Darya-i-Noor Diamond was once part of the Shah Jehan's fabulous collection.

Charles the Bold, Duke of Burgundy in the fifteenth century, was the first man known to commission Louis de Berquem to cut diamonds for him. He was the owner of the Florentine Diamond as well as many other famous diamonds.

for small sums of money, no one recognizing its real worth. Pope Julius II is said to have owned it briefly.

Then in 1657 the Medici family showed it to that redoubtable traveler Jean Baptiste Tavernier and at last it was restored to its true honor. Tavernier noted it weighed 137.27 carats, and its cut was a double rose of 126 facets with an irregular nine-sided outline and had it sketched among his favorite diamonds. From the Medicis, the Florentine passed to the House of Austria; it was now conqueror's loot, or at least that is my explanation of why Anna Marie Ludovica, the last of the Medicis, willed it to Francis of Lorraine, who had become the ruler of Florence in 1737.

Francis of Lorraine had married Maria Theresa of Austria, an arrangement which soon brought him into great power in central Europe. By 1743, when he actually received the Florentine Diamond, he was Holy Roman Emperor; but his jewels were part of the Austrian Crown Jewels.

The Austrian house—the Hapsburgs—held their jewels and a considerable amount of power until World War I when their empire fell and the family was sent into exile. Then, as impoverished kings are likely to do, they began there to sell their treasures, but they had little luck. A lawsuit complicated the sale, a too-cunning adviser disappeared, and the Florentine, among other jewels vanished. Many thought the adviser had taken it when he scuttled off to South America. Today there is no public knowledge where the Florentine is and rumors only confuse the question. After World War II a bright public relations officer in the American Third Army reported that American authorities had found and restored the missing Florentine to Vienna after finding it in Nazi hands. They had indeed found a large yellow diamond—but not the Florentine; it was the Austrian Yellow, a brilliant once in the Hapsburg crown. On another occasion it got mixed up with the Shah of Persia, a pale yellow cushion-cut diamond of 99.52 carats, long owned by the Russians.

We speak of these vanished diamonds because it is quite possible for them to turn up again; unlike the kings who owned them or the buildings and crowns they have adorned, they never die, fall apart, and only rarely are they buried in the dust of the ages. Sometimes they are cut to smaller diamonds but even that is a memorable occasion; their history is rarely lost in this manner.

One great diamond which had been "lost" for many years turned up not too long ago in a very strange place indeed. It is the Nizam, a rough-cut glittering rock of 277 carats. It was one of the last of the Indian diamonds mined, found in 1835 in Hyderabad, home of the historic mines of Golconda. Then it was 440 carats, but either it was dropped and it split along a cleavage or when it was cut, it broke. In any event its facets are irregular and its beauty lies chiefly in its impressive size.

What is it worth? Because today large diamonds are rare indeed and because few can afford really great chunks it would first have to be cut and then divided. But its owner does not really care what it is worth anyhow, for he is the Nizam—or administrator—of Hyderabad and reputedly the richest man in the world by far. As well as gold, land, and precious jewels of all sorts which have been part of his family heritage, he has more than his share of diamonds. But still it chagrinned diamond collectors elsewhere to learn in 1934 from *The New York Times* reporter Herbert L. Matthews that the present Nizam allowed the past Nizam—his father—to use the Nizam diamond as a paperweight.

There is one diamond, however, which will never turn up again and that is the Pigott, an Indian gem which got its name from Lord George Pigot (the proper spelling) who received it as a gift when Governor of Madras in 1763. It was a "small" diamond variously reported at 45 to 85 carats but handsome, a nice tribute to have; but it brought neither him nor his family luck. Pigot, after some sort of skulduggery, died in prison, his family put the diamond up for lottery, and the winner sold it for a fraction of its worth. Probably he needed a little cash more than he needed a lot of diamond. It then came into the hands of Rundell and Bridge the London jewelers who were smarter and they sold it for $150,000 to Ali Pasha, a noble of the Turkish court and the tyrannical "lion of Janina" ruler of Albania, when Albania was an important power. Ali Pasha was said to have kept the Pigott in a pouch tucked in his sash, but it was no aid to his fortune. The Sultan of Turkey sent an emissary to bring him back to Istanbul for excessive ambition; he fought back and was fatally wounded. He requested permission to die in his own throne room, in his own fashion, and upon being granted this last request, he ordered that his two most precious possessions be destroyed: his beloved diamond, the Pigott, and his wife, Vasilikee. A captain crushed with mighty blows the diamond to powder before his eyes but while his wife awaited her destruction, Ali Pasha died.

It is possible, of course, that other diamonds of note have been destroyed by men as possessive as Ali Pasha. But it is not likely to have happened in secret. Great diamonds were always recorded; they do not turn up as surprises in an old attic. It is more likely that in some immense vault or some other guarded retreat of the rich the so-called vanished diamonds rest in small cloth bags blinking in the light only on grand occasions.

We now have a few more great names in the diamond world to add to our collection. I would put Shah Jehan and Nadir Shah among the diamond users but Aurangzeb among the adorers—Ali Pasha being an extremist in this category. But we have spent enough time among the old diamonds, however fascinating, and must move on. The Indian diamonds have the most eventful history; they have come through the most sanguinary battles as clean and as shining as the day they were first washed. But the newer diamonds have their romances too, especially those from Brazil and South Africa.

The first of size and repute to come from the Brazilian mines was the Star of the South (Estrella du Sud)—261.88 carats—and it was also the largest diamond by far to have been discovered by any woman anywhere. The finder was one of the slaves imported from Africa, who worked at the Bagagem mines and when she found the giant diamond in 1853 she received her freedom plus a lifetime pension. At first the Brazilians had trouble marketing the gem; Indian diamonds were held to be far superior. It brought $200,000 in the rough but some years later, after it was cut at the great Coster plant in Amsterdam, to 128.50 carats—it was found to contain an inner fire of beautiful pinkish color and a Paris syndicate took it and publicized it under the name Star of the South. In 1867, they got their reward—the Gaekwar of Baroda bought it for $400,000. It stayed in his family almost a hundred years and in 1934 was part of a necklace of delicately colored diamonds, another of which being the historic Dresden Green.

Whether the necklace was broken up or whether it was sold in one part we do not know, but today the Star of the South is believed to be owned by Rustomjee Jamsetjee of Bombay.

The largest gem diamond found in Brazil, and the third largest known to have been found anywhere, is the Vargas, 726.60 carats in weight when a poor farmer stubbed his toe on it in the Santo Antonio River in 1938. Sold first for $56,000, it was bought by Harry Winston for $600,000 and cut into twenty-three gems, eight of which were emerald cuts weighing from 17 to 48.26 carats each. The largest of these retained the Vargas name—after Brazil's president—and it is now believed to be owned by Mrs. Robert W. Windfohr, wife of the oil millionaire of Fort Worth.

Brazilians discuss other of their diamonds by name but these are the two which have received world attention. Will there be others in the future? The mines at Minas Gerais are almost exhausted, but there are still prospectors working the Brazilian river beds and still stories told of diamond finds to lure on the adventurous.

South Africa is today's home of the diamond. The first diamond found there—the one which started the first diamond rumors in 1867—is now known as the Eureka—meaning "I found it" in Greek—but for decades it was known simply as the O'Reilly. The man who found it was Schalk van Niekerk who also found the second, a rough diamond of 83.50 carats which he sold for $56,000 to Louis Hond, a diamond cutter. Cut into an oval, three-sided brilliant of 47.75 carats, it was christened the Star of South Africa and resold for $125,000 to the Countess of Dudley, who had it mounted with ninety-five smaller diamonds as a brooch for her hair.

It was this diamond which persuaded the world there were really diamonds in South Africa and set off the great Diamond Rush.

There were other lucky diamond finders in those rough-and-ready days of intense excitement. Antoine Williams found his big one when his pick bounced off a rock so hard it leapt from his hand. He was just another adventurer; his "partner" Robert Spalding had got up the cash—$150—for a cheap site along a creek running into the Vaal River for him to work on. For two days after his find Williams couldn't eat; the stone was 296 carats in the rough. It was first named after Spalding, who sold it for $30,000 to a Port Elizabeth merchant named Stewart, who renamed the stone Stewart and sold it, still in the rough, for $45,000. It kept Stewart's name: it was cut to a brilliant of 123 carats but where it is now is not known. Streeter may have owned it in the nineteenth century.

The Tiffany, the Excelsior and the Jubilee were found more routinely; they were all mined. The Tiffany, the largest golden diamond in the world, was mined in the famous Kimberley mines in 1878, a 287.42-carat chunk, and sold to Tiffany's of Fifth Avenue the following year. They had it cut in Paris by George Frederick Kunz to a cushion-shaped brilliant of 128.51 carats with 90 facets—32 more than the standard brilliant cut—and it is these extra facets which give it the effect of a pool of pure sunshine or a smoldering fire.

It has been shown at several world's fairs and in between is on display at Tiffany's shop—sometimes in the window, like a golden star, and sometimes inside in a case. For seventy years no one wore it; then it was mounted in a necklace and worn at the Tiffany Ball in Newport in 1957. Allegedly it is for sale for $500,000 but no one has even been urged to buy it.

The Excelsior was found in the Jagersfontein mine in the Orange Free State in 1893, almost a half-pound in the rough—995.20 carats—and shaped like the famous half-egg Tavernier handled. It was plucked by a worker from some gravel he was shoveling; in reward he got a saddled riding horse and some cash. At the time it was the largest diamond in the world and a true blue white. For ten years it was kept intact and then in 1903 was cut by Henri Koe of Asscher's in Amsterdam. The resulting gems—twenty-one in total—were sold separately and namelessly, many of them by Tiffany's to customers who also preferred to remain nameless.

The Jubilee was also found at Jagersfontein, two years later. It weighed 650.80 carats in the rough and originally was named the Reitz Diamond after the then President of the Orange Free State. It was cut, however, in 1897, the year of Queen Victoria's Diamond Jubilee, and from it—now a cushion-shaped brilliant of 245.35 carats—it got its new name. Today it is owned by the Paris manufacturer Paul Louis Weiller, and he now and again lends it out for exhibition. It is particularly admired by gemologists who consider it perfectly cut; its facets are so exact that it can be balanced on the culet—or point—which is less than two millimeters across. It is also, because of this perfect refraction, pure white in color, great in depth, and particularly brilliant.

Among the diamonds found in the modern period the Cullinan is the most famous. It was found by chance in the Premier mine in 1905, the largest lump of gem-diamond crystal known to have been discovered: 3,106 carats, or about one and one-third pounds.

The Premier is the world's most de luxe mine, opened in 1903 some three hundred miles northeast of the Kimberley mines, where the diamond rush to South Africa originally took place. It is the De Beers showplace, a masterpiece of technology and was named for Cecil Rhodes, the diamond genius who founded De Beers and who was Prime Minister of the Cape Colony at the time the mine was planned.

The giant Cullinan came as a surprise. The mine superintendent, Frederick Wells, on an inspection trip, saw it sticking out of one of the side walls reflecting the setting sun. At first he thought he was being tricked by a lump of yellow glass but he pried it out anyway. It turned out to be not only genuine but huge—with three natural faces and a cleavage face, suggesting it had once been an even larger lump. He got a reward of $10,000 when he turned it in to De Beers. The company named it after the man who had opened the mine—Sir Thomas Cullinan—and sold it to the Transvaal government for $750,000 two years later.

The government in turn presented it to King Edward VII on his sixty-sixth birthday, mailing it to London by parcel post while publicly a dummy stone was shipped off as a decoy with great publicity and a couple of burly guards.

King Edward was of course delighted, and he sent it to Asscher's in Amsterdam to be cut, promising that it would be kept among the British Crown Jewels. In February, 1908, J. Asscher, after months of study, cleaved

The late Queen Mary of England in 1910 wearing the four major Cullinan stones as pins.

Crown of Queen Mary of England with Cullinan III in top and Cullinan IV in band. The big stone in the middle is cut rock crystal stone set there in 1937 when the Koh-i-Noor was transferred to Queen Elizabeth's (the Queen Mother) Crown.

British Imperial Sceptre set with Cullinan I, the largest cut diamond in the world.

British Imperial State Crown with Cullinan II in band

the diamond; the first steel blade broke against it while the Cullinan did not. On the second try, it cleaved as planned. It was then divided and subdivided, resulting finally in nine major gems, ninety-six small brilliants and 9 carats of polished fragments.

Two of the major gems are today the largest cut diamonds in the world. The largest is named the Great Star of Africa, but generally spoken of as *the* Cullinan: it is 530.20 carats and is mounted in the British Imperial Sceptre and on permanent display at the Tower of London. The second largest is called Cullinan II, a square-cut brilliant of sixty-six facets weighing 317.40 carats, and is set in the Imperial State Crown and like the Great Star/Cullinan is one of the British Crown Jewels.

The cutter, Mr. Asscher, got the other gems in payment for his nerve-wracking, highly skilled work, but he did not keep them around as trophies. A small one—the Cullinan VI—of 11.50 carats, cut as a marquise, was bought back immediately by Edward as a gift to his wife Queen Alexandra, and it is now a drop on an emerald-and-diamond necklace which Queen Elizabeth II wears.

Then in 1910, the Union of South Africa bought the other six name stones as a gift for the then Princess of Wales—later Queen Mary—when she came to open the Union's first parliament. Her father, Edward VII, died and she couldn't go after all but they mailed them to her instead. Two she put in her crown—Cullinan III, a 99.40-carat pear shape, and Cullinan IV, a 63.60-carat square brilliant. Set together, they were also detachable as a brooch. The other four she had made into personal jewelry: Cullinan V, an 18.80-carat heart shape, was first in a brooch, but when the Koh-i-Noor was removed from her crown and placed in her daughter-in-law's, she put the Cullinan V in its place. Cullinan VII and Cullinan IX she continued to wear. Cullinan VII, an 8.80-carat marquise, she used as a pendant on an all-diamond brooch: Queen Elizabeth II wears it now. Cullinan VIII, a 6.80-carat oblong brilliant, she put in the center of the all-diamond brooch. Cullinan IX, a 4.40-carat pear shape, she had mounted in a ring with claw setting. Queen Elizabeth II inherited it, too, along with the others but is rarely seen wearing it; her usual diamond is her 3-carat diamond engagement ring—the most modest stone in her truly magnificent collection of diamonds.

It is rare indeed today when a large diamond is found outside a mine—even in South Africa—but the discovery of the Jonker suggests it can still happen. Jacobus Jonker, a diamond miner by trade, found it on his day off, right in his own backyard like the legendary bluebird of happiness. It was after a heavy rain in 1934 that he went out to see what the storm had turned

The Jonker Diamond in the rough compared in size with a large hen's egg.

The twelve stones cut originally from the Jonker. Jonker I is in the center as it was when it was emerald cut to 142.90 carats. Later it was recut to a 58-facet, 125.60-carat oval

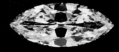

up and picked up the egg-shaped stone, washed it and discovered he had a millionaire's dream of a diamond.

It was then 726 carats. He gave it to his wife and she put it in a stocking, tied it around her neck, jumped into her featherbed and hid there for three days while Jonker went out to sell the stone. He got $315,000 for it from the Diamond Corporation, but what he did with the money, we don't know.

The stone went to London by ordinary mail (at a cost of sixty-four cents) and the news of its discovery went before it. Harry Winston cabled for an option on it and then flew to London to see it. After studying it for a month he bought it and shipped it to the Museum of Natural History in New York. Millions queued up to see it there; more millions saw it when it went on tour across the country. Two years later, he had Lazare Kaplan cut it; twelve gems came from it, the largest of all being an emerald first cut to 68 facets and 142.90 carats in an emerald-cut which kept the Jonker name. Later Winston recut the stone to 125.65 carats and 58 facets to give it a more oblong shape.

Several of the smaller diamonds were sold but the Jonker went back on exhibition again until in 1949 it attracted the eye of King Farouk of Egypt who bought it on credit for almost $1,000,000. When he went into exile briefly no one knew where it was although they were pretty sure he had not left it behind like his throne for the United Arab Republic. In 1959, it was learned that Queen Ratna of Nepal had bought it from him when he needed money more than diamonds.

Large and beautiful diamonds continue to come out of South Africa. There is the Niarchos, a brilliant pear-shaped diamond of 128.25 carats which was cut from a rough of 426.50 carats found in the Premier mine in 1954. The work was done by Bernard de Hahn in Harry Winston's Fifth Avenue diamond workshop and salon. De Hahn first called it the Ice Queen because it looked so like a large ice cube in the rough; its present name comes from its owner, Stavros S. Niarchos, the Greek shipping magnate who bought it from Winston's for $2,000,000 in 1956. It has the standard 58 facets for brilliance, plus an extra 86 around the girdle for splendor, and what Harry Winston likes to call "the Winston look."

Famous diamonds also come from other African mines: the Williamson, or Elizabeth Pink, is a 23.60-carat brilliant of a true rose-pink color, found in the rough—weighing 54 carats—in the mine of the late John T. Williamson, who gave it to Elizabeth for a wedding present in 1947. She wears it as a brooch; it is mounted in the center of a stylized Alpine rose with five white diamond petals.

And there is the Sierra Leone II, picked up in a creek in Sierra Leone by

The Star of Arkansas Diamond found recently in Murfreesboro, Arkansas, by a feminine Texan rockhound.

The Uncle Sam Diamond, the largest diamond found in the United States, now owned by Peikin of Fifth Avenue, New York.

a thirsty—and sharp-eyed—truck driver scooping up a handful of pebbles along with some water. It was 175 carats in the rough, flawless, and was brilliantly cut by a cutter trained in Puerto Rico in Operation Bootstrap, Gerald Colon. It is now owned and often displayed by F. J. Cooper and Sons, Philadelphia.

Any diamond found in the United States is famous simply because it is found here but the largest is the Uncle Sam, discovered in Murfreesboro,

Arkansas, in 1924. It was then 40.23 carats in weight; it was cut to a 12.42-carat emerald shape. It is owned by Peikin, a Fifth Avenue jeweler.

Another stone found in the "Crater of Diamonds" fields in Arkansas was named the Star of Arkansas—but it is kept in Texas because it was a Texas rockhound who found it: Mrs. A. L. Parker of Dallas. It weighed 15.31 carats in the rough, is of a clear water-white, and was cut to an 8.27-carat marquise by a New York cutter. Mrs. Parker paid the $1.50 fee demanded in 1956 to hunt at the Diamond Preserve, did her "mining" by hand and found the diamond when it glinted a beam of reflected light at her while she was collecting her lunchbox.

Another American diamond is the Punch Jones, named for the boy who found it near Peterstown, West Virginia, in 1928. It is 34.46 carats, still in the rough, and for years it was in the Smithsonian Institution's Gem Hall in a case near the Hope, loaned by Punch Jones' parents after "Punch" himself was killed in World War II.

And so we come to the end of our stories of historic diamonds, back in the museums again. A few more are listed in the glossary; many more are in the files of the Gemological Institute of America. And there will be more to come—any day, any moment may bring another prize from caverns yet undiscovered, ocean beds untouched, vaults unopened, and river beds unsearched.

5

Diamonds in the World of Fashion

Parson, ring and bride's bouquet
For these three things the groom must pay.

Old Rhyme

The United States, developing as it has without royalty or court circles, has not seen quite the fantastic eras of great jewelry that Europe and the Far East have, but it has not been without its moments of splendor, and despite its Puritan background, has never been without diamonds entirely.

Even in the Massachusetts Colony where the wedding band was frowned upon as being too pagan and ostentatious for good Puritans, the French-born family of Paul Revere was permitted to operate a gold and silver smithy. There is no record that either of the two wives of Paul Revere owned even one ring but it is well known that both he and his father sold gold rings to others, fluted the silver spoons they made and even adorned children's porringers with lacy handles.

In New York, the Dutch were less austere. Even before 1700 jewelry stores were growing up along The Broadway to Boston, not far from the Maiden's Path—a little footpath where a boy could meet a girl on her way to the river with the laundry—and by 1743 jewelry of some importance was being brought in from Europe. The New York girls liked diamond earrings glittering below their little Dutch caps and fancy bosom-buttons to hold their bodices tightly together and the men liked silver seals for stamping wax monograms on their letters and shiny buckles for their evening shoes.

Lockets were worn by the young, a parent's picture in some, in others a lover's. Hoop rings of small diamond "sparks" set in yellow gold were first an engagement ring and then later became "keepers" of the wedding band. Men began wearing fancy buttons on their waistcoats as they became prosperous and their wives took to stay hooks, silver things that fastened on the corset and were used for securing their purses. The first solitaire sailed in on a packet ship to New York in 1764 and was advertised along with some other diamonds, but whether it was intended for a man's wig bag or a lady's lavaliere we don't know. It was not yet an engagement ring stone.

By 1763 the Maiden's Path had become a commercial street and the sign of the Teapot and Tankard was out in Maiden Lane—not a saloon, but a silversmith's shop, later to be called The Teapot, Tankard and Earring, the first of the many jewelry shops that were to make the street famous. It was owned by one Oliver Bruff, who had his own lapidary mill where he cut diamonds and other stones, engraved hearts and doves, and worked hair into birds, figures, and cupid fancies for "true lovers' knots." Did he make money? We don't know. He advertised he had "put himself to great expense sending to London for diamonds" but he was in competition with a Dutch importer and engraver who specialized in gentlemen's knee buckles with mottoes on them, shoe buckles of diamond, and hat buckles. Canes were made by jewelers then and Yankee Doodle Dandy carried one with long silken tassels on its gold head. Men were the jewelry sporters in those days but their ladies were not neglected. Even during the blockade of 1812, First Lady Dolley Madison's clothes and jewels came through successfully from Paris. Reared a Quaker but excommunicated when she married the non-Quaker James Madison, Dolley lost no time in replacing her plain grey bonnets with a colorful variety of turbans—some say she had five hundred. Adorned with aigrette feathers or jeweled bangles depending on the hour or the occasion, she wore a turban indoors and out, day and night and at White House receptions and galas, she decorated her best one with a brilliant diamond crescent.

The First Ladies who followed this redoubtable party giver, matchmaker and fashion leader were quieter women; not until the 1840's when John Tyler's daughter-in-law Priscilla presided over the White House do we find satins, silks, and diamonds sparkling again at government balls. Priscilla Tyler brought her daughter out at the White House; dressed as Queen Titania with a wand in her hand and a diamond on her forehead she received all the elite of Washington. Life grew even gayer when the widowed President married the young and beautiful Julia Gardiner, toast of the country, nicknamed by reporters "the Rose of Long Island." She was not content with the traditional White House receptions and established a sort of court where, surrounded by twelve maids of honor, she received her guests on a raised platform. On her hair, she wore a headdress resembling a crown in the daytime, at night a tiara of diamonds. As First Lady, the press called her "Her Serene Loveliness."

A new store was opened during the Tyler administration along lower Broadway, near A. T. Stewart's great emporium. It was called Tiffany and Young, and boasted of its fancy yard goods from France, England, and the Far East. It was not far from Maiden Lane where there were now two dozen watch importers, six watchmakers, twelve jewelry manufacturers and one oddball who made gold pens which he said were better than goose quills. Tiffany's became a jewelry store partly by chance: while John Young was in the process of purchasing silks in Paris he was informed that there was a group of royalists who wished to sell their diamonds. He cabled Tiffany on the newly laid under-ocean cable about it and Tiffany cabled back to get all he could and bring them home for sale. It was the start of the great jewelry business that one hundred years later was to adorn Fifth Avenue's most fashionable corner.

But the jewelry boom of the mid-nineteenth century was nipped in the bud by the outbreak of the Civil War. Although Mrs. Lincoln had a passion for clothes and jewels—she even slashed her gloves to display her rings—most people stopped their clothes buying, jewelry displaying, and party giving. In Maiden Lane they said the jewelry business was dead, that the young artisans and designers had dropped work to enlist, and that only the stores selling military equipment were busy. Tiffany advertised swords "warranted to cut iron," "cap ornaments and gold lace from Paris," "epaulettes from London," and refused to ship mail orders to the southern states. After the troops settled down in camps, jewelry peddlers sought the boys out on payday and business picked up a little: the boys sent home lockets, jeweled combs, and even engagement rings. Rings made of "Californy gold" were particularly in demand, the gold rush of 1848–50 having now become an organized business. Hoop skirts were the rage then and luxury money went for them, or for feathers, flowers, or bows. Even a fine lady during this period was content with a single-strand necklace, a pair of matching gold bracelets (which she wore *over* her gloves), jeweled combs, a gold wedding band, and a keeper ring of sparks. Queen Victoria's fussy taste for ornate decoration did not begin to make itself felt in America until the post-war period—although pre-war she herself was already wearing diamond earrings so wide they had to be suspended from the *tops* of ears, bangle bracelets and by 1850 a brooch set with the massive Koh-i-Noor.

With the post–Civil War boom that built up to the Gay Nineties, however, jewelry of all kinds and especially diamonds began to blossom in both profusion and blatant extravagance. As new money battled with old to gain

The year was 1832 when Bailey and Kitchen founded the first jewelry store in Philadelphia on an old dirt road known as Chestnut Street. Later known as Bailey, Banks and Biddle, it is still on Chestnut Street.

Interior of Bailey & Co.'s jewelry establishment, 819 Chestnut Street, Philadelphia, 1860.

Among the early jewelry firms in America was Tiffany and Young. This is their first building, located at 259 Broadway, which they occupied from 1837 to 1841.

A woodcut of Tiffany's diamond room at their store on Union Square at Fifteenth Street published in 1879. The caption said that Mrs. Brown was completely overcome by the dazzling array of brilliants.

a spot in the social limelight a fever for enormous houses, expensive parties, fine clothes, glittering jewels, and a whirl of pleasure raged through the world of the new rich.

The result was what can only be called an era of ostentation. The men competed with palatial residences, stables of horses, ocean-going yachts, and Old Master paintings. William H. Vanderbilt's block-long Fifth Avenue brownstone mansion cost $3,000,000 to build and decorate, which was understandable enough, considering its French tapestries, Florentine doors, African marble, English china, and its Japanese parlor of bamboo walls studded with jeweled bugs and butterflies. His brother William K. outdid him, however, with a French chateau a few doors away, and the Astors, Goulds and others competed with similar ventures, some of which, like the Frick Museum and the Morgan Library, still stand today. When space ran out on Fifth Avenue they built what they called cottages in Newport, Saratoga Springs, and eventually Palm Beach.

Few of the men, however, now wore jewels except in their cufflinks or scarfpins. One exception was John Warne Gates, better known as "Bet a Million" Gates, who started as a barbed wire salesman in Texas and wound up a steel titan and gambler. He wore, even in the daytime, three biggish diamonds on his shirtfront and three smaller ones on each suspender buckle.

Another exception was the man who was probably the greatest diamond collector of modern time, "Diamond Jim" Brady. Diamond Jim Brady had a different set of monogrammed jewelry for each day in the month—diamonds one day, emeralds the next, turquoises, rubies, sapphires, cat's-eye—thirty-one different sets of studs, cufflinks, belt buckles, scarfpins, tie clips, watch fobs, and chains. His most famous was his bizarre transportation set studded with a total of 2,548 diamonds. Each piece was a different railroad car: a tank car, a coal car, a caboose, etc. It was freight cars which made him rich; like Gates, he was a salesman. He kept his sets in a jeweler's vault, and sent a messenger around each morning to pick up that day's set. His racetrack set he wore only on days he was going to the races, his Napoleon set—made only of jewels once worn by Napoleon—he wore only on grand occasions. It was believed he owned more than twenty thousand diamonds all told, that sometimes he wore as many as $250,000 worth on a single day, and that he purchased another several thousand for the actress Lillian Russell.

His display was considered somewhat of an expensive joke, however, and no doubt helped to encourage the rule that it was poor taste to wear diamonds in the daytime. Not that all the proper people adhered to this; it is said that when one young lady was told by a dowager that her handsome diamond brooch was out of place at lunch, she answered crisply: "I thought that too until I got it." Too, Mrs. Evelyn Walsh McLean wore her fabulous Hope Diamond day and night—indeed because she even wore it in swimming, a detective always swam beside her at Bailey's Beach, *the* place to swim at Newport.

But the big display of diamonds in the seventies, the eighties and the nineties was at night. For a long time the dog collar was the most stylish neckwear, layers of tight ropes of pearls fastened by diamond clasps, nicknamed because they looked like the collars used in Paris for poodles. Consuelo Vanderbilt started the fashion: her dog collar had nineteen rows of pearls with high diamond clasps, which she said years later rasped her skin, but which at the time set off her swanlike neck to perfection. She also had a diamond belt, a gift from her first husband the Duke of Marlborough and for New York and London opera and balls a diamond tiara which her father William H. Vanderbilt had given her.

The pearl dog collar soon gave way to diamond dog collars and then, probably because few had both money and necks as slim as the teen-age American Duchess, to bibs of diamonds. Set in gold, heavy and elaborate, these were something of a chore to wear, but extraordinarily impressive to look upon.

Many bibs were of old historic diamonds picked up at auction, others of newly cut diamonds from the booming African mines, but never was a diamond necklace bought "off the rack," or in this situation, out of the case. First the purchaser, usually a father or husband, told the jeweler in general what he wanted—a sort of vague request asking for something with two rows and pendant or four rows and no pendant. Then the jeweler's designer submitted a sketch, and the secret was out, because few men took the risk of buying such an expensive gift without their lady's approval. Now the search for matching flawless diamonds began; assembling the stones might take months. Once assembled, the stones were then laid out on a thin sheet of wax and tried on the would-be wearer's neck. If approved, the necklace was now made up and delievered by armored car, often with a matching replica in paste to be worn when traveling.

Luckier were the ladies whose millionaire husbands, fathers, or lovers bought up old royal necklaces at auction, like the Hapsburg diamonds that the first Commodore Vanderbilt picked up for a golden song. A few ladies also avoided the tedium of fittings by wearing their necklaces in long chains, diamonds if the chain was solely for show, jet beads if it carried a fan, lorgnette or glove buttoner. A few chains reached to the knees, most to the waist.

Two ornate diamond pieces owned by the fabulous "Diamond Jim" Brady, known to everyone in the social, theatrical and financial worlds of the "Gay Nineties." He was reputed to have bought nearly $2,000,000 worth of jewelry. Right, a diamond camel tie clip; left, a diamond-set belt buckle.

There were other uses for diamonds. Mrs. Potter Palmer of Chicago wore aigrette feathers in her hair set in a diamond-studded clip. Mrs. Jay Gould, like Mrs. Cornelius Vanderbilt, preferred her feathers set in gold and her diamonds in brooches that looked like swallows, insects, butterflies or ducks, and her daughter Helen had a fan chain of two hundred graduated diamonds.

The diamond engagement ring—a large solitaire—was beginning to come into fashion now, but not yet the diamond set wedding band. Few owned diamond belts or stomachers but many had belt buckles—and in the Midwest, many wore their diamonds on their garter buckles, a specialty of Peacock's in Chicago. There were also diamond-studded button hooks, for shoes or gloves, diamond-set lorgnettes and opera glasses and even diamond-studded jewelry cases to keep your diamonds in, such cases being particularly nice to have when showing off jewels to a friend, a custom rarely followed today but considered in the past a seal of friendship.

The acme of diamond wearing in this period, however, was the tiara, the true crown of a lady's jewel collection. Some tiaras contained as many as a thousand diamonds; almost all were convertible, that is, they broke up into sections, the center usually being a brooch, the side sections being clips, bracelets, or pendants. Prices began at $25,000 and went up—and up, and up and especially so if they came from Cartier's, which had recently opened a branch of their Paris firm in New York.

Lillian Russell, light opera star of the Gay Nineties. Like Mrs. Cornelius Vanderbilt she was said to wear as much as $1,000,000 worth of diamonds at one time.

Diamonds across the footlights. Opera singer Geraldine Farrar's matched tiara and dog collar in diamonds and pearls were said to have been equalled only by those of Mrs. Jay Gould. Like other divas she wore her own jewels in operatic roles. New York, circa 1895.

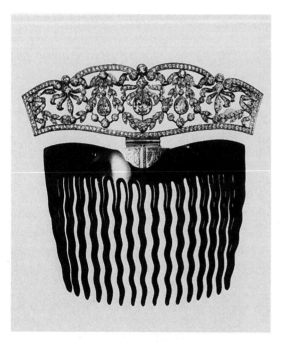

A tortoise shell comb set with brilliant-cut diamonds from Tiffany.

Two lorgnettes, one for reading and one for theatre-going, with a holder set with diamonds, from Cartier's.

Gay Nineties' earrings for pierced ears imported from France. Metal is gold, the diamonds almost three-eighths of an inch in diameter.

A brooch with eight interlacing fish made of diamonds and enamel by the French goldsmith Lalique.

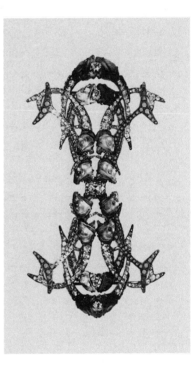

Ring of pear-shaped blue diamond and pear-shaped black pearl in a hoop set with diamonds in a snakeskin pattern.

Few pieces of jewelry are as beautiful or as becoming as a diamond tiara. Take the $1,000,000 Whitney tiara, a Hapsburg relic of enchanting flowers and sprays—or the Gardiner tiara, treasured for generations, a half-circle crown with radiating beams of diamonds that shoot off in graceful array like so many beams of the sun. These exquisite pieces are seen now only rarely but what a sight they were then, glittering by the score in the newly discovered electric light, adorning a woman's high pompadour, set off by a dark sable collar or a broad expanse of pink powdered bosom and shoulder.

Nor were places lacking to wear one. As well as opening night of the opera in New York, Philadelphia or Boston where all tiara owners of course had boxes in the Golden or Diamond Horseshoes, there were scores of elaborate private parties. Along Fifth Avenue during the fall season, at Palm Beach in January, at Saratoga Springs in May, at Newport in July or August, there was always a dinner or a fete or a masked ball—parties with a hundred guests or more, a footman for every couple, and ten-course meals set on solid gold services. A single ball might cost $250,000 without including the cost of clothes or jewels, and the latter were a necessity. Mrs. William Backhouse Astor, *the* Mrs. Astor, led the fashion. For any party larger than one hundred guests, she wore a diamond tiara on her black pompadour; for smaller, more intimate gatherings of a mere eighty or ninety, she wore a three-strand diamond necklace, a dazzling diamond stomacher, and several chains of diamonds. Indeed, once dressed in white and "resplendent in diamonds," she was described by a friend as a "walking chandelier." Mrs. Cornelius Vanderbilt, *the* Mrs. Vanderbilt, countered with her famous "headache" band—a diamond-studded velvet piece she wore low over the forehead—and a huge diamond flower spray she wore on the left shoulder like an epaulette. But she could not outshine Mrs. Astor.

Aided by her two "social secretaries," Ward McAllister and Harry Lehr, and supported by the $80,000,000 of tax-free money earned by her almost invisible husband, Mrs. Astor ruled the billionaire society of nineteenth-century America for almost four decades. There had never been another woman with such social power outside a royal or official court. Coincidentally with her withdrawal into a make-believe party world of her own, the Gilded Age went into a slow decline. It had ignored Queen Victoria's distaste for display; it had lived through panic and prejudice, vulgarity and boredom, but as the new century dawned, it was clear that its day was all but done. Affluent echoes were to be heard again in the Roaring Twenties and the Fabulous Fifties, but never again was so much owned and displayed by so few.

Now the spotlight of fashion returned to the great capitals of the

Queen Alexandra of England, wife of Edward VII, in her famous diamond-trellis necklace.

The Astor tiara with the famous Sancy Diamond goes with American-born Lady Astor to the ceremonial opening of the British Parliament in London after World War II.

Western world. In 1901 tiny, old Queen Victoria died and the handsome Edward VII and his Danish-born Queen Alexandra ascended the British throne. As the Prince and Princess of Wales they were well known for their love of sport, horse racing, the theatre and yachting, and as the new King and Queen they set a pace of luxurious pleasure difficult for even an American mogul to follow. Their style fast became legendary, but writing of Alexandra in her memoirs, Consuelo Vanderbilt Balsan showed her a natural leader. "As everyone knows, Queen Alexandra was a beautiful woman. Like the Empress Eugenie she had sloping shoulders, and her breasts and arms seemed specially designed for a fabulous display of glittering jewels. . . . She was most often dressed in white with the blue ribbon of the garter. On her head glittered a tiara, pearls and diamonds cascaded from neck to waist. . . ."

Soon she was being credited with the change-over American diamond lovers made from gold settings to platinum. Platinum was first found in Russia near the end of the century and almost immediately thereafter in Canada. As valuable as gold, if not more so, it was more easily worked, lighter, and because of its whiteness, gave an extra gleam to diamonds. Many diamonds from Britain's old royal necklaces, brooches and rings were reset in platinum because of Alexandra's eagerness for the new styles, and new cutting methods often were employed during the process. Old elaborate cuts, particularly the rosette, began to die out, and the square cut came in; single stones, heavy and chunky, began to replace clusters and the solitaire became the engagement ring stone most in demand.

Spurred on by Alexandra, too, young girls now began wearing diamonds in the daytime—as studs and cufflinks for their shirtwaists, as copycat stickpins of men's scarfpins. Single diamond lavalieres, tear-shaped, on a thin platinum chain, were their answers to their mothers' bib necklaces; a circle brooch, a specialty of Bailey, Banks and Biddle of Philadelphia, their replacement for the bug and bird pins so beloved of the Victorians.

In Washington, meanwhile, America boasted its own "princess"— bright, quick and lovely Alice Roosevelt, daughter of President "Teddy" and a newsmaker on her own. Because of a furor over how to rank her, she was not permitted to attend Edward VII's coronation but she was consoled with a series of trips to Puerto Rico, New Orleans, the St. Louis World's Fair and in 1905, to the Orient, where she was presented to the Japanese royal family and the old Empress Dowager of China. Also on the trip was Nicholas Longworth, whom she married in the White House two years later, surrounded by wedding gifts from royalty the world over—including a $25,000 pearl necklace with a diamond clasp, a chest of Chinese silks, a French tapestry, antique Spanish jewelry, and a diamond and pearl pendant.

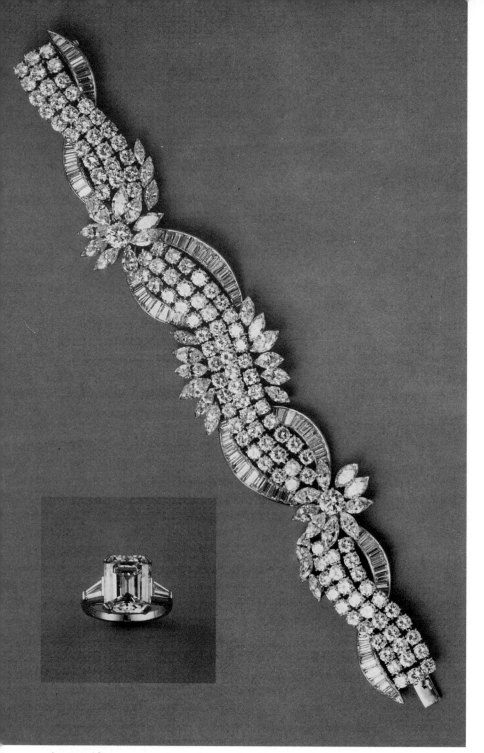

A magnificent emerald-cut diamond with tapered baguettes set in platinum, and an all-platinum bracelet with perfectly matched marquise, baguette, and round diamonds are examples of today's jeweler's art. From the collection of Bailey, Banks and Biddle of Philadelphia.

More interested in politics than pomp, Alice Roosevelt Longworth never seriously challenged Alexandra as a fashion leader but along with her youth and wit she brought a happy sense of style to Washington's official circles.

As World War I slowed luxury traffic from European centers, more and more American jewelers now became known for their particular contributions. In Kansas City, home of the wheat millionaire, Jaccard's introduced special rings to be worn for specific occasions: an echo of the old Roman custom. There were dinner rings, lunch rings, and reception rings, soon to be called cocktail rings. In their St. Louis store, Jaccard's had long been known for elegant diamond crowns for the Veiled Prophet ball, easily the biggest social event of the Midwest.

In Chicago, Peacock's work with platinum was attracting attention; a wartime call-in of gold pushed the demand even higher, and some of the new, slim, white wedding bands were set with diamonds. In Boston, Shreve, Crump and Low sold diamond-studded barettes until the late war period when short hair came in, and fancy barettes began to be replaced by the bobbie pin. Galt's of Washington were known for their monograms of diamonds set in watch fobs until the diamond bracelet watch replaced the watch-brooch and fobs for ladies went out.

The new demand for bracelets reflected the lack of demand for sleeves. Skirts were still long during World War I, but sleeveless dresses grew steadily in popularity, and with them bracelets of all kinds—solid gold, linked gold, shimmering platinum, wide, thin, flexible, or filagreed. Only a few bracelets were jeweled: diamonds were still largely evening wear, pearls were too easily smashed and the scarab bracelet of Egypt was not to become a vogue until the twenties—and the opening of King Tutankhamen's tomb. A few bracelets carried pendants; the charm bracelet was just beginning to be talked about.

It was Everts Co. of Dallas who first made charms a big part of their business. Since people wore anything at all, amulets and charms have been part of human adornment: the small cross worn around the neck is the most lasting evidence of this in today's world. But not all charms have been religious: President Cleveland cherished a ring made of Lincoln's hair; Sarah Bernhardt, the great tragic actress, wore always on her wrist a diamond pendant sent her by Victor Hugo—who said it was the tear he cried during one of her moving performances.

Mrs. Robert McCormick, Chicago's social queen, liked to say that she launched the charm bracelet fashion in this country, that she saw the first one—she called it a "bangle bracelet"—on a trip to South America in 1909 and thereafter collected charms representative of each country she visited. Everts, however, had their charms going strong much earlier; they started in business in 1897 with a basketfull of pearls from the Coronado river, twenty dollars in capital and a willingness to copy or set any lucky charm any frontiersman brought in. As the Texans grew richer and richer, Everts became more and more imaginative, making miniature oil wells in gold, creating small bejeweled beer carts, and putting diamond eyes in monkeys and rattlesnakes. Some Texans wore their charms on their watch fobs, some carried them loosely in their pockets, a growing number presented them to their wives to wear at their wrists on a chain. Today diamonds are the jam of the American jewelry business, and charms are its bread and butter. Whole firms are devoted to producing them in quantity and rare is the charm that today can't be found ready made. But in those days you found your own and then took it to a jeweler to enhance it, copy it or frame it. It was part of the growing democracy of American life that this should be so.

For slowly jewels, once the prerogative of kings, were becoming a part of everyone's life in the United States. In the boom of the twenties that followed the war, the great dowager jewelry lost its power. With short dresses, short hair, motor cars, modern art, flaming youth, working women, and a shortage of royalty, jewels became baubles and the wearing of them more of a game and a pleasure and less of a serious display of wealth and importance.

Young girls liked their brief frocks spangled with sequins, their bracelets banging at the wrists and their newly discovered cigarette holders long and glittering. Fake junk jewelry was not yet perfected but onyx and jade had come into vogue during the war when more precious stones were hard to get. Cigarette cases were large gold things, sometimes with a monogram of diamonds, sometimes made in combination with a "vanity"—a compact powder case. A true flapper also had her lipstick case bejeweled; it was thus both daring and dazzling to color your lips in public. With the new sheer silk stockings, black satin lady's pumps with fantastic jeweled buckles came in, a plain steal from men's dress shoes, which now sported nothing but a black faille bow. Diamond earrings were now worn in the daytime and the diamond wristwatch replaced the tiara as a badge of prosperity. Very important, however, even to an avowed career girl, was the matching set of platinum rings that came with marriage: the thin wedding band, engraved inside, and the thicker engagement ring sporting as large a solitaire as possible.

Soon, too, the great new motion-picture industry began to catapult actors and actresses into the world of money and fame that had previously

Arlene Francis, television star, with diamonds in a photograph of the 1960's.

Lily Pons, the opera singer, wearing a diamond bib necklace of the 1940's.

Claudette Colbert, the movie star, in a matching diamond and ruby necklace, earrings and diamond cocktail ring.

belonged to more serious businesses. Mary Pickford, America's Sweetheart, early brought a dimpled wholesomeness to the fore, but quickly she was overshadowed by the popularity of Mack Sennett's sultry bathing beauties: Theda Bara, Clara Bow, Gloria Swanson. Erratic weather drove the studios from the sheds of Long Island and New Jersey to the creation of a new city, Hollywood, about 1915 and by the mid-twenties, what Hollywood wore, did, said or displayed exerted a tremendous influence on fashion.

With only a few stars—such as Greta Garbo—standing aside, the mad scramble for status that goes with a change of power began. The biggest houses, the finest furs, satins and jewels were collected and a new symbol was added—the swimming pool. Merle Oberon was known for her twenty-seven diamond bracelets, five diamond necklaces and three diamond roses— and a sixth necklace of diamonds and emeralds, with earrings to match, once owned by Napoleon Bonaparte. Joan Crawford, rising fast, stuck to one trademark: a ring with a huge star sapphire surrounded by diamonds. Mary Pickford, growing up and marrying Douglas Fairbanks, celebrated her newfound sophistication with an elaborate diamond necklace that broke into five pieces, a clasp for her hair, a bracelet for her wrist, two clips and a brooch.

The stars of Hollywood had no rules about when or how to wear diamonds; they wore them with their bathing suits, their slacks and their negligees, on their ankles and even, at times, on their toes. But they did not take up the tiara. "Movie queens," they might be called but they lacked the regality necessary to carry off crowns.

And they could not put Society entirely in the shade. Although Newport's formality was passé, Palm Beach's informality was just coming into its own. Sunny, luxurious and full of games and sport, the Florida resort attracted a rich, pleasure-seeking crowd from the business weary the world over. Five years was said to be the length of an average Palm Beach marriage; five hours the average length of a bridge game.

Probably the most successful and certainly one of the richest and most glamorous of the women in this group was the then Marjorie Post Close Hutton, heiress to the Post cereal fortune and wife of the stockbroker E. T. Hutton. When it came time to choose between her Palm Beach house and her yacht, however, she chose her yacht, the famed "Sea Cloud," which cost her some $20,000 a year in crew uniforms alone but was the yacht which took her and her third husband, Ambassador Joseph Davies, in impressive American style to Russia. Today she is Mrs. Herbert May and a part owner of Tiffany's in New York. Her jewels have long been as famous as her ageless beauty. She keeps them in a walk-in vault in twin metal filing cab-

The marriage-coronation diadem of young Queen Geraldine of Albania sold by the former court jewelers, now Ostier, Inc., of New York City.

Emerald and diamond bracelet made in Russia at the end of the eighteenth century and presented with other pieces to Louis XVIII of France, then exiled to Warsaw by Napoleon.

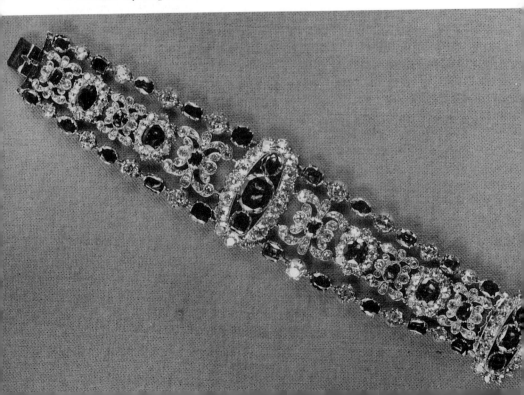

inets with eighteen drawers in each section, each lined with beige velvet, each thirty inches wide and each devoted to one kind of jewel—pearls, sapphires, emeralds, etc. Her diamond drawers contain some magnificent pendant earrings that the hapless Marie Antoinette once wore and some charming diamond-studded Easter eggs made by the great Russian jeweler Fabergé, along with an incredible number of bracelets, rings and brooches.

Another well-known Palm Beachite was Mrs. Harrison Williams, the daughter of a horse trainer from Kentucky who married her first husband (of four) at eighteen. Perennially on the list of the best dressed, she was impressive not only for her clothes but also her jewels—one bracelet and necklace, indeed, was said to have consisted of 129 sapphires, 144 emeralds, 79 pearls and 762 diamonds.

Mrs. E. T. Stotesbury of Philadelphia was the party giver at Palm Beach: she kept three secretaries, seventy-five servants, her own personal fashion designer, forty cars, and displayed her fabulous jewelry on neck mannikins atop a giant showcase–dressing table in her upstairs sitting room. Her husband, unlike many, liked parties as much as she did: he had 150 fancy dress costumes—and it was he who ordered the gold door knobs and gold faucets that adorned their house—and he who ordered up the detective who accompanied them on their honeymoon because he wanted his bride to take all her jewels along.

The depression put an end to a lot of public wearing of jewels, but at the same time it brought a lot of jewels out of hiding. In Philadelphia, for instance, where the greatest fortunes of the post–Civil War were made and where life has always been more familial and less familiar than in other large cities, thousands of old mine diamonds were taken in to Caldwell's, Bailey's and F. J. Cooper's in the thirties to be turned in for cash. As Hollywood cried for more diamonds, Philadelphians yielded theirs up; once one of the great diamond-owning cities of the United States, Philadelphia lost out slowly thereafter to Los Angeles and Dallas.

And by one of those strange quirks of fate, the dreary thirties escorted into the limelight one of the great jewel wearers of history: the Duchess of Windsor. Although this Baltimore-born girl failed to become queen because of her two divorces and was never received by her royal in-laws, she took readily to royal prerogatives. In the jewel-wearing world, she is best known for her large, pictorial pins against a simple straight dress. I remember her well in the Bahamas, where the Duke was Governor General during World War II, wearing a white sheath with an elegant, amusing flamenco pin four inches across. Its feathers were ruby; its body, diamonds; its bright eye, an emerald. The earrings that matched it were another bit of ruby

feather. Van Cleef and Arpels then only in Paris made most of her jewels,
although some she claimed to have designed herself. She liked big sprays of
flowers, gadgety birds whose heads nodded on platinum springs, peacocks
whose mother-of-pearl feathers shimmered, sprays of wildflowers that mixed
diamonds and turquoises and rubies. Sometimes the small beanie hats she
fancied then were sequined or pearl sewn, others were plain but adorned
with jeweled clips. Her favorite jewel seemed to be the frosty blue sapphire
ring that matched her frosty blue sapphire eyes, but her engagement ring
was a blinding 20-carat rock of a diamond and her finest single piece a
diamond necklace that had once belonged to Queen Alexandra.

Because of the publicity she received and because Mainbocher always
designed her dresses with a sketch of the jewel she would wear with them,
the Duchess had a tremendous effect on jewelry wearing, although not quite
the way in which she might have hoped. For it was the Duchess who made
junk jewelry acceptable. Few could afford ruby and diamond flamencos like
hers but many could have amusing pins in the brilliant new synthetic stones
Europe and the United States were now producing in steadily increasing
quantity—and many were the designers only too happy to make them up
soundly crafted and imaginatively worked. The designers now outshone the

The Duchess of Windsor with
one of her well-known diamond
and turquoise flower pins, the
leaves of which match her
beanie-hat clips, the blossoms,
her earrings.

jewelers in many cases and New York talked about Fulko de Verdura, Jean Schlumberger, Marc Koven and Paul Flato instead of the merchants in whose firms they worked.

It was a great jewel-wearing period, in short, but not an expensive one. Many more women wore elaborate pieces than before, but few followed the Duchess's lead and had their amusements done up in real rubies and diamonds. They preferred to look but not leap at these. When the World's Fair in New York opened in 1939, the House of Jewels drew an amazing crowd, largely to see the $1,000,000 worth of diamonds that were collected in a handful of showcases. Earlier the 726-carat Jonker diamond had been exhibited in the rough around the country by its owner Harry Winston to massive audiences.

Behind the scenes major diamond history was being made. As Hitler entered the lowlands, twenty thousand diamond-cutters were scattered to go to work wherever and however they could all over the world. New York got the most—it started with three hundred cutters and wound up with thirty-five hundred. With the refugees came not only diamond skills but diamonds too; the Rothschilds alone brought in thousands to England and America.

The retail business in diamonds as war swept the whole world was in engagement rings. Here any business could play: the department stores moved in on the jewelers, Bergdorf Goodman leading the way with showcases of diamonds, others like Nieman Marcus of Dallas following fast— and soon even Sears Roebuck was selling diamonds by mail.

In 1943, diamond sales reached a new high—$78,000,000 worth were sold that year—largely in engagement rings, some of them new, some of them redesigned old mines turned up during the depression, some of them slipped through Hitler's barbed wire in the lining of a coat, the toe of a shoe, under a bandage. Macy's became a diamond brokerage; there you could not only buy diamonds, you could sell them: bring in your old, advertised the store, and we'll take them in trade on something new.

Earrings were in vogue as well as rings, and so were military insignias— small anchors or air arms in diamonds and gold for her, important gold buttons and bars for him. As World War II progressed jewelry grew at once more sentimental, and, more providential, a diamond frequently being a nest egg, a hope of escape from prejudice, hunger, and pain.

With the end of the war, and slowly the end of tension and horror, the chance for ornamental jewelry wearing came again. But times had changed. A single event illustrates the complex upheaval in fashion that had occurred with the power and money revolution that began at the turn of the century and culminated in two world wars. The place was Sotheby's, the great auction house in London, the scene there was routine—an estate was going under the hammer. But one piece made it stand out: a sixteen-section tiara of 1,240 diamonds, a treasure of the great British House of Westminster. Once the tiara had been loaned to Princess Margaret, often it had been worn in court, and at least twice it had been present at a coronation; now the family "crown" was sold to the great American diamond merchant and collector, Harry Winston, for $308,000. As a family jewel it would exist no more: like the Koh-i-Noor, it would henceforth be primarily a museum piece—and an American one!

Today the rich and social wear their great elaborate jewel pieces rarely; except for their huge engagement diamonds they are more likely to be in vaults than on their hair or around their waists and necks. The opening of the Opera in Philadelphia may bring out three tiaras—the Assembly twenty. In New York the annual Tiara Ball brings out them all (plus a gaggle of detectives) but whether the wearers are the owners is a closely guarded secret; today tiaras can be "borrowed" at all the important jewelry stores. What is the explanation? In part, of course, the income tax explains it: the purchase of a diamond tiara or stomacher cannot find its way into an expense account with the ease, say, of a new office building. Partly too, tastes have changed: glittering jewels are no novelty today, in some cases (although not with diamonds) only the experts can tell the real from the fake. There is also a greater fear of robbery today than there was in the days when the rich were walled in by an army of servants, soldiers or slaves.

But probably most important is the fact that since World War II the rich have been traveling fast, far, and light. In the nineteenth century, the rich moved sedately at a precise pace; there were seasons of several months in several spas for which those who cared adhered to closely and prepared for with diligence and detail. By the middle of the twentieth century there was a new kind of travel, international in scope, faster than sound in speed, and a new social set to enjoy it: the jet set. Early in the fifties it was dominated by the late Ali Khan, the Near Eastern monarch; it included the mid-century billionaires—the Greek shipping merchants like Niarchos, a lot of homeless French and German royalty like Prince Hohenlohe and the usual bevy of beautiful women, rich and not so rich, from anywhere and everywhere. Some have joined it for the skiing, winging their way to Switzerland or to Colorado's Aspen at a moment's notice. Some have preferred the sun-bathing along the Riviera, at Marbella, in Barbados or the Bahamas, at Palm Springs, in California or the islands off Greece. Fashions reflected the new pace: in the fifties and sixties short evening dresses were in, tail-coats went out, pants for women were worn day and night, and uncrushable knits and drip-dry nylons and tie silks replaced satins and damasks. With these went only a few, basic pieces of jewelry which were as good on the beach as in the ballroom.

Recently, Constance Bennett, her leg in a cast from a ski accident at Aspen, received her Manhattan dinner guests in a tangerine silk blouse, black slacks, a huge diamond pin and two diamond rings, a costume which would have horrified Mrs. Astor and Queen Alexandra but which was not unimaginable on Princess Grace of Monaco or Princess Margaret of England.

Not so long ago, about a century, "naked without her jewels" meant not having a full set for each important costume, and a set (or parure) was two bracelets, one comb, one necklace, two brooches, two stickpins and a hair ornament of some kind. In mid-century Euro-America "naked without her jewels" meant something far different: the everyday set being a string of pearls, a diamond engagement ring, matching wedding ring, a diamond and platinum watch, two or three charm bracelets of gold, rubies and diamonds and a pair of earrings. There may be also earrings and/or necklaces for each costume, there may be a ring of sapphire or emeralds, or a priceless bracelet that one wears with a special dress. There may be a chest of beads in a variety of stones, shapes, and colors. But the junk and the jewels mix and match together with gay abandon and any jewel and any piece of junk can go anywhere, anytime one feels inclined—without need of detectives, for more valuable pieces are kept in the vault. The etiquette authorities complain in vain; when *Women's Wear Daily* said Elizabeth Taylor committed a "fashion crime" by wearing her diamonds with a gingham dress, the actress only laughed. Once, and this was a mere half-century before, invitations noted how formal a ball was with the word "Tiaras" engraved at the bottom left; today, such a notation has gone the way of the buttonhook and the carriage and quite often the notation in its place is likely to be: "Tickets twenty dollars," since most recent big balls have been for charity.

Not only were more ladies wearing fewer diamond pieces but so were gentlemen. The diamonds once owned only by kings were now flatly ruled out by the etiquette experts who grudgingly said that if a man must have a diamond, let him have it set in his cigarette case, not in his shirt front. Those who ignored such a dictum included the followers of "Diamond Jim" who wore diamond studs in their evening dress, plus a handful of old timers who fancied having diamonds set in their teeth—*not* as fillings but as sparklers in the middle of each tooth, granting thereby a guaranteed, built-in glittering smile.

Having said that there were fewer great diamond wearers and collectors in the fifties and sixties than there had been previously, it must now be added

The late President and Mrs. Kennedy leave the Quai D'Orsay for a state dinner June 1, 1961 at the Château of Versailles. Mrs. Kennedy wears diamond clips in her hair.

that there are, however, a great many more diamonds about in the sixties than there have ever been before: like all sorts of other privileges and perquisites, the diamond became democratized in the twentieth century. While at the turn of the century only the dowager queens across the United States owned diamonds, in the Fabulous Fifties it was a poor woman indeed who hadn't a single diamond to her name. Indeed a survey in mid-century showed that three out of four brides received a diamond engagement ring, most of which carried less than a .50-carat stone but a good number of which held a 1-carat diamond or larger.

And no fashion or social leader of this period was without important diamonds. Jacqueline Kennedy during her brief but glorious reign in the White House was reluctant to discuss her diamonds, but she owned and wore at least a dozen pieces of importance. There was a pair of chandelier earrings, diamond pendants, often worn with a crescent brooch with a single row of diamonds in her dark hair. Another diamond pin in a fan design she wore sometimes on her dress, sometimes in her hair. She had a diamond and ruby clip, another of diamonds and emeralds, and two diamond bracelets. There were small emeralds in her diamond necklace, matching a diamond and emerald bracelet. She also received two gifts of jewels: a pearl necklace

with a carved golden pendant set with diamonds, rubies, emeralds and turquoises from the President of Pakistan when she visited there, and from the
city council of Paris, a thin diamond-sparked Cartier watch.

Curiously neither the second Mrs. Nelson Rockefeller nor the first
cares much for jewelry despite the great family wealth. Among the Republi-
can women of the sixties, Claire Boothe Luce, who earned a lot of her
wealth herself, cast the most glittering light. Her charm bracelet of twelve
diamond crosses is one of her best known pieces; she also has a superb necklace, several bracelets of diamonds and sapphires, and a large ring. Princess
Grace of Monaco is another diamond lover of the sixties, the tiara that she
wears at royal functions is as valuable and beautiful a diamond piece as
any in the world. Because of her cool blonde beauty, she believes that diamonds suit her better than any other stone. Her wedding gift from Prince
Rainer was a parure of diamonds: a three-stranded pearl necklace clasped
with diamonds, a matching bracelet, the clasp of which was a diamond blossom, a ring which was a twin to the clasp on the bracelet, and a pair of
earrings, pearl on the lobe, a leaf spray of diamonds up the ear. Her engagement ring was a 12-carat emerald-cut diamond solitaire; her wedding ring,
diamonds on platinum.

Both Queen Elizabeth and Princess Margaret have access to an enormous treasure of diamonds, but neither has had a great influence on American fashions. Perhaps Margaret's most copied jewel was a pair of diamond
butterflies she wore clipped on a velvet band in her hair at informal dances.

More diamond engagement rings were displayed—and sold—than any
other single style, but diamond bracelets, earrings and necklaces were great
favorites. Fancy rings were seen in abundance and the anniversary diamond
was becoming almost obligatory in well-to-do circles. Sometimes this was
given on the twentieth anniversary—sometimes the sixteenth, nineteenth, or
twenty-seventh. It was the diamond's symbolism of true love that counted—
not the number of years. The stones were usually solitaires, like the engagement diamonds that preceded them and between 1962 and 1964 the stone of
3 carats and pure white doubled in price with the demand. Smaller ones were
set with rubies or emeralds—or in the round cushion-clusters fashionable in
the mid-sixties.

Anniversary rings were more often than not surprise gifts picked out
by the husband and the jeweler, although gift necklaces and earrings might
be chosen by the woman herself, sometimes by designs, sometimes from the
case. Personal fittings of paste or wax were a thing of the past but "trying on"
was more fun than ever. Great care was taken by the makers of great diamond pieces that necklaces fitted the neck of the wearer or suited the earlobe

A portrait of the young Queen Victoria, from Sully's sketch in color. She is wearing a diamond crown and her favorite branched diamond earrings. Painted at Buckingham Palace, London, 1838; now in the Metropolitan Museum of Art, New York.

Queen Elizabeth II of England in a necklace of 647 diamonds and 12 aquamarines, a coronation gift of the President of Brazil. Her tiara is also set with diamonds.

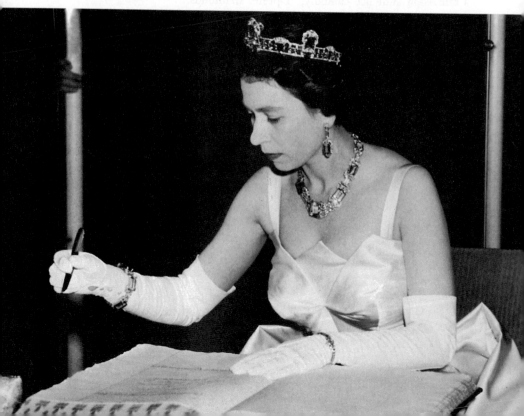

of the receiver, but no jeweler was above letting a customer try on a variety. A few women shopping in America requested certificates of quality with their diamonds but this was still more of a European practice and there a practice used largely by mistresses who feared that when their lover left them, they might be cheated out of the true value of their jewels.

By the sixties the United States was purchasing more gem diamonds than any other country in the world and girls from fifteen to a hundred and five were wearing them. Some liked them small and some liked them bold but all wore them now in the daytime or nighttime, at the beach or in the ballroom, with slacks and with satins, on jets and in jalopies.

Because of the plenitude of small diamonds—and money—fads abounded. The headache band of Mrs. Vanderbilt—a diamond-studded band of velvet worn low over the forehead—was shown as the latest thing on Fifth Avenue. Add-a-diamond brooches appeared—flowers or thistles with small gold wires on which one or more diamonds could be set like so many dew drops. A vogue for piercing the ears swept through the teen-age group and rich American youngsters, copying the Latinos, wore very small diamonds in their ears to school. Ringo, the drummer in the Beatles quartet who took his name from his passion for rings, summed up the American dream of the sixties: "If you want to give me a ring," he told a television audience candidly, "I prefer diamonds."

6

The Romance of the Bride's Ring

Julia I bring
To thee this ring
Made for thy finger fit
To show by this
That our love is
Or should be, like to it.

ROBERT HERRICK
(1591–1674)

*R*are is the archeological dig which does not turn up at least one ring: it is thought now that only the most primitive of men and women were without them: in gold at Mycenae and Troy, in ivory in Africa, in iron in Italy. Certainly there was never a period where the circle was not important: first drawn on the ground like a wall, to keep evil spirits out, later tied in fur or grass or twigs around the wrists, the ankles, the nose, the head, the ear and the fingers to keep the soul, the life spirit, in.

It took time, but not too many centuries, for symbols to replace knots and circles, for the earring, the nose ring and the finger ring to develop. Today there are many groups who prefer the ear or nose ring—South Americans the ear, Africans, Indonesians the nose, Hindus the toe ring—but since the beginning of history, the Mediterranean and European world has preferred the finger ring. Gold, bone, brass, iron, copper, silver, and platinum replaced the first grasses, but the form remained the same.

The early Celtic rings are a good example. The Celtic hunters were, off season, great basket weavers and their first rings were obviously of grass, for the rings found in their graves are copies of grass work, done in plaits

The marriage of Bacchus and Ariadne being performed by Venus. The ring
figures prominently in the ceremony. From a painting by Tintoretto (1578)
now in the Doges Palace, Venice.

and twists of thin gold wire. Were they already love rings? It was the Britons who gave us the love ring tradition. When a Briton wooed and won his maid he gave her a ring as a pledge of his protection: "wed" was his name for pledge and "wedding ring" became our betrothal ring.

Can you imagine the lovers' tryst? He wrapped in skins and perhaps still in his blue warpaint, she in a shift perhaps of grass, perhaps of fur. Did she have a choice of lover? She went as wife not only to him but to his younger brothers and his father too, Caesar tells us, but her children belonged to the man who brought her into the family. He was her husband, her protector. Their meals were of milk and meat and a few fruits; their entertainment the "song of innumerable birds," and the rituals of the tree-worshipping religion to which they belonged. The rich knew pearls and gold, the poor only flint and bronze. When the wife died her wedding ring went with her into the burial fire, thus surviving her. What did that ring mean to her?

Did she twist it on her finger when alone, waiting for him, worrying about him? Was there time for love? There was time to dance around the maypole in the spring, to teach pet geese tricks, time for ballads and crude flutes made of reed. When attacked—and after Caesar and his troops landed in Britain, they were repeatedly attacked—she and her children went into the swamps and stood there for days, often with only their heads above water. They had a courage and hardihood, these early people, a family life and a tribal life; it is not too credulous to believe their rings spell love.

The Mediterranean and the Oriental civilizations were far more advanced than the Britons at this time, just before the birth of Christ. The glory that was Greece was all but gone. Troy had been rebuilt for the eighth time. The Romans had baths and heating for their fine houses, they wore robes of silk and gold and sandals of leather. And they were crazy about rings. A rich man or woman might wear as many as fifteen or sixteen rings; even the thumbs were adorned. The Sybarites went to bed with fatigued hands from their many rings. But the third finger left hand was for them the finger where the love or marriage ring went. The Egyptians early had decided that and the Greeks had passed the custom along to the Romans. Master embalmers though they were, the Egyptians were romantic students of anatomy and decided that a "vein of love" ran directly from the heart to the tip of the third finger left hand. Pledges were made first by extending this finger towards one's partner until it touched his love finger, and then sealed with the placing of the ring. No hate could stick to this finger; no false pledge ring would fit it. It is amusing to think that so strongly was all this believed that the Romans called this finger "Medicus" and insisted that it and it only be used to stir potions for ailing loved ones—this on the

FROM REED TO RING

1. Plaited grass or rushes; earliest known type of troth ring.
2. Thong of leather as improvised by Roman soldiers in Europe.
3. Colonial diamond hoop called a "keeper" ring.
4. Bouquet cluster of large diamonds, nineteenth century, with a "rose" in the center.
5. Half-hoop with six matched diamonds in a row. Also made with three, five, or seven stones. Mounting of yellow gold.
6. Diamond solitaire in Tiffany prong-setting. The classic engagement ring since about 1890.

grounds that were there venom or poison on this finger it would go first to
the owner's heart. "Medicus" had another scientific use: the doctors claimed
fainting women could be revived by massaging it.

Roman rings were made of various metals. When in mourning, retire-
ment or if poor, they were iron; gold was preferred by the rich and social.
Engraved rings, studded with gems or adorned with cameos, were found in
the ashes at Pompeii; amber was well known and a great favorite for the
engraver's art. Glass, ivory, jet, and stone made up the cheapest rings; pearls
and rubies set in gold marked the beringed man or woman of property.
When a group of Romans got together for an evening's entertainment, each
might proffer a ring to pay the lute player or dancing girls. On birthdays
special rings were worn, designed for the day. Equally special was the matri-
monial ring.

Both the Romans and the Hebrews used a wedding ring and our customs today have in them echoes of theirs. The Romans' wedding ring was
an espousal or speaking-for ring; when a Roman of the freeman or noble
class wished to marry, he went to the girl's father or protector for permission
and then, in the presence of bride and bridegroom, her parents and his, a
marriage agreement was drawn up. This paper listed which possessions she
would bring and which he would bring to their union. When it was signed,
or sealed, the man gave to his fiancée a ring—perhaps the same one he had
pressed to the parchment as his seal, perhaps another. Giving and accepting
of the ring in this manner had a two-way meaning: that he gave his house-
hold into her keeping and that, in accepting it, she agreed to take care of
his house and possessions, his "lares and penates." Some of the earliest
marriage rings were of iron with a small key sticking out of the top, but
whether the keys were useful or merely symbolic we can only guess today.
Others were engraved with such words as *"ama me"*—"love me," or *"amo te"*
—"I love you." The ashes of Pompeii revealed many love rings of gold,
one has an engraving of a man and a woman holding hands, another a
double ring with two green stones in each circle.

The early Hebrews married under a canopy, just as Orthodox Jews do
today, signifying that the husband and wife entered a world of their own.
They also used a ring but the wife did not wear it after the ceremony. While
the Roman ring appears to have been symbolic, the early Hebrew ring was
more precise; it was expected to be of a specified value and fully paid for
at the time of the wedding. Traditionally it was large, heavy and gold.

The early Christians took over these customs but added a blessing to
the use of wedding rings and chose the third finger left hand as the marriage
finger. All groups insisted the ring be of some worth; a man who wanted to

Jewish wedding rings in various designs, elaborately worked and often inscribed with *Mazel Tov* or *Good Luck*.

His and hers sixteenth-century betrothal or wedding rings. Called a gimmal or twin, the inscription is visible only when the rings are separated and placed side by side: *Quod Deus conjunxit homo non separet*— Let no man separate what God has joined together.

marry a woman with a ring of grass or reed was mocked out of the community. Valued slaves of the Romans, however, might be given iron or even thin gold rings by their masters so that they might be properly married. While there is a lot of romantic legend about the necessity of the metal being durable "like married love" there also seems to have been the sensible thought that inasmuch as a wedding signified a man's protection for the woman and responsibility for her children, the wedding ring symbol ought to be more than a mere trifle—that only a good solid piece of gold or iron meant the man was dependable, or in the old phrase that he "carried some weight."

As Rome declined in power and decadence set in, greater and greater emphasis was placed on the outward forms of stability. The rings grew heavier and more valuable, the inscriptions more redolent of eternal passion, the contracts of marriage longer and more exacting. Form was replacing substance. Inevitably, it was in this period that we get our first diamond as a love-pledge ring—and also inevitably, that we find that pledge broken.

The story of the first diamond ring given as a love pledge is in verse. Written by the satirist-historian Juvenal, it tells how Agrippa, appointed king of the Jews by that malevolent Roman emperor Caligula, fell in love with his own sister and, greedy and possessive, pledged her to fidelity with the gift of a diamond ring. The sister Berenice, however, broke with both him and the diamond's power and ran off to live with Titus; in revenge, Agrippa ripped the ring from her hand and placed it in public view for all to see. The horror of both the pledge and the breaking of it comes out in the lines which speak of a young girl looking at the diamond in shocked fascination:

> One gem is there whose scintilating light
> Too strong temptation! Captivates her sight!
> The same (they tell her) the authentic stone
> That once on Berenice's finger shone
> The pledge which on a guilty sister's hand
> Agrippa placed.

This story was enough to ruin the diamond as a love pledge for years and perhaps it did. It is more realistic to think, however, that the gap in diamond ring history between the late Roman period and the beginnings of the Renaissance was due chiefly to a lack of diamonds among the populace. As Pliny noted, in Europe diamonds were in the first century A.D. only in the possession of kings and emperors; as the power of the Christian Church

Two medieval lovers wearing matching betrothal rings apparently set with garnets or rubies. Jeweled wreaths adorn both their brows; she wears a necklace, he fancy garters. Painting is of the Swabian School, circa 1470, and is in the Cleveland Museum of Art.

deepened and its control spread over Europe, sumptuary laws prohibited the wearing of any jewelry by men other than nobles or the clergy, and forbade trade with the infidels who handled diamonds. The Church took over the pagan myths and declared each gem had its own religious meaning: the diamond, fidelity to God and Christ; the ruby, glory through sacrifice—as with Christ's blood; and the emerald, peace and happiness, as given by God, like the green grass.

Now diamonds adorned chalices, priestly robes, and crosses; if a poor man or a merchant came upon one, he wore it in a small bag around his neck as a charm against the Devil, handling it stealthily as one must secret wealth and magical power.

But as the population grew and spread and dogma was shaken by scientific curiosity, the diamond slowly came to be displayed as an ornament of status, of beauty, and of worldly love. It is sometime in the fourteenth century that the first experiments in cutting and polishing the diamond succeeded in bringing out inner radiance—and in the fifteenth we get the first woman not of royal rank recorded as wearing one. She was, as we have seen, Agnès Sorel, mistress of the melancholy Charles VII of France, fashion model for the great financier Jacques Coeur and known to the people of Paris because of her fair skin, tranquil smile and blue eyes as the Dame de Beauté, the Lady of Beauty. As well as her own fabulous jewel-studded robes, she made for the King a waistcoat embroidered in pearls and precious stones which he liked so well he wore it hunting 250 days in a row—or until it shredded from his back begrimed with sweat and dust. Her only diamond ring, however, was neither a gift from the King nor a loaned showpiece from Jacques Coeur; it was given to her by a courtier who some whispered was in love with her, Etienne de Chevalier whose portrait was painted with hers on a paneled screen by the French artist Fouquet. Chevalier was going into a tournament wearing her colors when he presented her with the diamond ring. She was pleased, she showed it to the Queen, to whom, as the King's mistress, she acted also as a Lady in Waiting. The Queen looked at it a moment and then said with royal sarcasm: " 'Tis nice; you had need of a ring."

The diamond was brought by Jacques Coeur into first place as a personal ornament both through his fashionable display and the cuttings he encouraged. Within thirty years it had become also the royal betrothal stone. In 1477 the court counsel of the Archduke Maximilian of Germany ordered him to prepare for his marriage to Mary of Burgundy with two rings, one set with a diamond as an engagement—or betrothal—ring, the other a gold band, the wedding ring.

Henry VIII of England wearing three rings which exactly match the jewels on his collar and sleeves. Portrait was painted by Hans Holbein, also the royal jewel designer.

Elizabeth I, the last of the Tudors. She had three thousand dresses, countless diamonds and pearls, but her "wedding" ring was the State Seal of England. Portrait is by an unknown painter of the sixteenth century, now in the Metropolitan Museum of Art, New York, gift of J. Pierpont Morgan, 1911.

Francis I of France who
with Henry VIII of Englan
extravagant gift-giving and
jeweled robes. His favorite
was a pointed diamond g
for writing flirtatious mess
on palace windows. Portra
by Titian, now hangs in
Louvre, Paris.

Marie Antoinette, Queen of
France from 1774 to 1793. Her
diamonds were many and royal
but her two love rings were
simple and secret until a century after her execution. Portrait is by the Court painter of
her time, Madame Vigee-Le
Brun, now hanging in the Musée de Versailles.

Doubtless the not-too-highly regarded court of Germany was seeking status with the ancient court of Burgundy through these costly gifts, but happily for the diamond engagement ring, Maximilian gave his alliance with Mary a romantic air. Bold, popular and reckless, he was called later the last of the knights and he immortalized his troth with his queen in a love ballad. His diamond meant lifelong faithful devotion to him and it is sad to relate that she was a frail beauty; within four months of the marriage she was dead.

The diamond engagement ring lived on, however, its popularity growing fast. By 1502 we find an otherwise unknown young woman in England, one Marion Chambers, writing in her diary that her "marrying ring" was of gold and had "a dyamond and a rubie therein." Martin Luther's "marrying ring" had only a ruby; when he broke his vow of celibacy as a priest to marry a nun, he chose a gold ring displaying Christ on the cross, with a blood-red droplet of a ruby set over His head. Similarly the Tudors of England placed in the coronation ring a ruby signifying divine marriage of state and religion.

But the Tudors of England also encouraged the symbolism of the diamond; they gave away diamond rings as love and loyalty pledges with extravagant profligacy. Henry VIII was recklessly generous—he passed out diamonds to the nobles who supported him in his marriages, divorces, and executions as if they were daisies. And then he got more for himself. His own jewel case was a good-sized room in the palace and he boasted one diamond "as big as a walnut" and a robe with a forty-yard train sparkling with smaller ones. His hands, like those of the rich Romans, were fatigued with his many rings—several on each finger and usually one on his thumb—and his drinking cups were so bejeweled they were almost impossible to lift. He imported the famous Belgian artist Hans Holbein as his personal jewel designer; Holbein in turn imported his own personal diamond-cutter. His subjects liked rings too, preferably ones with pointed diamonds which could cut messages on the glass windows being installed in the best houses. Some called them Tower rings, a reference to the prisoners of the Crown who had cut farewell messages into the rock and glass of the Tower of London.

In France the French court of Francis I was almost as resplendent. At Fontainebleau—the summer palace—it was said that the ladies carried the "wealth of lands, forests and châteaux" in the diamonds pinned, sewn and draped in chains on their bosoms, and King Francis himself rivaled King Henry VIII in bejeweled splendor: when he and Henry met on the Field of the Cloth of Gold in 1532 Francis was said to be wearing the finest diamonds ever seen anywhere. His designer was Benvenuto Cellini and his wife's jewels included a great necklace of eleven diamonds.

The tag end of the Middle Ages and beginning of the Renaissance was a strange period. It was a time addicted to such morbid practices as picnicking in cemeteries, the curing of the bones of dead friends by boiling off the flesh, and the bestowing of memorial rings via wills with death's heads or even coffins upon them. But it was also a period of incredible extravagances, of sumptuous living (for the rich) with such unbelievable displays as gilded ships' masts, nobles' suits sewn with silver florins, and "holy" pilgrimages that were week-long frolicking orgies of merry-making. Extremes seem to have been the rule rather than the exception; either you had a dozen diamonds—or had only heard of one. Either you were in luck—or in trouble.

Yet it was also a simple period: every house, bell, and diamond had a name and was spoken of fondly as he or she, never "it." The Beau Sancy was named in this period. Success in war, hunting—or that mock war, the tournament—was considered the apex of manliness, knights pledged themselves to either kill for justice or die. Their ladies, adorned with their signet rings, encouraged them. The love of the simple shepherdess was celebrated in poetry and song but the rich were too restless, too beset with the problems of ruling to have much time for it themselves. So while nobles and kings passed out diamond rings, the simpler people echoed them with a less expensive mode of romantic expression: the poesy or posey ring.

This was of gold and inscribed with a small poem, some doubtless made at home by loving minds, others probably purchased with the ring. Favorites varied. "A vertuous wife a happy life." "As God decreed so we agreed." "In love linked fast while life dost last." A few were decorated with hands clasped in troth, a few with hearts, some of which were topped with coronets—but most spoke simply with words. "Forget not he who loveth thee." "Oh dear to me as Life can be." "Endless bee my love to thee." That most famous chivalric poem in France, *The Romance of the Rose,* starred a faithless flirt, but, like the Roman rings, the poesy rings of the late Middle Ages tell of the widespread yearnings for a gentler, more familial story.

The third finger left hand was still the marriage finger, the thumb was still popular for rings and the second finger left hand—the Digiter Infamous of the Romans and our middle finger—never decorated. Upper joints as well as lower joints might be ringed but few of the ladies slashed their gloves as did the Kings to show their jewels. Some think there was a proverb that a diamond in the wedding band was bad luck: it interrupted the circle of eternity. It is more likely this was sour grapes: the diamond was still too rare for commoners to own.

Even Queen Elizabeth I, who inherited her father's talent for sporting jewels along with several of his diamonds, gave a sardonyx as her love stone. Set in a ring she gave it to the hapless Lord Essex, promising him that if he ever needed her aid, he would get it if he sent it back to her. When he was in the Tower charged with treason, she waited in vain for it. Too much pride, she thought, not enough love—and she let his execution take place.

Elizabeth, a forceful woman with a separate house for her voluminous jewel-bedecked gowns, her wigs, and her iron corsets, said she was wife only to England, and wore as her wedding ring the seal of state. The wedding ring —a plain gold band—was part of church ceremony now. 'With this ring I thee wed, with my body I thee worship and with all my worldly goods I thee endow," read the *First Book of Common Prayer* in 1543. An engagement ring was a matter of choice—or wealth. Some of Shakespeare's lovers exchanged them; some did not. As defined in Dr. Johnson's pithy dictionary they were not too desirable. The ring, he said, "was a circular instrument placed upon the noses of hogs and the fingers of women to restrain them and bring them into subjection."

Diamonds were incredibly costly things in that period. They were now coming in from Europe by the new route opened up in 1498 by the Portuguese Vasco da Gama—no longer was it necessary that Christian ships pass through the swords, arrows and burning oil of the infidels who held the eastern gateway to the Orient; now it was possible to bring diamonds directly into Antwerp and to the diamond cutters assembling there by going around Africa to the coastal Indian ports of Madras and Goa. But they were still not plentiful; not until the French diamond merchant Tavernier came back to Louis XIV in the mid-seventeenth century with literally pounds of diamonds do we hear of diamonds being sold in batches. The Sun King's collection of diamonds was magnificent, vying only with the jewels of the Moguls of India, but we will not deal with it here because while it too pushed further upward the popularity and status of the diamond, Louis XIV did nothing whatsoever for rings. Whether this was superstitution—ugly hands —the hated memories of the Medicis' poison rings—or a lesson learned from the bankruptcy of the ring-giving Tudors we don't know. Diamonds, the kings of France had in great abundance—but not diamond rings.

Even Marie Antoinette cared only for two modest rings. She was a diamond lover; she wrote her mother she had a "fantasy for diamonds—a passion" and she had great numbers of them. Her dowry contained her portion of the Crown Jewels of the Hapsburgs; King Louis XV gave her a casket of family trinkets when she married his weakling son. She was fourteen then and he fifteen; she was young and beautiful and full of playful, frivolous yearnings for the gay and glittering, and he weary with his own crippled impotence and the burdens of kingship too early. Parties, charades, clothes and jewels became her way of life; the royal jewelers visited her at least twice a week offering her new baubles she rarely could resist and although her dignified mother begged her by letter and messenger to be more serious, she showed no inclination to follow her advice.

But as she grew older, she fell secretly in love and in the two rings that long after her violent death revealed that love, we find the serious heart of Marie Antoinette. First there is the ring she had made for herself, the one she wore constantly after her fourth child was born, after she felt she had done her duty by the royal marriage arranged for her, and after she had found true love. It was gold and the bezel held the Swedish coat of arms, a signet of her secret lover, Axel de Fersen. Inside, unseen until her executioners stripped it from her in the dungeon before they carted her off to the guillotine, was the inscription in Italian: *"Tutto a te mi guida"*—"Everything leads me to you."

Then there was the ring she sent the faithful Fersen when she was imprisoned in the Tuileries. Twice he had banished himself rather than bring harm to her, her family, or her reputation. Once he had tried to rescue her, her children, and her husband, the King, but he had been foiled. Now she had banned him from Paris but she could not, she wrote him, "live without writing to him"—and she wanted him to keep in touch with her. The ring she sent him had on it the fleur-de-lis, that simple, thornless flower sent by God to the first French kings. She had worn the ring herself, she wrote to him in cipher, to warm it with her blood. Inside was the inscription "Faint-heart he who forsakes her." But this message was not quite the invitation to hazard all that it seems at first glance; when on receiving it, he immediately got a letter through to her that he would visit her in prison, she replied that he must not—that her happiness at seeing him would be nothing beside the risking of his life. "I live only to serve you," he wrote her in return and wigged, costumed, and carrying a forged passport, he slipped into Paris, into the Tuileries, and saw her for the last time. The Affair of the Diamond Necklace she never owned rocked the whole world; the story of the two rings she possessed was her secret and his for more than a century when her letters to Fersen were discovered in Sweden.

Others were more overt with *their* "secret" rings; the eighteenth century was also the period when message rings began. Some were political, some signified belief, some were romantic. None, however, used words: if you wished to say "dearest" with a message ring you spelled out the letters with the stones representing them; the diamond was *D,* the emerald *E,* the amethyst *A,* the ruby *R,* and so on. Lovers still use these codes today but it has been some time since a word such as "repeal" was set in jewels—as it was during the days of the hated Corn Laws passed by England. By 1782 just before the Revolution, ring-wearing had reached such popularity that an essayist wrote gloomily that holding a lady's hand was like "clasping a quantity of stones."

In New England during this same period, the late eighteenth century, land and freedom were the prizes, not jewels. The Puritans indeed frowned upon what they called the pagan ostentation of even a wedding ring; the Quakers in Philadelphia prided themselves on their plainness. But the Virginia cavaliers and the New York gentry, especially those of Dutch ancestry, felt differently. There was always a group in New York and Virginia who imported their fashions from Paris and loved frivolous things. As early as 1743 New York had its own lapidary mill and jewelry makers and importers.

The fashion leaders were as likely to be men in this period as women, however. While the New York women prized their simple wedding bands with their "keepers" or guards set with small diamonds they called sparks, the gay young blades along the Hudson wore big diamonds on their shoe buckles, carried two watches and had their coat buttons studded with jewels. These were the Macaroni, the lads who had gone to Europe for the grand tour and had returned home to become the Yankee Doodle Dandies mocked in the long-lived ballad.

But they were not ring-wearing dandies. We hear little of rings in the America of this period. George Washington gave his wife a watch with diamond hands for a wedding present, although he did give rings to his faithful officers, a particularly nice one going to Lafayette. Perhaps the hands of the colonial ladies were too busy for rings; the first glimpse we get of any of importance comes with the Currier and Ives prints of the affluent mid-nineteenth century. Here the brides are shown in long-sleeved white satin dresses, with bracelets over their cuffs, and a diamond ring on the middle finger of the right hand.

Did the artist choose this finger because it displayed the ring better? Was the young lady going to switch it to her left hand after the ceremony? We do not know. Which finger the betrothal ring and the wedding ring are worn on has varied throughout history. Many early Roman Catholics wore theirs on the left hand, probably because the Church wears its rings on the right. Some Protestants but not all have worn theirs on the right hand; the Germans still do. England has been inclined to stick to the old Roman-Egyptian-Catholic custom of third finger left hand; so have Americans.

The Currier and Ives ring is of yellow gold studded with a fairly large diamond, apparently a marquise-cut, that is, an oval with 58 facets, the same number the first Venetian brilliant had. It was quite unlike the favorite diamond ring of England of this same period, a band of gold with three to five sizable diamonds mounted across the top, and called the princess ring.

Other love rings in this time were simpler; orange blossoms were a favorite engraving; plain inscriptions of names and date and often the words "with love" were inside the band, not out, as they had once been.

Some were elaborate. Queen Victoria's wedding ring, and one gathers from history she picked it out herself, was a gold serpent with its tail in its mouth, an ancient symbol of eternity, and was studded with twelve small diamonds. She craved ornament but frowned on wearing diamonds in the daytime. Even after Britain had bought the new South African diamond mines, she wore them only at night, like the Roman wives who wore iron rings around the house and gold ones to parties.

On the fiftieth anniversary of her reign she found a diamond necklace by her breakfast plate, a gift from her children, and out of courtesy she felt she had to wear it to church. When she returned, however, she took it off, confiding to her diary that it made her feel "too dressed up."

The American billionaires' wives claimed they felt the same way about diamonds, that they were evening wear, but apparently they never felt too dressed up. Their splendor at the opera in New York, Boston, or Philadelphia was the talk of the world; only in royal processions had so many diamonds been seen as blazed under the new found electric chandeliers that lighted up the opera's Golden and Diamond Horseshoes, those famed half-circles of expensive balcony boxes in New York. With tiaras on their pompadours, necklaces at their throats, brooches on their bodices, and large rings flashing from their fingers, the Gay Nineties' dowagers were blinding in their brilliance. Newly rich and greedy, they demanded and received the trappings of royalty. If the family wealth had not come along in time for a diamond engagement ring, no matter, better to have it late than never beside the breakfast—like Queen Victoria's diamond necklace. Other Americans, following the wheat, copper, sugar, and railroad society through the ever-excitable American press, quickly followed suit. By 1900 the careful *Ladies Home Journal* announced solemnly that a diamond engagement ring was in just as good taste day or night as a pearl one, and far better than an opal, which was deplored as bringing bad luck.

The South African Dutch discovered the new diamonds and the British took the industry over but it was the *nouveau riche* Americans of the nineties who took these jewels to their hearts and hands in pride, affection and esteem.

Almost all engagement diamonds of this period were round, only a few were oval, and only those set in France, marquises. The ring itself was yellow gold and the diamond sat well inside the bezel with little but its top facets showing. Only rarely was it a large stone; big, 3- and 4-carat stones were used for necklaces, pendants or tiaras, but the small ring stone was often surrounded by others to make it look larger.

In South Africa diamond production was keyed to the number of engagements expected in England and the United States; it was, the great diamond king Cecil Rhodes declared, the "symbol of licit love." Only on the continent of Europe was it also the symbol of illicit love: there a joke circulated that a man bought three diamonds in his life—the first for his bride-to-be before their marriage, the second for the mistress he took after his marriage, and the third for his wife when she discovered his mistress.

Until after World War I, it was still the jewel of the rich or sophisticated and as the diamond engagement ring became as much a part of courtship as the wedding ring was of marriage, rituals developed about it. First it was held that the man bought it; the girl had no voice in the matter. Indeed, she was expected to be surprised to receive it, just as she was surprised at being proposed to. ("This is so sudden," was the ladylike answer to "will you marry me?")

If the man was reasonably sure of being accepted, he might be prepared with the engagement ring already bought and present it to her when she said: "Yes." But this was considered romantic, even a little off-beat; it was generally held to be wiser to wait not only upon the girl's acceptance but also upon her parent's approval; parents had a strong voice in Victorian marriages. Advice might be sought from the father-in-law–to-be about the ring; the ability to purchase a handsome engagement ring spoke well for a prospective husband.

But the ring was not presented with any but the loving couple present; somehow the chaperons, the ever-loving parents, and the pesky little brothers were to be avoided for a romantic presentation.

Once given and received, the ring was then shown formally to the parents and, after the engagement was properly announced, to friends. Despite all this elaboration, however, the superstition that a diamond engagement ring must never be taken off did not grow up until later—until after a lot of luckless ladies had lost their rings removing them to wash, to sleep, or just because they were heavy.

As the peak of the Victorian era passed and the fussy, brilliant little queen left more and more of her public appearances to her dashing, handsome son Edward, Prince of Wales, and his beautiful wife, Alexandra, engagement rituals became less rigorous and diamonds that went with them more charming and less formal.

The introduction of platinum at the turn of the century spurred on the

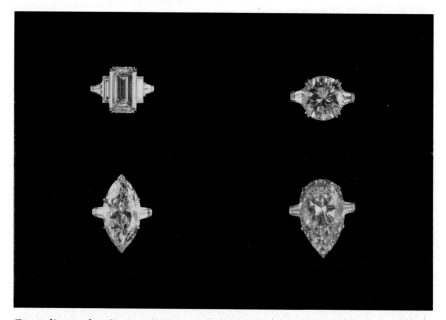

Four diamond solitaire shapes: upper left, a 3.50-carat emerald cut; upper right, a 5.38-carat brilliant; bottom left, an 11.17-carat pearshape; bottom right, a 6.76-carat marquise. Stones of this size and quality cost from $2,500 up per carat in 1964 and were in demand by the rich of all countries. All stones were purchased and sold by Harry Winston, Inc.

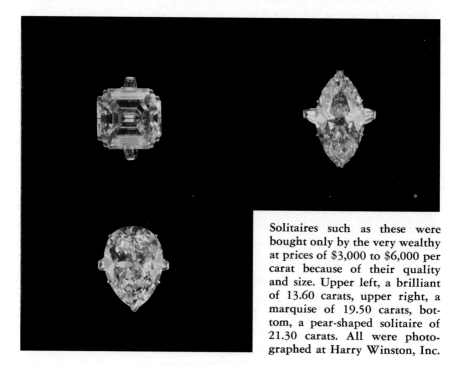

Solitaires such as these were bought only by the very wealthy at prices of $3,000 to $6,000 per carat because of their quality and size. Upper left, a brilliant of 13.60 carats, upper right, a marquise of 19.50 carats, bottom, a pear-shaped solitaire of 21.30 carats. All were photographed at Harry Winston, Inc.

informality; now the diamond became more dazzling in its new white setting (approved of by Alexandra) and the once silent engaged girls spoke up in covetous praise of it. Etiquette authorities fell into line; it was agreed the girl should have a voice in choosing the ring, and that it would indeed be wise if she tried it on before letting her fiancé purchase it. New ways of cutting developed, adding brilliance to the stone itself; smart American girls learned something about diamonds and went along to help when their fiancés shopped.

In general, however, the rituals lasted well into the twenties. World War I gave platinum a boost—after gold was requested by the government, platinum was considered patriotically chic, although some sentimentalists preferred a mixture of gold and brass. With the rise of the flapper, the popularity of the Tin Lizzie, the smoking of women and other evidence of feminine emancipation, the parental role in engagements grew less and the young girl's role larger. Matching engagement and wedding rings grew in popularity under feminine demand for the ornamental as well as the sentimental. The diamond ring salon, where a couple could examine engagement rings in privacy, began to be talked about. Soon couples were openly wandering through jewelry stores together—and during the depression, when even the rich ignored the engagement-announcement party, it became quite acceptable for a girl to announce publicly her coming marriage with the flash of a diamond, third finger left hand.

By the 1940's a marketing survey revealed that three out of five American brides (or 60 per cent) received a diamond engagement ring sometime before marriage. The average size of the diamond was less than 1 carat but those who could afford them bought big solitaires: the Duchess of Windsor's ring of 20 carats lit the way.

In the British commonwealth, too, more and more diamond engagement rings were being worn. Despite her vast collection of jewels, the one diamond that the then Princess Elizabeth—now Queen—wore around the clock was the 3-carat brilliant which Prince Philip of Greece had given her when their marriage was agreed upon. In Canada, Australia, Bermuda, and the Bahamas, her subjects-in-love followed royal example. Like the Duchess of Windsor's ring, Elizabeth's was an emerald-cut solitaire—the rectangularly shaped cut for diamonds that had been launched in Paris with Cubism and the art of the rectangular. Its supporters declared it made the feminine finger look dainty in comparison with the stone's bulky brightness; its opponents clung to the round brilliant of tradition or compromised with an oval or marquise.

What difference did it make that the engagement ring was now much

With her diamond engagement ring the bride wears a serpentine necklace from Cartier's of baguettes, marquises, pear shapes and round diamonds as her bridal headdress. Irregular snowflakes with the same diamond cuts are the motif of the earrings.

more expensive than the wedding ring? Apparently none at all. It was the first gift of value a man gave a girl and it was more than a gift—a promise of good things to follow, of trust and faithfulness embodied in a pledge of obvious worth.

And a high credit rating! Aiding in the twentieth-century democratization of the diamond was the ever-increasing number of jewelry stores—fine and not so fine—who offered credit. Etiquette authorities differed on how much credit *should* be sought for the purchase of a love pledge; but none felt that a ring bought on credit was any less sentimental than one bought for cash.

Because of the popularity of the "matching" wedding ring, many wedding rings were now bought on credit too. Some of the wedding rings were diamond studded but the most popular continued to be the traditional gold wedding band, especially among those who wanted a double-ring ceremony with similar rings for man and wife. Men of the twentieth century did not accept platinum wedding rings with the pleasure their brides did; a man's wedding band of platinum was rare.

By the affluent fifties a remarkably high percentage of American women owned at least one diamond—and that was an engagement ring. Many owned more than one; baguettes in a brooch bought to go with a special costume, perhaps, a pendant stone, a pair of earrings. Others were receiving the love tokens that once only kings gave their queens and their mistresses— diamonds marking a wedding anniversary, a rise in status, the birth of a child. Big stones were in demand but hard to get and expensive; for many the answer was the chunky clustering of small stones or *pavé*—a French method of setting small diamonds so closely that the metal was almost invisible. Others turned in their solitaires of the twenties and thirties for the larger ones of the sixties.

Personal though these gifts seemed to both the man and his love and personal though they were, they were all part of the long history of love rings and pledge rings, of legend and truth, of power and perquisites, of fidelity and hope: the ring remained the love token that spoke not only of the present but of eternity. Only the poor, the Bohemians or the whimsical preferred other tokens of love—or none.

How deep this goes is revealed by a strange, sad incident in the life of Jacqueline Kennedy. After President Kennedy was assassinated his widow stood by his coffin for a last moment. When their baby Patrick had died, together they had put in his small coffin a gold St. Christopher's medal Jacqueline had given Jack when they had become engaged. Now she stood alone beside her husband's coffin wanting to give him something, something that was hers, something that she loved. And so she slipped her wedding ring from her finger and placed it upon his finger.

The word of what she had done sped around the world. In the Senate, it became part of a poetic eulogy to the slain president. "And she took a ring and placed it on his hand . . ."

But Jacqueline Kennedy was troubled.

"Do you think it was right?" she asked her husband's dear friend, Kenny O'Donnell. "Now I have nothing left."

That night, late, Kenny O'Donnell went to the hospital and retrieved her ring for her. She put it on her finger again and whispered "Thank you." Death had parted them but their symbol of love, their circle of faith, embraced her still.

7

Purchasing the Sentimental, Ornamental and Providential Diamond

Then on my finger I'll have a ring
Not one of rush but a golden thing
And I shall be glad as a bird in Spring
Because I am married on a Sunday.

English Ballad, *circa* 1550

*F*or some decades now it has been considered quite proper in America for a nice girl to have a voice in the purchase or procuring of her engagement ring. In 1881 the thought was first voiced when *Social Etiquette in New York* not only advised engaged girls to assist their fiancés in the choosing of their rings but suggested that they be clever about it. "Choose a flawless diamond for the stone," the book stated. "There is a haunting superstition about the perfection of this symbol that is not without its uses."

At the turn of the century Emily Post, the great etiquette arbiter, went even further. She declared it was not only proper but mandatory that an engaged girl help choose her rings—engagement *and* wedding—saying: "The man who produces a ring from his pocket the instant a girl says 'yes' never existed outside of novels."

Mrs. Post also agreed that if a diamond were chosen it should be flawless, but with her usual forthrightness declared that she did not consider any engagement ring, much less a diamond, a necessity.

"The engagement ring is not essential to the validity of a betrothal," she stated so firmly that her publishers italicized the sentence. "Countless

The majority of engagement rings are purchased by the young couple together, a practice that Emily Post termed mandatory.

The new fiancée modestly shows off her new ring. The diamond tells the rest of the story.

wives have never had an engagement ring at all; many another has received her ring long after marriage."

She continued realistically suggesting that it was vulgar to go into debt for a large diamond—and unbecoming to wear a small one. If a ring was desired but diamonds were too expensive, she suggested birthstones, noting that a clear large aquamarine looked remarkably like a diamond anyway.

Apparently most brides accepted her advice to help choose the ring but rejected her attitude that diamonds were for the rich only. Today it is generally held by jewelers that most engagement rings are bought with the girl present, that most of these choose diamonds, and that most are quite happy with small stones.

Indeed, half of all engagement ring purchases are made by the couple together, jewelers report. Only 3 per cent are made by the girl shopping with her mother, and another small group of girls purchase their rings alone. About a third bring in inherited or gift stones to be set or reset. Only about one out of four of mid-twentieth-century brides choose a stone other than a diamond—and out of this small group only about one in ten foregoes an engagement ring entirely.

But for all this wise and proper picking and choosing of diamonds by not just one person but two, it is generally agreed by jewelers that of all the purchases people make the buying of a diamond is the most unstudied.

Over and over again jewelers mourn the foolhardy way in which the engagement ring is bought and shake their heads over the lack of foresight and care which prevails among their youthful customers.

It is said that diamond purchases generally are made in one of three attitudes: sentimental, ornamental, or providential—and most are sentimental. Diamonds for centuries have exerted a strange influence over the emotions of man. More than likely a man's first diamond purchase is made in such a sentimental mood that he might as well make it blindfold.

"We want young diamond customers. We like them," a chief diamond salesman at Tiffany's on Fifth Avenue said. "But it is worrisome when couples come in and the man waves his hand expansively over our case of diamond engagement rings and says to his girl 'Choose what you like, darling.' He doesn't mean it and she knows he doesn't but neither of them know what they mean.

"We've got diamonds of 15 points to 15 carats—from $80 to $280,000. No couple can possibly make a proper choice among them in literally a fog of sentiment."

Any diamond no matter how small should be purchased only after some study is made of both the diamond itself and the reason for its being purchased. Just because the first diamond is likely to be a sentimental diamond commercial caution and care should not be flung to the wind. And just because the girl has the final choice, no man should forego his own perogatives of getting beauty and delight for his money.

It is the experts' present advice, therefore, that before any couple decides to purchase a diamond ring together, the man should come in and first make some study of diamonds in general, and second study the diamonds available to him at the stores of his choice. Then and then only should he bring in his fiancée and allow her to choose which one of the several diamonds *he* likes and can afford.

Every jewelry store provides literature on diamonds and all good ones have salesmen who are more than happy to educate customers on gems. The difficulty is that so few people know even what questions to ask; diamonds are too often either a once-in-a-lifetime purchase with rather mysterious overtones, or gifts accepted gracefully but with little knowledge.

One of Harry Winston's repeated plaints hinges around this gift aspect. He is a diamond lover as well as merchant and quite frequently falls in love with one of the stones he is selling—like the 426.50-carat diamond cut in his own shop and sold to the Greek shipping merchant Niarchos. For months he kept that stone on his desk, now rolling it like a marble, now turning it in his hand and studying it with his eye loup.

"Some of the women I sell to get the thrill of a lifetime out of a diamond's beauty," he said. "Others don't appreciate half the stuff they get. They'd wear diamonds on their ankles if it was stylish—and look at them only when they tossed them in the jewelry box. A diamond on the third finger left hand ought to be a diamond really worth looking at."

What makes a diamond worth looking at—and therefore worth purchasing? Although each diamond is as unique as a thumbprint there are four qualities which pertain to all diamonds which should be heeded whether they are purchased sentimentally, ornamentally, or providentially. Jewelers have summed them up as the four C's and it's a useful phrase.

The first C is carat weight. This plays a large role in the retail price. The carat is so small a unit that it takes 142 to make an ounce. One-hundredth of a carat is called a point; thus Tiffany's smallest ring of 15 points weighs .15 of a carat. There are tricks to making a small diamond—one less than a carat—look larger but nothing changes its actual weight. The national average size of an engagement diamond is a half carat or less: the average suburban woman with her own car has a diamond a carat or more in size.

The second C is cut. This refers both to the shape of the stone—round, square, oval—and the facets upon it. The most popular shape is the round brilliant with 58 facets; the most fashionable in America are the marquise or boat shaped and the emerald or rectangular. Proper faceting is a precise art, but it is possible to glimpse something of the faceting caliber by turning the diamond to catch the light.

If it lacks fire or brilliance, it is obviously poorly faceted or poorly proportioned, although only an expert can tell you in what manner its workmanship is in error. The most usual mistake (sometimes made under orders by the cutter to save weight) results in the spread stone—that is, a stone in which the table is too large for perfect refraction. In the trade this fault is called swindling—possibly because it is believed such a diamond is swindled of its beauty in an effort to bring more profit through its weight, possibly because the customer is being swindled of diamond beauty.

The third C is color. The traditional engagement diamond is expected to be as flawless as true love and as white as the bride's gown. The best way to check for color is to look *through* the stone rather than down into it, either in daylight or light approximating daylight. Yellowish tints reduce the value of a diamond; to be a champagne diamond, a canary, or a blue, the color must be clear and strong. The most famous colored diamond is of course the Hope Diamond. It is rare when a diamond is that vivid a blue but there are many beautiful steel blues available to those who love them. At Baumgold Brothers, the great New York brokers, I saw one of 18 carats, cut in a pendant shape, a pool of twilight blue water.

The last but not least C is clarity, meaning the absence of carbon spots, inner flaws, or surface blemishes. Truly flawless diamonds are rare; tiny inclusions invisible to the naked eye are frequent. A really top quality 4-carat diamond may sell for as much as $3,000 a carat. A good jeweler will tell you when a diamond has flaws and how important they are. Gemologists use a magnifier of at least ten power to spot flaws; so do fine jewelers.

The four C's are what make up value in a diamond and are basically what determine cost. But in considering them none can be considered without the usually unmentioned fifth C—the customer. The customer may prefer a big stone somewhat flawed to a small perfect one—he may even like a swindled stone and not miss its lack of brilliance. It is also possible for a customer to decide that a perfect diamond in his price range is so small as to be not worth buying. Gaining knowledge of the diamond, each customer must integrate it with his own desires and needs to get the diamond that is closest to his own heart's desire.

Then, having harmonized these things, he must prepare to place his trust in a good jeweler, his attitude properly cautious, but not suspicious. Two remarks illustrate the necessity for a middle-of-the-road position.

The first remark is an echo of the old *caveat emptor* of the Romans: Let the buyer beware. At the Diamond Dealers Club in New York there was a phrase used to refer to men who had made poor diamond buys because they were talked into them by glib salesmanship. Such men, it was said, "bought the salesman, not the stone." Each customer should be prepared to make inquiries about the diamond itself, never taking the salesman or his store for the value of the stone.

The second comes from an American representative of one of the large Dutch diamond firms who deal aggressively with tourists. In these after a view of the diamond works, tourists are pressed to purchase a diamond or two. Are they rooked—as tourists so often are? "Not if they put themselves in our hands and ask us what the best values are. But if they're Mr. Smart Aleck and expect to cheat or be cheated, we hate to disappoint them," said the Dutch salesman.

In order for a customer to achieve the perfect posture of trustful intelligence, it is necessary that he select his jeweler with as much care as he would his doctor. How does one discover a good jeweler? As a general rule of thumb, time will tell something; that is, a long-established firm is likely to be more trustworthy than a new one simply because if any firm is in the habit of cheating its customers even slightly, the news would bankrupt them quickly.

Picking a store because it was the store where father got his engagement ring, however, is not always a sure test of tried and true ownership. Some opportunists buy an old name along with the merchandise and while presenting an appearance of stability actually are just passing through town. Others may be one of a large chain. A few queries at the Better Business Bureau or your local newspaper may bring an old store's ownership up to date, and provide information on a new one's reputation.

Another test can be made by finding out which jewelry stores or jewelry departments are members of the American Gem Society. This is a society of jewelers dedicated to high standards and the education of their members and the public. Specific titles are granted the staffs of stores which qualify. Registered Jeweler, for instance, means that a man has made some study of diamonds and other gems. Certified Gemologist is higher: it means, among other things, that the knowledge of the member holding such a title is such that he or she can distinguish between such look-alikes as a brilliant, clear white topaz and a brilliant, clear white diamond, or determine exactly the number of flaws in an apparently flawless gem. It is astonishing how many jewelers do not know how to test precisely for quality—and if such men get cheated in their purchases, it is expectable that they will pass their losses along.

Can a bargain be had from a wholesaler? Of course it can if the wholesaler is a reputable man with a stable relationship to his community. But it is not likely any wholesaler can give you a *great* bargain. The mark-up on cut diamonds from wholesale to retail is about 50 per cent (of retail) but not all of this goes into chandeliers and carpets. Part goes into the equipment necessary for viewing and testing the diamond, part into designing the settings, some into the education of the staff, some into the time given each customer. It is possible to get a stone at 20 to 30 per cent off retail price at a wholesaler but the customer must pay for his bargain with his own time and trouble or someone else's and the odds he faces are worthwhile only in special situations, such as a relative in the business.

Are diamonds much cheaper in Europe or Africa where they are nearer the source? Theoretically they should be; actually they are only when they lack certain standards taken for granted in the United States. When the gemologist and jeweler Elaine Cooper of Philadelphia went to Johannesburg in South Africa a few years ago after going to the mines she went into the stores to see what was being sold. The diamonds available she found astonishingly poor. "Good diamonds go where there's a good market," she reported later. "The best come to the United States."

It is also much more difficult to return diamonds to foreign salesmen, wholesalers, and fly-by-nights.

Why must the problem of returning a diamond come up before a diamond is even purchased? Because since diamonds after all *do* live forever they are frequently returned or resold. Perhaps it is a matter of needing the cash more than the stone—a matter which we will discuss more fully when we discuss providential diamond purchases—often it is a need for a new setting or a larger stone.

Impossible as it may seem when the diamond ring is purchased, engagements do get broken and it is a rare man indeed who wants to keep a returned ring in his dresser drawer. If the ring is bought from a reputable jeweler it may be returned very simply. A "Dear John" letter is necessary from the girl in most cases—because jewelers and judges take the position that once an engagement diamond is bought, it belongs to the girl, not to the man, even though he purchased it. Legally she doesn't have to give it back to him even if the engagement is broken.

Will the man then get his money back? Most of it, at a good store, although not all. Probably the ring has been sized to the girl's finger. Possibly it has been engraved. Perhaps it has been flung across the room and the setting is damaged. It is a *used ring,* in short, although not a used diamond.

There is also the problem of the divorced woman. Her wedding ring she usually throws in the river, hides in a corner, or pawns in a hockshop but her engagement diamond is something else again. Perhaps she will want it resized for her right hand. Perhaps she will want it clustered with small diamonds or turquoises to disguise its original use. Perhaps she simply wants to sell it.

Whatever she wants to do, it is easier for all concerned if the jeweler from whom it was purchased is neither distant nor disappointing in his help.

There is always the possibility, of course, that she won't want to return it at all but rather wear it on her third finger left hand where she is used to it. The television star and jeweler Zsa Zsa Gabor wore three large rocks on her engagement finger even after she was divorced. "Who cares where I wear them?" she asked. "Thees is the finger they were made for."

Some husbands and wives also like to return the first engagement ring for a larger one after they have been married several years. Recognizing this, Sears Roebuck guarantees in its catalog that any diamond purchased from them can be returned as credit on a larger stone. Others, because of current scarcity, are advertising to buy any quality diamonds of more than a carat. Although most jewelers don't see the need to advertise this so frankly, all major stores follow the same pattern. None however grants full credit for the ring and the setting once it is used, only the stone itself.

Should return be discussed at the time of purchase? I would think not, unless the discussion hinges around the hope of purchasing a larger diamond or an anniversary diamond later. It would not be either well-mannered or pleasant to discuss any other reason for the diamond's return during an engagement.

Should the wedding ring be purchased at the same time as the engagement ring? That depends on the kind of ring bought and the place where it is bought. If a girl knows she is going to want a gold band on her wedding ring instead of platinum (which today is more popular) she may feel it is more attractive to get a gold-banded engagement ring. Similarly if she is choosing her ring from a set of matched rings, the wedding ring should be sized and set aside at the same time—although rare is the girl who wants to try it on before the wedding day.

Similarly, if the diamond is purchased in a small store without much stock it is advisable to secure the wedding ring at the same time; in a large store like Tiffany's, Nieman Marcus, or one of the Zale chain there is no need to pick the wedding ring until later since there will always be one to

ration with ammonia in it, and rub. Some jewelers sell a prepared diamond cleaner. Winston's cleans its diamonds by boiling them but this is not recommended for general use. Any stone but a diamond will shatter in boiling water, and even a diamond may if it goes from cold to hot too rapidly. There is also a risk of damaging the setting.

The actress Natalie Wood had a very special problem recently which may concern a few diamond lovers. She was ordered to remove her 14-carat diamond engagement ring received from Arthur Loew, Jr., during the shooting of the motion picture *Sex and the Single Girl*. She refused. Briefly it looked like breach of contract in one form or another, but the director compromised by letting her turn the stone inward and covering the band with pink tape.

Whether a ring is worn constantly or kept in a jewel box at night, it is wise to insure it separately from other belongings. A brief description from the jeweler of weight, cut, clarity, and color will provide the agent with enough information to grant total coverage in the case of loss, theft, or damage: about $20 will pay the "all risk" diamond policy for three years on rings with a 1-carat diamond.

Must the same engagement ring be worn forever or until death do you part?

The First Lady, Ladybird Johnson, still wears the modest diamond ring she and President Johnson picked out together in Austin, Texas, in 1934 a month before their marriage, even if they have become multi-millionaires since then. The band is yellow gold, the brilliant less than a carat and the wedding ring that accompanies it was ordered from Sears Roebuck for $2.98.

But many other women—and their husbands—see no reason for clinging to the same ring on purely sentimental grounds. Indeed, one woman who prefers to be nameless, has received a new engagement ring every year of her married life, each stone a trifle larger than the last, each one bought by turning in the previous one as partial payment. Engagement rings are a personal and private matter. And, as everyone knows, a woman has a right to change her mind about anything.

Some prefer not to change the diamond but simply the setting. To some husbands this is as upsetting as getting a new ring—until their brides persuade them that it's the diamond that was the love token, not its setting. There is no happiness or romance in a love token which doesn't please— and some men charm to the thought that a woman is still so fond of her engagement diamond that she wants it in a more perfect setting.

It is bad form after marriage to suggest that the original diamond be used in another piece of jewelry and a new diamond bought for a new engagement ring? It is quite possible that a married couple outgrows the engagement ring, especially when circumstances demanded then that it be a small stone. There is no reason whatsoever against using the original diamond in some other piece of jewelry or resetting it with other larger stones in a new engagement ring. Sometimes the husband is eager to have this done and the wife is unhappy; a discussion with the jeweler on the many possibilities may solve the question of how to have sentiment and ornament too.

Should a diamond engagement ring be bought on credit? It can be, for they are offered everywhere on varying terms. It is my feeling that the payments should be arranged to terminate before the marriage, however, the sentiment's sake if no other. Certainly no girl should have to expect to pay for her own engagement ring and no man should either ask her to or permit it.

Are there other problems of etiquette in the choice of an engagement ring? There are few rules; the chief thing to remember is that while both the man and the girl should be pleased with their decision, the choice of how much to spend is the man's and the choice of how to spend it is the girl's. One man I know was told flatly by his fiancée he should produce a 10-carat diamond or nothing. He produced nothing. It was not up to her to pick the size—that was setting the cost. It was up to her only to choose the stone and ring she liked within the bounds of cost he had set.

Another girl faced a different problem. Her fiancé's mother offered her an emerald for her engagement ring. She wanted a diamond. She asked if she could have the emerald set with two small diamonds on each side. The mother said no, she thought an emerald made a nicer ring than a diamond, and besides it was traditional in the family that the fiancées wore solitaire emeralds. The girl politely refused it. The mother in this instance erred in giving the girl no choice. Fortunately for the couple she was not backed up by her son.

If the girl *wants* no choice, however, that's a different matter. If he says to her, "The family has a diamond in the vault" and she says, "That's fine with me," it is quite all right to give it to her as is.

Reginald Gardiner of the New York Gardiners Island clan went to the family vault alone for the heirloom diamond he gave his bride, put it in his pocket and then forgot it until they were both in Bergdorf's for a fitting of the bridal gown. "Here, darling," he cried as she came out of the salon. "I nearly forgot your ring." It was a 7-carat solitaire and while the salesgirls nearby shed tears of mixed sentiment and envy, he slipped it happily on her third finger left hand.

The Gardiner diamond needed neither recutting nor resetting but many old diamonds do. Most rings that have been used before should be resized and cleaned professionally: grandmother's diamond may also be vastly improved at a small cost by recutting.

Should a diamond ring from a broken engagement be used again for a second engagement? This is a question that only the couple themselves can answer. It would depend on how well known the first engagement was, how often the ring was worn, how unhappy the break-up. There are few girls who want a ring rejected by another woman, however beautiful it is— but there *are* some.

What if a man can't afford a diamond? Some men take Mrs. Post's advice and suggest other stones, and some promise a future diamond and suggest a diamond substitute in the meantime. While diamond substitutes have little long-term value, they can be real stones—like the spinel or the zircon—or be compounded of minerals like the strontium titanate imitations. More than one diamond lover owns these substitutes; some, indeed, prefer to wear well-cut fakes while their real diamonds rest in the safe.

Does a girl ever give her fiancé a diamond? She can if she wishes but here she should be as considerate of his tastes as he is expected to be of hers. He may prefer his love token set in cufflinks for evening wear rather than a ring. Here *she* must decide what *she* can afford and *he* must indicate what *he* will cherish.

In short, the diamond symbol to be lasting should be ornamental as well as sentimental. Sooner or later a girl will regret it if the ring she chooses does not suit her hand and her personality.

The ideal feminine hand is long, slender, and not too large; all rings should be chosen to bring hands not so ideal closer to this perfection. A small, cuddly hand, for instance, will just look overburdened with an elaborate ring—a large hand will seem enormous surrounding a tiny diamond in a tiny setting.

Similarly, stubby fingers demand slenderizing and lengthening designs that seem to extend the finger rather than cut across it: a marquise, for instance, or an oval solitaire is a good cut for such a hand, while the princess ring with its cross-finger row of three diamonds is taboo. Long but efficient-looking hands look particularly good in emerald cuts, the larger the better. Hands with prominent finger joints demand wide ring bands—some of the new bejeweled wedding rings are so wide they stretch almost from the base to the knuckle. Romance may demand that the engaged girl keep her reasons of choice to herself but a candid look at her hands is imperative before she chooses the ring.

And, if the girl feels strongly about it, there is no reason why a ring has to be chosen at all for the diamond setting. Martha Washington preferred to get her engagement diamond in a watch and wear her wedding band solely with a keeper. If a girl likes her diamond in a pendant or a brooch or a necklace, why not? It's not as sentimental or traditional—but it's her choice.

Much, however, can be done with the setting of a diamond in a ring to make it suit the hand. Tiffany's introduced the prong setting almost eighty years ago and it remains the most popular diamond setting but it is not always the most complimentary. Illusion settings—that is, settings of white platinum which are built up around the diamond make a small stone look larger and flatter a large hand; *pavé* settings are not traditional but they make the whole ring glitter like a single circlet of diamonds. Clustering small diamonds around a larger one increases the brilliance of a ring and while not as fashionable as a solitaire can be more ornamental. New non-symmetrical matching wedding bands and engagement rings are excitingly different.

Not all diamonds are bought as engagement presents, however, although the large proportion are. There is a steady demand for diamond pins or brooches, bracelets, earrings, necklaces, and now hairpins, and a sporadic demand for tiaras and shoebuckles.

Many of these diamond ornaments are picked out by women but most are paid for by men. Here, however, ornament—the taste and appearance of the feminine wearer is all important. How taste varies! A fashionable woman will want a fashionable piece of jewelry, even if the value of the stones is foregone to pay the designer. A woman who cherishes precious stones will not want a diamond set with manufactured gems, no matter how chic they are. A girl who leans toward flower pieces will not want an amusing conversation piece—a lover of modern pieces will never grow ecstatic over a Victorian sunburst. A woman whose life is spent in suits will only be startled by a pair of pendant diamond earrings—while a girl who only gets up at noon will shudder at a lapel pin no matter how beautiful it may be.

How then to get the proper ornamental diamond? It would seem sensible to adapt the etiquette of the engagement ring purchasing to this procedure: that first the man selects the pieces he likes and can afford and then the woman he's getting the piece for accompanies him to the store to pick out the one of these she might like.

But how then does she choose? She does not, of course, have to make her decision on the spot. Although spontaneity might contribute to the gaiety of the occasion, if none of the pieces selected by the giver really satisfy her, she can beg for time. Then, with the co-operation of the jeweler, she can

FROM THE DIAMONDS-INTERNATIONAL
AWARDS COLLECTION

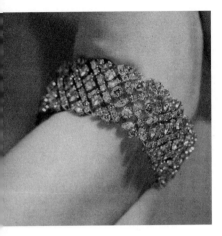

Over 30 carats of diamonds set
in platinum produce a length
of lace for the wrist by Calder-
oni of Milan, Italy.

Weaving and overlapping
strands of diamonds and emeralds climb up the wrist in
this design from Schilling Jewelers of Stuttgart, Germany.

Overlapping diamond feathers
of various lengths make this
pin by Kenneth Brown Jewelers, Inc., of Beverly Hills, California, an award-winning piece.

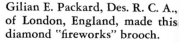
Gilian E. Packard, Des. R. C. A., of London, England, made this diamond "fireworks" brooch.

Granat Bros. of California created this ring with an emerald-cut diamond in the center and twenty-four baguette diamonds in the rippling frill.

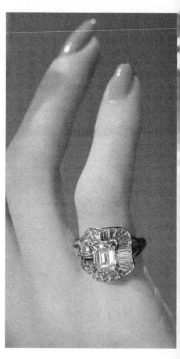

A diamond spray on a finger band of translucent green onyx was designed by Lindemann Jewelery Co. of San Francisco, California.

Twin leaves of diamonds in
platinum earclips created by
Marianne Ostier of New York
City.

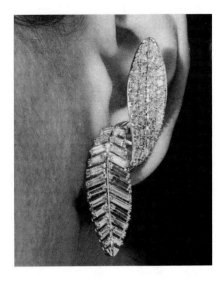

Three free-swinging pear-
shaped diamonds are suspended
in this earclip designed by
Charles Walker of Petit Musée
of New York City.

Pear-shaped diamonds set in
complementary levels and angles provide depth in a continuous wreath necklace designed
by J. Ortman of New York City.

"The Pagoda," a detachable diamond-necklace clasp was designed by Barbara Anton of Edgewater, New Jersey.

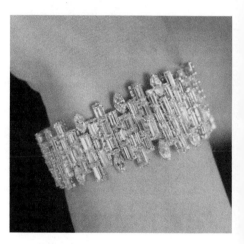

Patek Philippe of Geneva, Switzerland, created this diamond bracelet with an inner-secret timepiece which reveals itself at the touch of a marquise diamond.

Omega Watches of New York City received an award for this diamond and gold-loop lapel watch.

make a more lingering study of the pieces within her man's general price range to find the one she wants.

Those women who can choose jewels as most choose accessories—that is, they look for whatever they need to enhance themselves—face these decisions. Sometimes it is a matter of already having one stone—a fine ruby, say—and wanting it set with diamonds in a special piece to honor a particular party. Here it will be advisable for the woman to select a good designer to help with the task; there are designers who will work over as many as fifty sketches to provide the perfect piece of jewelry for a single customer.

It is also possible in some stores to bring in your own designs—a remembered piece of a relative's, perhaps, or a modification of something seen elsewhere. Everts Co. of Dallas makes a speciality of making up pieces from customer's ideas; F. J. Cooper's of Philadelphia and Hardy's of Norfolk enjoy working with both old and new designs.

It is important to note here that as well as the cost of the jewel and the setting, there is the cost of the designer. A good design may double the price of a piece of jewelry. For this reason some people ask that the stones other than the diamond be either lesser stones or imitations. Some firms will not work in response to such demands. No Chatham (manufactured) emeralds are set with diamonds at Tiffany's although in other stores on Fifth Avenue they or the Linde Stars (imitation sapphires) will be surrounded with as many diamonds as desired.

To avoid designer costs, many women—and some men—haunt auction houses and estate sales. Here charming Victorian brooches and pendants go relatively cheaply—the designer having long since been paid off. Pawnshops provide another source of jewelry for those who either know diamonds or care more about the more ornamental charms of a piece than its sentimental attachments.

Is it possible here to get a fake instead of a diamond? It is against the law to misrepresent any merchandise; if a salesman anywhere says a stone is a diamond and it isn't, he is in trouble with the law. However, it is not illegal to fudge a little. An auctioneer can, without violating any law at all, call something "a brilliant" which is actually a piece of well-cut glass; a pawnshop proprietor or even a jeweler is perfectly within his rights in advertising a ring as "the perfect engagement ring—at the perfect price" even though the stone in it is paste. If there is any doubt at all whether a stone is a diamond, the customer should ask for a forthright declaration from the salesman.

Where can a man get a stone appraised when he needs to? Any fine

A spectacular 187.93-carat diamond necklace from Harry Winston, Inc., consisting of 137 brilliants of 149.1 carats, 43 marquises of 36.37 carats and 2 pear-shapes of 2.55 carats.

jeweler will appraise a stone whether the gem comes from his store or another's. Lacking a fine jeweler locally, the public is encouraged to take or mail gems to the Gemological Institute of America (11940 San Vicente Boulevard, Los Angeles, California, or 580 Fifth Avenue, New York City). No prices will be quoted by the GIA but all qualities will be tested and reported upon and current market values for diamonds quoted. The fee for certifying the quality of a diamond is $15.

Is it worthwhile having an old stone recut? For beauty, yes. For a price rise, maybe. The price for old diamonds was low during the depression and many got the impression old diamonds were not worth much. Since then the price of diamonds has risen again and any stone of more than a carat is worth considerably more than it has ever been. The older the cut, however, the less the value per carat, not because of the cost of recutting for beauty (which is small) but because of the loss of weight recutting demands.

An old mine diamond, for instance, will probably lose half its weight while receiving twice the brilliance. These diamonds were cut prior to 1900; they are recognizable by their facet-placements, as related in Chapter 3. When clean and viewed face down they have a yellowish tinge or a sleepy look; the face is lusterless and the pavilion is too short.

The mounting of a diamond will also reveal its age but this is much easier to change. Diamonds were set in silver or yellow gold prior to 1900, when platinum came in; there were no imitations except glass which was rarely set in a good piece of silver. Ring settings were high and usually pronged between 1895 and 1925, and usually were of yellow gold; the solitaire in open-work platinum came in about 1917; during the early years of World War I gold and silver were blended to save gold and a greenish tinge dates the metal.

Diamonds set in flower pieces of yellow gold, especially those with bow knots, may be pieces of old French or Georgian-English jewelry of the 1700's or early 1800's. Birds, bees and butterflies in yellow gold are distinctly Victorian. The diamond sunburst, the horseshoe and the circle brooch date from the Gay Nineties but are still being made; here the metal is the important factor in determining age.

Any fine jeweler can tell you generally whether it's worth recutting an old diamond; it is a relatively simple matter to pry a diamond out of its prongs or even its cement. If it is larger than 2 carats, it is worth doing financially. Tiffany's catalog of 1899 offered diamond rings for as low as $10; in 1917 a pendant watch with ninety-three diamonds was offered for $1,250. Either would bring about ten times as much today. And is money the point? The flame of a diamond burns eternally; finding this hidden fire in an old diamond provides a real thrill.

Those who count cost too precisely or those who instinctively want diamonds appraised before they purchase them should seriously consider whether they are not more interested in a diamond for its investment value than for its sentiment or beauty. Since the twenties it has been held in song and story that a diamond is a girl's best friend, but if this is taken generally to mean that the purchase of a diamond is as wise a way to insure a nest egg as the purchase of a blue chip stock, it can be very misleading.

To illustrate this vagary of the providential purchase: a fashionable New York woman confessed recently to her jeweler that upon her divorce in the late twenties she had taken in alimony, instead of stocks or bonds or cash, some diamonds. Now she needed cash. She presented a handsome bracelet appraised at the time of the divorce for $47,000. The jeweler shook his head thoughtfully and retired to his microscope to look at the diamonds more carefully. He returned to offer her about $15,000. She was horrified and unhappy and she stood looking at the bracelet as if it had betrayed her. On her right hand she wore a large solitaire of about 12 carats. "For that," said the jeweler, "I think I could give $40,000 or $50,000." "But it isn't worth that much!" she cried. "Nothing like!" He smiled. "Big, clean stones of the whiteness necessary in an engagement ring have become much harder to get because so many people want them," he said. "While the smaller stones like those in your bracelet have become much more plentiful and much better cut."

Could this switch of value have been foreseen? Possibly but not probably. The gorgeous bracelet was much the more expensive when it was bought; to be expensive now it would have to be broken up, its diamonds recut, its style refashioned. The shining well-cut solitaire was and is in such increasing demand that it had quadrupled in price since it was bought.

Certainly, if a diamond is purchased primarily for investment purposes it should be purchased in stones, rather than in jewelry. Fashions change in jewelry faster than in diamonds.

It is also better to purchase a fairly large stone, provided, of course, the cut is either good or can be remedied, and the diamond is a fine one. If the stone is set at all, it should be set as simply as possible in a brooch or a ring, with as little money as possible put in the setting. And, even when dealing with the best jewelers it would be wise, if a lot of money is involved, to have the stone studied by the GIA. There it can be certified for quality: graded on international scales for flaws, imperfections, color, clarity, cut weighed to the last hundredth of a point and its quality related to market trends.

Does this say a fine diamond is as good an investment for the money as a share of blue chip stock? This is a complicated situation; on the whole the answer is no. But there are situations where diamonds are the only investment that *is* sound for the diamond is the chief form of lightweight, portable international currency.

When the Castro Revolution occurred in Cuba in the late fifties, many prosperous Cubans who opposed it swiftly turned a good portion of their cash into diamonds and abandoning their homes and businesses fled to the United States or South America. Jewelers say that for the most part they got between 75 and 100 per cent of what they had paid for their diamonds. What would have been better? They might have bought prize American stocks and allowed their American broker to keep them for them. Then there would have been no hiding of the diamonds in their teeth or in the linings of their coats and no fret about being searched—and probably the full price of the stock, *plus* the dividends. But it would have been necessary to have some knowledge of American stocks, some acquaintance with a broker, and some time to pick and choose and to sell.

The plight of the Hitler refugee was similar. It was impossible for many in Germany to foresee either that they would have to get out or if they did where they were likely to go. Collecting diamonds was like putting gold away in a sock and a lot wiser because when the knock at the door by the SS threatened, the diamonds could be swiftly hidden and the fugitive was ready to flee. "A man can always withstand emergency if he owns diamonds," Alphonse Rothschild of the European banking family reportedly remarked after the Rothschild family fortune was moved from both Germany and France largely through diamonds.

When a government is in trouble, when the stability of the currency is threatened, when a minority group is in danger of being dispossessed of its holdings, diamonds as portable wealth come into great demand. They are the traditional hedge against inflation, the prized nest egg for sudden flight, the historic bribe against ill will and injury.

But for the majority of Americans—are they a good investment?

The consensus among experts is that they are not. They note that the price of diamonds fluctuates with the market just as does any other commodity and even the experts cannot say certainly what return can be expected from a purchase at any given moment. In 1961 *The New York Times* interviewed Harry Winston and William Lusk, president of Tiffany's, as to what kind of a diamond they would advise a customer to buy *if* he were buying it solely as an investment. Mr. Winston suggested something small but perfect and flawless—that a 2-carat stone of the highest quality would

always find a quick market. Mr. Lusk preferred a larger stone, of perhaps 5
carats, of good but not exceptional quality. "There might be some time lost
finding a buyer," he said, "but in due course such a stone would be sure to
sell."

In the intervening three years since their advice was given, both stones
have increased in price. Both men were clearly right. But whether their
advice holds good today is another matter. As of this writing diamond prices
are higher than they have ever been; even a minor stone that cost $300 in
1961 costs $360 today. And the demand for perfect stones and stones of
more than 3 carats is such that dignified Fifth Avenue stores are running
advertisements stating that they *buy* as well as sell diamonds. A threat of
scarcity hangs over the diamond world, partly because of the sharp increase
in demand, partly because the original De Beers' mines are nearing their
hundredth birthday.

Is it ever a good investment to buy at the top of the market? And, when
is the top of the market? Harry Winston and William Lusk stand firm
on the basic premises of their advice to diamond investors: their two diamonds will, as they stated, serve a man well as portable currency and will
always find a buyer. But while agreeing that diamond prices are up and
diamond demand increasing, they hold fast to a basic position that it is far
wiser for Americans to buy diamonds because they like them than as money
makers.

More diamonds are bought as security than as ornament. In Europe
men and firms with bank accounts of a million or more dollars try to keep
at least one sixth of their wealth in diamonds held in Swiss vaults—obviously a precaution against political upheaval.

But no financial advisors have ever recommended a similar freezing of
their assets to American millionaires—who are much more prone to drape
their women in jewels as they get richer than they are to hide such jewels
away.

And so the answer to the question "Is the diamond a good investment?"
remains, yes and no. Certainly it is if you want to have your cake and eat it
too; while a Cadillac declines in value each year, the diamond holds it
beauty, its charm, and its basic value. But while a blue chip stock not only
climbs but provides dividends, the diamond's dividends are in the pleasure it
brings, the beauty it adds to life.

You can't display a share of AT&T around your neck and you can't
look into the face of a gold ingot and see the colors of the rainbow flashing in the sunlight. The diamond is unique. It gives thrilling delight, obvious status, and a certain measure of security all in one beautiful bundle.

But it cannot be guaranteed to make a man any richer in the future than he was the day he bought it.

We have discussed in Chapter 2 the position of broker's investments in diamonds. But there remain a few questions the average customer may ask himself.

What threat is synthetic diamond production to the value of gem diamonds? Very little. Possibly in several decades a gem diamond might be produced synthetically successfully but to date the process is far too expensive. The only diamonds produced synthetically now are industrial grit-diamonds about the size of a grain of sugar (and sugar is what they can be made from). Too, if previous experience with other synthetic jewels means anything, fakes don't harm the market for the real thing. Chatham emeralds, for instead, have neither lowered the price nor the demand for real emeralds.

What if India, say, floods the market with its vaults of diamonds? The price won't go down but it may even go up. Those traveling gemologists who

The diamond, from digging to demoiselle. Its success is due to the unstaled custom of love, the uses of industry, and the most expert salesmen in the world.

have seen some of these treasures say that the stones have an unmatched luster—as well as a special sort of romance. Why would anyone want to lower diamond prices? The basic secret of De Beers' success in stabilizing the diamond market is said to be the fact that everyone—customer and seller both—wants to keep the price of diamonds up.

The cost of a diamond has become part of its charm. This is not commercial chicanery: it is commercial fact.

And so whether you are buying your diamond sentimentally, ornamentally or providentially, the basic advice remains the same: choose the diamond you want and then relax and enjoy it. "Mazel un b'rachah" as the old phrase goes in the diamond world: Good luck and prosperity. In this symbol of radiant love, this piece of dazzling ornament and infinite usefulness lies an everlasting reminder of the graceful gifts of nature, of sunshine and fire, of strength and power, of simple, elemental beauty enhanced by human skill.

8

A Glossary of Diamond Terms

di'a·mond . . . Native carbon crystallized in the isometric system (often in the form of octahedrons with rounded edges), highly valued, when transparent and more or less free from flaws, as a precious stone. H., 10. Sp. gr. 3.52. Usually colorless or nearly so, often tinged with yellow; but some specimens are green, blue, red or pink, etc., all exceedingly rare and the variety carbonado is black. . . .

Webster's International Dictionary
Second Edition

A

AGS. See American Gem Society.

AGS color-grading system. One of three color-grading systems, it is the chief system used by the American Gem Society for determining the amount of yellow in a diamond. Scores range from 0 to 10, the higher ones showing more yellow; zero thus means a pure white or colorless gem.

acira. A Sanskrit word for diamond, meaning fire or sun.

Agra Diamond. A pink diamond said to have belonged to Baber the Mogul of India which was smuggled out of Delhi in 1857. Originally 46 carats it was cut in Paris to 31.50 early in the twentieth century and sold to an unknown buyer.

Ahmedabad Diamond. A 157.25-carat crystal purchased by Tavernier in India, later cut to 94.50 carats and sold in Persia, now Iran.

Akbar Shah Diamond. Also called Shepherd Stone. See Chapter 4.

Alaska black diamond. An inaccurate name for hematite.

Alençon or Alenoon diamond. An inaccurate name for rock crystal.

alluvial deposits. Many gems, including diamonds, are laid down on land by erosion, or the action of water. Wet diggings, river bed finds, and chance finds are likely to be alluvial deposits, since water either carried the gems there or revealed them through erosion. The original deposit, however, probably occurred through volcanic action or underground pressure.

Angola. Also called Portuguese West Africa. An important diamond producing country, the deposits of which are along the Kasai River and its tributaries. Exclusive mining rights are held by the Companhia de Diamantes de Angola. Modern production methods have increased the Angola yield to an annual million carats, more than half of which are of gem quality.

Anton Dunkels Diamonds. Fancy colored and black diamond drops in a diamond brooch exhibited at Christie's in London in 1959 and named for Dunkels, head of the firm of A. Dunkelsbuhler and Co., one of the original members of the Diamond Syndicate formed to purchase rough diamonds from De Beers in 1890.

Antwerp. The most important diamond-cutting center in the world and a major distribution place for polished stones. All sizes and shapes of diamonds are cut there and a special agreement with the Diamond Corporation, Ltd., ensures a continuance of variety.

appraisal. An evaluation of something in monetary terms. Appraisals of diamonds are usually made for insurance or estate purposes. A *good* appraisal is one which provides pictures or detailed descriptions, with color and clarity grades, listed proportions, exact measurements, and flaws of the diamond or diamonds under evaluation. See Chapter 7. The appraisal value is usually less than the purchase price but more than the resale price.

Arcot Diamonds. Two pear-shaped stones weighing a total of 57.35 carats given Queen Charlotte of England in 1777 by the ruler of Arcot, a district of Madras, India, and sold on her death by the crown jewelers, Rundell, Bridge and Co. Bought by the Marquess of Westminster for about $55,000 in 1837, they were remounted in 1930 and set in the family tiara with 1,421 other diamonds and a 32-carat brilliant. In 1959, the tiara was auctioned off at Sotheby's to Harry Winston for $308,000.

Arkansas. The only state in the U.S. where diamonds of any amount have been found. They were discovered there by John Huddleston in 1906 on Prairie Creek near Murfreesboro in Pike County. Altogether four pipes have been found, the principal one being called "the Crater of Diamonds" in which the public may search for a fee.

Arkansas diamond. Watch out! This is usually rock crystal from Arkansas.

Astryl. A trade name for synthetic rutile.

Atherstone, William Guybon (1813–1898). A brilliant South African geologist, who identified the first diamond found in South Africa in 1867, encouraged the workings at Jagersfontein and pointed out the diamantiferous pipes at Kimberley.

Alpine diamond. A misleading name for pyrite.

American cut. Also called ideal cut. Precisely used, a label for the way of cutting of diamonds first worked out by trial and error by American cutters and later confirmed mathematically by Marcel Tolkowsky. Generally, a mode of cutting designed to reveal fire and brilliance rather than save carat weight.

American Gem Society. A professional society of fine jewelers in the United States and Canada whose purpose is to promote high ethical standards in business dealings and to encourage gemological education among its members. The Society awards the titles of Registered Jeweler and Certified Gemologist to qualified members and member firms. Membership is usually announced by a window seal. Members include firms as large as Tiffany's in New York and as small as Hardy's in Norfolk, Virginia. Established 1934; headquarters: 3142 Wilshire Blvd., Los Angeles, Calif.

Amiti Diamond. A 31-carat diamond named for Amiti Runyon Coffin, formerly Mrs. Damon Runyon, which was stolen in 1949.

Amsterdam. A diamond-cutting center which has declined in recent years but which has several centers open to tourists. See Chapter 3.

Australia. About as important a diamond producer as the United States although there is some production of industrial diamonds along the rivers in New South Wales.

B

baguette. A French word meaning rod and pronounced "bag-ett" which refers to a style of step-cutting small rectangular gemstones, usually diamonds. Called *baton* in England.

Ball, Dr. Sydney H. (1878–1949). A noted American geologist who specialized in the study of diamonds. He led the expedition into the Belgian Congo which found the first diamond there; he also worked in Angola. His writings include *A Roman Book on Precious Stones,* which included a translation of parts of Pliny the Elder's essays, and the *Annual Review of the Diamond Industry.*

Ball, Dr. Valentine (1843–1895). No relation to the American geologist; an authority on the economic geology of India and a translator of Tavernier's *Travels in India.*

ballas. Masses of minute intergrown diamond crystals; a very hard and tough industrial variety of diamond.

Barnato, Barnett (1852–1897). An English trader and speculator who came to Kimberley in the South Africa diamond rush. See Chapter 2.

Baroda Gem. A trademarked name for a glass backing that makes something else look diamond-like.

base. That part of a faceted diamond or other gemstone which is below the girdle—the same as pavilion.

baton. What the British call our (and the French) baguette cut.

Baumgold Bros. Diamond brokers and cutters in New York who have handled many large, famous stones.

bearded girdle. Also called fuzzy girdle, this is a phrase for a poorly rounded diamond girdle with fuzzy edges due to hairlike fractures.

Beau Sancy Diamond. See Chapter 4.

Berquem, Louis de (or Bergham, Ludwig, Lodewyck or Luigi). A fifteenth-century diamond cutter of Bruges credited as the creator of a "revolution" in diamond cutting. See Chapter 3.

bevel cut. A variation of the step cut which produces a large table joined to the girdle by one or sometimes two bevels. If the bottom is the same as the top, it is called a double-bevel cut.

bezel. In general, the part of a brilliant cut above the girdle, or the crown. Specifically, only that small part of the diamond just above the girdle, or the setting edge. The bezel is also the groove or cup made in a setting to receive the girdle.

bezel facets. The eight large, four-sided facets on the crown of a round, brilliant-cut gem, the upper points of which join the table and the lower points the girdle. Also called top-main facets, quoin or top-corner facets.

black diamond. A dark grey or black diamond—perhaps opaque, perhaps semi-transparent. The words are also used to describe carbonado, a tough industrial diamond.

Black Orloff Diamond. A 67.50-carat cushion-cut gun metal diamond which once belonged to a Russian princess and is now owned by a New York gem dealer. It is mounted now with one-hundred-twenty small white diamonds and is often on exhibition, sometimes under the name of the Eye of Brahma Diamond, a reference to the legend that it was once an 195-carat idol's eye.

blue diamond. Can be any shade of blue but diamonds that are blue in both daylight and incandescent light are rare; most show blue only in daylight. Some blues are induced artificially. The most famous blue is the Tavernier Blue or the French Blue, from which was cut the Hope Diamond. See Chapter 4.

blueground. An everyday name for kimberlite, the blue-gray rock that contains diamonds in the South African pipes.

body color. A professional term meaning the color of a diamond as observed when examined under diffused light against a white background free from surrounding reflections.

bombarded diamond. A diamond which has been subjected to bombardment by fast electrons, neutrons, for the purpose of making the color more attractive. The bombardment occurs in a cyclotron and is also called cyclotron-treated. Bombarded diamonds are not as valuable as natural fancies.

Borazon. The General Electric Company's trademark for their boron nitron industrial quality artificial diamonds. First produced by General Electric in 1957, tons are now being made annually and for some purposes are better than natural diamonds.

Braganza Diamond. This stone was found in Brazil in the eighteenth century by three outlaws who gained pardons with it. It is believed to be still in the possession of the Portuguese government. It weighs 1,680 carats but since it is not exhibited experts think it is not a diamond at all but a topaz.

Brazil. An important diamond producing source with about 200,000 carats coming out annually now, plus some smuggled. First discovered in 1725, the Brazilian diamonds include many beautiful gems of size. See Chapter 1.

brilliancy. The intensity of the internal and external reflections of white light to the eye from a diamond or other gem in the face-up position.

brilliant. Correctly, this refers only to a round brilliant-cut diamond, but it is often used incorrectly about any kind of round brilliant-cut gem.

brilliant cut. The standard round brilliant consists of 58 facets in total: one table, 8 bezel facets, 8 star facets and 16 upper girdle facets on the crown, plus 8 pavilion facets, 16 lower girdle facets and usually a culet on the pavilion or base. It is the most common style of diamond cutting; modifications of it are the marquise, half moon, pear shape, and others. It was confirmed (after trial and error) mathematically by Marcel Tolkowsky.

brillianteerer. The workman who places and polishes the secondary facets on a brilliant. See Chapter 3.

brown diamond. A reddish or coffee-brown fancy diamond, second in value among the fancies to yellow.

C

C. A very important letter in diamonds, C is an abbreviation for carat and a reminder that it is the four C's which made a diamond valuable—clarity, cut, color, and caratweight. See Chapter 8.

cabochon. A simple polishing of the faces of a diamond; more often used for stones of color.

Canada. A few diamonds have been found in British Columbia and prospectors are out hunting right now around Quebec, but nothing has really turned up there to support the theory that the diamonds found in the Eastern United States came via the glaciers from Canadian pipes.

canary diamond. A really yellow diamond, a fancy.

cape. A yellow diamond.

Cape May diamond. Rock crystal from the beaches of this New Jersey resort town.

carat. A unit of weight for diamonds and other gems, named for the seeds of the carob tree in India. The carat formerly varied from country to country but today is standardized at 200 milligrams; 142 carats equal an ounce. In England carat is used interchangeably by some with karat but in the United States and most other countries, karat refers to the amount of gold in gold alloys and carat is reserved for gem weights.

carat goods. A parcel of diamonds, each of which weighs about a carat.

carbonado. The toughest form of industrial diamond, usually black or gray and principally found in Brazil.

Cellini, Benvenuto (1500–1571). The gold, silver, and diamond worker famed for his art. A Florentine by birth, he was constantly fleeing or being chased out of one city or another because of his strong passions, brawling, or womanizing. He worked for Pope Clement VII and Francis I of France and, as well as his engaging *Autobiography,* left several fine works of sculpture and jewelry.

Cellini Green Diamond and Cellini Peach Diamond. These two diamonds of
Francis I were described by Cellini as the most beautiful in the world. The
Cellini Green, he said, "was green like a pale green emerald but it shone
as no emerald has ever shone." The Peach, which Cellini described as the
second most beautiful, was "flesh colored, tender, most limpid and it scin-
tilated like a star."

Certified Gemologist. A title awarded by the American Gem Society to jewelers
who have completed specified courses in gemology or passed examinations in
gemological knowledge. One test is the accurate identification of twenty-gem
stones. The title ranks higher than Registered Jeweler and is usually displayed
when held.

champagne diamond. A greenish yellow to yellow-green diamond of pronounced
color.

Charles the Bold Diamond. Described as "a great pyramid" it was supposedly
more than a half-inch at base and its point was a four-ray star. First known
in 1476 and thus possibly one of the diamonds brought in by Jacques Coeur
to his cutters in Bruges, it was sold to King Henry VIII by a Nuremberg
broker, after which it vanished in Spain.

China. Some diamonds of value and quality have been found in the Shantung
province.

chip. A chip diamond is usually a small rose-cut diamond or single-cut melee,
but it can be any irregularly shaped diamond. As a chip *in* a diamond it is
usually a break on a diamond's edge. The Spanish call it *chispa.*

clean. Jewelers, although they are not supposed to by regulation, call a diamond
clean when it has no obvious internal imperfections or only a few.

cleavage. Used to cover many diamond situations: (1) the tendency of crystalline material to break in certain definite directions leaving a smooth surface;
(2) the act of producing such a break; (3) one of the portions left after
cleavage is *the* cleavage; and (4) a break within a diamond—"It's got a
cleavage in it." Well-developed cleavage can occur in any of four planes because of the basic atomic structure of a diamond; the cleavage planes are
known as the grain of a diamond. See Chapter 3.

cleaver. The man who performs a cleavage, and often also the man who plans
the entire fashioning from rough to finished.

cleaver's knife. The tool the cleaver used for cleavage, an iron bit shaped more
like a large razor blade than a knife.

Cleveland Diamond. A 50-carat 128-facet diamond fashioned from a rough
twice the size. The first diamond cut in New York City, it was made in 1884
by S. Dessau of Maiden Lane, and named for the then new President Grover
Cleveland. Where is it today? No one knows. Minnie Palmer, a musical
comedy star of the 1880's, was last seen wearing it.

cloudy texture. A cottony look inside a diamond, perhaps a mere wisp, or possibly enough to ruin the brilliancy of the stone.

cloverleaf effect. Seen around the culet in diamonds which have been cyclotron-
treated for greenness.

cluster. A group of stones very closely set, sometimes with the aim of impart-
ing the illusion of one large stone.

Coeur, Jacques (1395–1456). Money master of France in the fifteenth century and importer of luxuries—including diamonds—into Paris. See Chapter 3.

collection color. A term used by the Diamond Trading Company for the finest color grade.

color grade. The relative position of a diamond's body color on a colorless to yellow scale. Diamonds with no yellow such as reds or blues, are called fancies; these are in the minority. Three major systems of judging exist, precise instruments are used as colorimeters, because color in a diamond is a basic factor affecting its beauty and value. "Extra river" is top in the usual retail scale, it is more colorless than "river" or "fine white."

commercially clean or commercially perfect. Don't listen. These are mumbo-jumbo terms prohibited in the best diamond circles.

conductometer. A device used by the GIA to determine whether a diamond is of the type that conducts electricity. Very few do.

Congo Republic, formerly Belgian Congo. The laregst single producer in the world today of diamonds—more than 50 per cent; but only 3 per cent of these are of gem quality.

critical angle. The angle of incidence in a diamond or other gem in which light refracts rather than reflects. In diamonds the critical angle is just less than 24 degrees 26 minutes. Diamond facets today are determined by this critical angle; the object is to first direct the light into the pavilion and then to return it to the crown to escape to the eye. See Chapter 3.

Cross of Asia Diamond. A champagne-colored diamond of 109 carats so cut that a Maltese cross is visible when you peer into it. It is owned by a charitable organization.

crown. The portion of a brilliant-cut gem above the girdle.

Crown Diamond. An 84-carat honey-colored stone that once belonged to the Czars but was sold in the United States to Baumgold Bros., Inc., New York jewelers, after De Beers exhibited it at the New York World's Fair in 1939. It has since been resold to Everts Co. of Dallas, where it is frequently exhibited.

Ct. An abbreviation for carat.

culet. The small facet that cuts off the sharp pavillion point of the diamond, the principal function of which is to reduce the possibility of damage to the stone. Pronounced "kew-lett."

Cullinan. See Chapter 4.

cushion cut. Another name for a squarish old mine cut and still used in Europe, an older form of the brilliant.

cutters and cutting. Any step in the fashioning of a jewel diamond from the rough is called cutting, including sawing, grinding, polishing, brillianteering, etc., and the men who do the cutting are called cutters. See Chapter 3.

cutting centers. The major cutting centers in order are Antwerp in Belgium; Amsterdam in Holland; Johannesburg, Capetown and Kimberley in South Africa; New York in U.S.A.; Tel Aviv in Israel. Early cutting centers were Paris and Bruges and very recently cutting centers have been opened in Puerto Rico, West Germany, France, England and the Navaho Territory in New Mexico.

cutting machine. The machine that does the girdling of a diamond.

cyclotron. A device by which subatomic particles are used as projectiles for the purposes of studying or changing the structure of matter. The cyclotron may be used to change a diamond's color; old-fashioned diamond lovers dislike the new cyclotron-treated diamonds; modern ones are beginning to enjoy their great variety. A small bombardment produces colors in the pink range, a greater, longer bombardment tends toward green tints. So far as is known the color change is permanent.

D

D is for Diamond, a gem without peer.

Darya-i-Noor. See Chapter 4.

De Beers Consolidated Mines, Ltd. The major firm (and factor) in the diamond industry. It has a controlling interest over approximately 80 per cent of all diamonds mined and sold throughout the world. See Chapter 2.

De Beers Diamond. A 440-carat yellowish octahedron discovered in the original De Beers mine in 1888; a 234.50 carat stone was cut from it which now belongs to an Indian prince.

Deepdeen (or Deepdene) Diamond. A 104.88-carat cushion-cut golden-yellow diamond owned by publisher Carey Bok of Philadelphia who named his estate after it, and who loans it for exhibit, usually to the Philadelphia Academy of Sciences.

diamant. French, German, and Dutch for diamond. *Diamantbort* is thus diamond dust, *diamantband* is diamond bracelet or necklace, *diamantwerker* is diamond worker.

diamandiferous. Diamond-bearing ground or rock.

diamond. A mineral composed essentially of carbon which crystalizes in the cubic or isometric crystal system. It is the hardest of all natural substances, (Mohs 10); has a high refractive index, 2.417, and a high dispersion .044. Specific gravity is 3.52. See Chapter 3 for explanation of these properties.

diamond anniversary. Correctly either the sixtieth or seventy-fifth annual anniversary of an important event. But the gift of a diamond can make any anniversary a "diamond anniversary."

diamond balance. A scale for weighing diamonds and obtaining their specific gravity.

diamond cement. The glue used for setting diamonds, usually a mixture of mastic and isinglass in alcohol.

Diamond Corporation, Ltd. The marketing organization for the diamond industry, organized in 1930 to replace an earlier organization known in the trade as "The Syndicate." See Chapter 2. It is owned 80 per cent by De Beers and 20 per cent by its subsidiary the Consolidated Diamond Mines of South-West Africa, Ltd.

diamond cut. A term applied to gemstones cut in the brilliant fashion.

Diamond Dealers Club. A non-profit organization for traders and cutters in diamonds, located on West Forty-seventh Street in New York City but national in membership. See Chapter 2.

diamond caste system. Diamonds were classified by the Hindus by caste, the finest—including the coral red and canary yellows—being the Brahmins, which were supposed to bring power, friends, riches, and general good luck; second, the military caste diamonds, the Kshatriya, which prevented aging; the merchant caste, or Vaisya, which brought success; and the Sutra, worker's caste, which brought good fortune.

"Diamond Jim" Brady. See Chapter 5.

Diamond Jubilee. The sixtieth anniversary of the British Queen Victoria's reign in 1897.

Diamondlite and Diamondlux. Two lighting methods for diamond viewing, patented by the GIA, the first being in use for color grading by comparison with master diamonds, the second for jewelry store illumination. Both shed a constant flow of light which is the equivalent of north daylight, but each has technical differences for their different uses.

diamond paper. A sheet of waxy paper folded seven times to form a pocket in which diamonds are carried.

diamond paste. Basically, a diamond powder mixed usually with olive oil for use in grinding and polishing diamonds.

diamond pencil. A cutting tool tipped with diamond.

diamond plow. A diamond-pointed tool for glass engraving.

diamond point. In modern use a stylus tipped with diamond. In medieval times, a method of fashioning a diamond into a tool or jewel by polishing its natural points and facets. See Chapter 3.

diamond-pointed. When point is used as an adjective, however, it means the diamond has been set in something to make a tool which is then called diamond-pointed or diamond-tipped.

diamond powder. Powder, grit, or dust made of diamonds and used to work other diamonds or forced into tools for industrial grinding, drilling, machining, and slicing.

Diamond Throne. In Buddhist legends there was a throne made of a single diamond one hundred feet in circumference near the famous tree under which Buddha was said to have received enlightenment.

dispersion. The breaking up of light into color; in a diamond, fire. See Chapter 3.

dop. The old Dutch word still used world-wide for any device used to hold a diamond during the cutting process. See Chapter 3.

Dresden diamonds. See Chapter 4.

drop cut. Any form of cutting suitable for use in pendants or pendant earrings, but usually pear shaped or tear-drop shaped.

E

edge up. A diamond position with the girdle head on; usually used to observe color.

emerald cut. A form of step cutting, rectangular in shape, with the number of rows of step cuts varying, but usually consisting of three steps on the crown and three on the pavilion. It is an excellent cut for emphasizing color or whiteness.

Emperor Maximilian Diamond. A 42-carat bluish diamond worn by the French

Emperor Maximilian of Mexico in a little bag around his neck to his execution in 1867. It was sent to his wife Carlotta who was in Europe trying to raise money to help him; instead it paid for her subsequent mental breakdown. It is now in the jewel box of a New York diamond collector.

Empress Eugenie Diamond. A 51-carat brilliant once owned by the Empress Catherine of Russia's favorite, Potemkin, but sold to Napoleon III for his bride, Eugénie, and after their downfall, resold to the Gaekwar of Baroda for $75,000. It is now in Bombay.

English round-cut brilliant. A style of diamond cutting fashionable in England in the mid-nineteenth century. It looks like a brilliant cut from above but because weight was then more valuable than beauty, it is lumpy.

English square-cut brilliant or double-cut brilliant. An early style having 16 crown facets, 12 pavilion facets, an octagonal table and a culet.

Excelsior Diamond. See Chapter 4.

extra facets. Facets in excess of planned symmetry, usually necessary to polish away nicks or chips and regarded as blemishes, but sometimes placed deliberately to add brilliance.

F

Fabulite. A trademark for strontium titanate.

facet. A plane or polished surface placed on a diamond or other gemstone.

faceting. The operation of placing facets on gemstones.

face up. A diamond positioned with the table toward the viewer, the usual position for viewing a mounted stone.

fancy. Any diamond with a strong, attractive and natural body color. Red, blue, and green are the rarest.

fancy cut. Any style of diamond cutting other than the round brilliant or single cut—including the marquise, emerald, heart shape, pear shape, keystone, half-moon triangle. Sometimes called "moderne cut."

fancy ring. Any diamond ring not an engagement ring.

fire. In a diamond this refers to the flashes of different colors seen as a result of the diamond's dispersion.

flaw. A general term meaning any internal or external imperfection on a fashioned diamond—be it a feather fissure, carbon spot, or knot—but not a blemish, which is only a surface imperfection.

flawless. A permitted term for a diamond without imperfections or blemishes when viewed by a trained eye under proper lighting and a corrected magnifier of no less than ten power.

Flinders diamond. Beautiful . . . but only colorless topaz from Tasmania.

Florentine Diamond. See Chapters 3 and 4.

fluorescence. The property of changing one kind of radiation to another. Under X-ray, ultraviolet or cathode rays, the diamond usually fluoresces blue, although occasional stones may glow red or yellow shades. If the fluorescence is sufficiently strong to change the color of the stone for any length of time, it is called fluorochromatic.

foilback. A thin leaf of metallic foil which is used nowadays to back up faceted glass or an inexpensive gemstone to make it look like a diamond. In the medieval period diamonds were sometimes set in foilback for brilliance or color.

Forty-Seventh Street (West). The street in New York which replaced Maiden Lane in the forties as the center of the diamond and jewelry industry of America.

four C's. An advertising phrase. See Chapter 8.

French Blue. See Chapter 4.

French cut. A square form of cutting with a variable number of facets and a square table.

G

GIA Jewelers' Camera. A special camera for photographing set and unset diamonds and colored stones.

Garry Moore Diamond. A 6.43-carat yellow diamond found at Murfreesboro, Arkansas, and named for the television personality when he visited there.

gem. Precisely, a cut and polished stone that possesses the necessary beauty and durability for use in jewelry, but also used for pearls and amber. Gemstone is a synonym generally speaking, but gem can be used alone as an adjective— as in gem quality or gem diamond, meaning precious or fine.

Gemological Institute of America. Also referred to as GIA. A non-profit, endowed, educational institution controlled by jewelers and maintained for the benefit of the industry and the public. GIA conducts courses in diamonds, colored stones, jewelry designing and retailing, and publishes books and periodicals as well as manufacturing testing instruments for diamonds and other gems. It also maintains laboratories where gemstones are identified and graded for the industry and the public. Headquarters are: 11940 San Vicente Blvd., Los Angeles, California, with an eastern office at 580 Fifth Avenue, New York City.

Gemologist. Properly used this refers to academically qualified specialists in gem knowledge.

Ghana. An important alluvial diamond producing country in Africa where diamonds were discovered in 1919. Some 2,000,000 carats are produced annually but the one-fourth that is gem quality has been in small stones. Formerly called the Gold Coast.

girdle. The outer edges or periphery of a fashioned stone; the portion usually grasped by the setting or mounting; the dividing line between the crown and pavilion. Almost always polished, not always faceted.

girdle facets. Sometimes called break facets, these are the 32 triangular facets (16 above and 16 below) that adjoin the girdle of a round brilliant-cut stone.

girdle thickness. In stones up to 2 carats, the girdle should appear to the unaided eye as a faint white line—if it is more than that the diamond is said to have a thick girdle. In stones of greater weight the girdle should appear in proportion to size.

girdling. The operation in which a stone is given its rounded shape, also called rounding, bruting, or cutting. This can only be done by another diamond. Once

it was a handrubbing job, today modern machinery speeds it up. It is still
diamond cut diamond.

Goa. A medieval diamond port in India owned by the Portuguese after 1500
and used by them also as a city into which the first Brazilian diamonds were
brought and then exported again. See Chapter I.

Golconda. The Indian city that was the center of diamond trading in the seventeenth century, and as such a synonym for riches in the drama and poetry of
this period. The term is often generously used to cover the ancient alluvial
diamond deposits to the south and east of the city along the Pennar, Kistna,
and Karnul rivers.

Golden Pelican Diamond. A 64-carat brown diamond named for the famed street
of diamond cutting in Antwerp and owned by Ginsberg and Sons of that
Belgian city.

grain. In a diamond this is the cleavage direction.

grease belt or grease table. A device for separating diamonds from other heavy
minerals using grease because diamonds, which shed water like ducks, adhere
to grease. See Chapter 2.

Great Mogul Diamond. See Chapter 4.

Green Brilliant Diamond. A 40-carat brilliant green diamond described in
1882 as a button in the plume of the King of Saxony's hat more than a century before. It is believed to be in Russia—part of the war booty from Germany in World War II.

green diamond. A diamond with a naturally green color, a fancy. A stone turned
green artificially should carry that information in its name. No naturally colored diamond of a true emerald green has yet been found, although Cellini
claimed to have seen one in the fifteenth century.

Grodzinski, Paul. An authority on diamonds who died in 1957; best known as
head of the Industrial Diamond Information Bureau.

Guinea. A major producer of alluvial diamonds but plagued by smugglers since
its break with French West Africa.

H

hardness. The resistance of a substance to being scratched. Diamond is 10 on
Mohs scale of hardness, and is 10 to 150 times as hard as emerald and ruby
depending on the direction in which the diamond is scratched—with the
grain or against it.

Harvard Diamond. A name given locally to the yellow 82-carat stone that was
part of the James Garland collection in the Peabody Museum at Harvard
University in Cambridge, Massachusetts, but was stolen with other diamonds.
It was particularly prized because of its flawlessness.

Hastings Diamond. A 101-carat diamond that created a political scandal in
England in 1876 when Warren Hastings, Governor General of India, gave
it to King George III. Hastings said it was a gift from the Nizam of the
Deccan; his opponents, who later impeached him, said he was trying to bribe
the King.

Hatton Garden. The center of the diamond industry in London, just as West
Forty-seventh Street is in New York and Pelican Street is in Antwerp.

Hawaiian diamond. Just rock crystal, alas.

Heart Diamond. Tavernier said this 35-carat heart-shaped stone was part of the treasures of Aurangzeb, but no one else ever reported it.

heart-shaped brilliant cut. First cousin to the brilliant but heart shaped, the round end being flattened and indented and the girdle widened until it is as long as it is wide.

heat. It is not true that a diamond won't burn but the fire must be exceptionally hot—in pure oxygen, 800°, in ordinary air, 875°. The result is not ashes but carbon dioxide. Blowtorch heat may scorch, but this can be corrected by polishing. Rapid temperature changes may also cause fractures to spread internally.

heat treatment. A stone previously irradiated may be heated for an extensive period as a sort of color treatment. If you don't like the green of your cyclotron-treated diamond, try again with a heat treatment in hopes of a better color.

hexoctahedral class. A name given to the highest symmetry class of the cubic or isometric crystal system; diamond is in this class.

Hope Diamond. See Chapter 4.

Hortensia Diamond. A 20-carat peach-colored stone worn by Hortense de Beauharnais, Queen of Holland, and stepdaughter to Napoleon, but originally purchased by Louis XIV. It is now on display in the Louvre in the Apollon Gallery.

Hyderabad. The modern name for Golconda, although Golconda's old fortress wall is actually seven miles northwest of the present city.

I

ideal cut. Those proportions and facet angles that were calculated mathematically by Marcel Tolkowsky to produce maximum brilliancy consistence with a high degree of fire in a round brilliant. Sometimes called American cut, because it was also approximated by American cutters by trial and error. It is rarely used precisely today, however, because in part it brings about a large loss of weight and because a larger girdle is preferred. The strict proportions are invaluable, however, to cutting plans and to the analysis of already cut diamonds. See Chapter 3.

Idol's Eye Diamond. A 70-carat sky-blue diamond said to have been once the eye in a sacred idol in the Temple of Benghazi but used by the Prince Rahab of Persia in 1607 to pay off a debt to the East India Co. It has since been sold and resold in India, Paris, and finally in the United States where it is now privately and anonymously owned by a collector who paid $375,000 for it.

igneous rock. A major class of rocks formed by cooling and consolidation from a molten state. Kimberlite, the source rock of diamonds, is an igneous rock.

illicit diamond buyer, also known as IDB. One who buys rough stones from thieves or smugglers, most of whom are also unlicensed miners. See Chapter 2.

imitation. Gemologically this ordinary word is used only to apply to glass, plastic, and other amorphous materials when they are used to look like another stone. A faceted bit of glass, for instance, in a dime store ring is an *imitation* diamond; a piece of real spinel stone used in the same way is not an imitation diamond but still is spinel. Trademarked diamond imitations include artificially produced strontium titanate and others.

imperfect. There is a precise, government approved scale that grades diamonds from imperfect to perfect, the imperfect diamond being the lowest because its flaws are visible face up to the unaided eye.

imperfection. Used interchangeably with flaw.

India. The most important producer of diamonds from 1000 to 1735 A.D. and prior to that the only producer of diamonds at all; India now ranks as an insignificant source. There is one kimberlite pipe located near Maggawan, southwest of Panna, town in central India, which is being worked and another recently discovered in the Bundkelkhand region. See Chapters 1 and 3.

Indian cut. A clumsy form of the single cut adopted by East Indian cutters.

Indore Pears. Two pear-shaped diamonds each about 50 carats which were given to Nancy Anne Miller of Seattle when she became the Maharanee of Indore in the 1920's. She divorced the Maharajah subsequently but stayed on in India living on the proceeds of the Indore Pears which she sold to Harry Winston. He exhibited them in his "Court of Jewels" for some years and then resold them privately.

industrial diamond. Generally speaking this is a term referring to all non-gem–quality diamonds suitable only for use as abrasives or tool points. Actually many gem-quality stones become industrial diamonds because of their hardness and flawlessness is important in the work demanded of them—notably in tool die work. Cleavages from fine diamonds also sometimes wind up as industrial diamonds, as may foreign cut diamonds unwanted in modern America as jewels.

Industrial Diamond Association of America, Inc. An organization of diamond-tool manufacturers and others associated with diamonds in industry. It promotes knowledge of industrial diamonds, encourages high ethical standards, etc. Headquarters: Pompton Plains, New Jersey.

inherent vice. If an insured diamond is said to have suffered damage, the insurance adjustor determines whether that damage is attributable to some weakness characteristic to that particular stone—to its inherent vice. If so, no pay off.

internal strain. A stress set up in a diamond or other gems as a result of structural irregularities or distortion.

Iranian Royal Treasury. The currency of Iran is unique in that it is backed not by gold reserves but by a huge collection of diamonds, pearls, and other gems. Some of the diamonds have no known recorded history; the Darya-i-Noor, however, is an exception. See Chapter 4.

irradiated diamond. A diamond bombarded by neutrons and electrons etc. for color change.

Isle of Wight diamond. Rock crystal again.

isotropic. Meaning singly refractive; that is, light passing through is not polarized but passed through in a singly refracted beam. Diamonds, like other gems in the cubic or isometric system, are isotropic. See Chapter 3.

Israel. A comparatively recent—since World War II—cutting center for diamonds.

Ivory Coast. An important production area of industrial diamonds, once a part of French West Africa. Properly called Côte d'Ivoire.

J

Jager. A term used for stones that display faint tints of blue, adopted from the Jagersfontein Mine because it produces so many of them. Its beginning "J" is pronounced Dutch fashion as "Y."

jahalom. Hebrew for diamond and still to be heard among Orthodox Jews in the trade.

Jehangir Diamond. An 83 carat which appears from its inscriptions to have been used by at least two Moguls to hold ceremonial plumes on their turbans —Shah Jehangir and Shah Jehan. Briefly owned by Niarchos, the Greek shipping merchant and diamond collector, it was resold to the Indian diamond collector, C. Patel, in 1957.

jig. A mechanical sieve with a plunger used to separate diamonds and other weighty minerals from lighter materials.

Jonker Diamond. See Chapter 4.

Jubilee Diamond. A 650.80-carat stone from South Africa in 1895 which was two years later (the year of Queen Victoria's Diamond Jubilee) cut to a 245.35-carat cushion-shaped brilliant.

K

K. An abbreviation for karat, but *not* carat.

Kaplan, Lazare. American diamond cutter. See Chapter 3.

karat. Once a unit of weight, this word now refers to the proportion of pure gold in an alloy. Pure gold is 24 karat; 10-karat gold is 10/24 gold. In England carat and karat are used interchangeably and must be read in context for meaning.

keystone cut. A four-sided form of cutting wider at the top than bottom, like a blunted triangle.

Khedive Diamond. A 43-carat champagne-colored diamond given by Egypt to the Empress Eugenie of France at the opening of the Suez Canal, 1869. Reportedly worth about $500,000, it is believed now to be in Belgium.

Kimberley Diamond. A 70-carat emerald-cut, flawless, champagne-colored stone from the Kimberley mine that was once a much larger rough belonging to the Russian czars. Baumgold Bros. of New York cut it down first in 1921 and then in 1958 cut it again to 55 carats. It has been widely exhibited.

Kimberley mine. Now a water-filled crater known as the "Big Hole." For what it once was see Chapter 2.

knot. In diamonds as in wood, this is a tough inclusion that resists working.

Koh-i-Noor. See Chapter 4.

La Belle Helene Diamond. An exceptionally fine, 160-carat, colorless diamond found in South-West Africa in 1951 which the Belgian purchaser named for his wife before he had it cut to two matching pear shapes and a small marquise. It is also one of the rare type II diamonds which have exceptionally unusual optical properties.

La Favorite Diamond. A 50.28-carat fine diamond which was put up for exhibit and sale at the Chicago World's Fair of 1934 for $1,000,000 but which went unsold.

lapidary. A cutter, grinder, and polisher of colored stones other than diamonds.

lapped. Same as polished. Dutch.

lapper. Also called blocker, this is the man who specializes in placing the first 18—and main—facets on a diamond. See Chapter 3.

Liberator Diamond. A 155-carat diamond found in 1942 in Venezuela and purchased by Harry Winston, gem merchant of New York City, who had it cut into three stones.

Light of India Diamond. One of two large diamonds which the late Boston art patron Mrs. Jack Gardner wore as hair ornaments, set on springs to be in constant motion. The other was the Rajah Diamond; the whereabouts of both are unknown.

limpid. A diamond is said to be limpid when it is without body color and very transparent.

loose goods or goods. Polished but unmounted diamonds.

lot. A group of rough diamonds offered for sale by the Diamond Trading Company to firms invited to view its sights, sorted or unsorted.

loupe. Sometimes spelled *loop,* this is American-used Dutch for any small magnifying glass; a hand loupe is held in the hand, an eye loupe fits the eye. In order to pronounce a diamond *flawless* or *perfect,* the viewing loupe must be corrected and of a specified power (10x).

louped. When a diamond has been louped, it has been graded by a proper loupe.

lozenge cut. A four-sided usually step-cut mode of fashioning a diamond that results in a shape like the diamond on a playing card.

luminescence. A general term used to describe the emission of certain wave lengths of light by a diamond or other substance when excited by radiation of different wave lengths.

luster. The appearance of a material's surface in reflected light; if it reflects the reflected light it has luster. The luster of rough diamond is said to be greasy; of fashioned diamonds, adamantine, from the Greek word for inconquerable. See Chapter 1.

M

made. A term used for a fashioned diamond when describing the quality of its cutting, as in *well made* or *poorly made.*

Maiden Lane. The New York City street which was once the center of the diamond and jewelry industry of America, now replaced by West Forty-seventh Street. See Chapter 7.

Major Bowes Diamond. A yellow 44.50-carat diamond owned by the late Major Bowes, onetime producer of a famous radio and television Amateur Hour. He willed it to Cardinal Spellman who sold it; it is now believed to be owned in Cleveland, Ohio.

make. A synonym in the diamond world for made—that is, *a good make* is a well-made diamond.

Mali Federation. The new African country which includes old Senegal and French Sudan and where a number of kimberlite pipes have been reported near the Faleme River.

Marie Antoinette Diamond Necklace. See Chapter 4.

marquise cut. A style of cutting in which the girdle outline is boat shaped; the facet-placing is along brilliant plans. See Chapter 3.

master diamonds. Fashioned diamond of known color grades used for comparison stones when grading other diamonds for body color.

Matan Diamond. A nearly colorless 367-carat stone discovered in Borneo in 1787 which is thought to bring good luck and is kept secreted in the royal treasury. Some think it is merely rock crystal.

mauve diamond. This has enough purple in it to rate as a fancy.

Maximilian Diamond. A 33-carat diamond probably stolen from the onetime Mexican emperor, which was confiscated by the United States when in 1901, two Mexicans attempted to smuggle it in. The U.S. government auctioned it off and it has since been held in private hands.

Mazarin, Cardinal Jules (1602–1661). A French statesman, diplomat, and prime minister under Lous XIV as well as Cardinal of the Church, but mentioned along with diamonds because of the collection he willed Louis XIV and the popularizing he gave the first brilliant cuts. See Chapter 3.

Mazarin cuts. Named for Mazarin, this is a form of cutting the brilliant only on one side of the girdle, or single form. See Chapter 3.

melee. A French word for confused mass but mispronounced in the diamond trade as "mell-ee" and used collectively to describe small, brilliant-cut diamonds—usually .20–.25-carat diamonds. Also casually used by diamond wearers to refer to all small cut stones embellishing mounted settings which are not placed so close together as to constitute *pavé.* Larger diamonds in a group may be referred to as *melange,* another French word but pronounced in Franglais, "may lange."

meteoric diamonds. Small to minute diamonds found in meteorites.

Mexico. No diamonds known there. Mexican black diamond is a misnomer for meatite, and Mexican diamond is rock crystal.

milky diamond. A diamond with a hazy interior.

Minas Gerais. The diamond mining area in Brazil. See Chapter 1.

Mirror of Portugal Diamond. A diamond that Elizabeth I of England got as a bribe from the Portuguese Prince Dom Antonio in return for a promise to support him in a battle for the throne in 1567. She broke her promise but kept the diamond; in 1644 Mazarin of France bought it and in 1793 it vanished from the French treasury with other royal jewels.

Mogul Dynasty. Founded by the great Baber the Mogul, this dynasty over northern and central India lasted from 1562 until 1957 and included such diamond lovers and owners as Shah Jehan and Aurangzeb. See Chapter 4.

Mohs scale. The most used scale of relative hardness of minerals.

Moon of Baroda Diamond. A 24.95-carat, pear-shaped diamond of a true canary yellow once a family treasure of the Gaekwars of Baroda, now believed to be held by a Detroit collector. It is unlucky for the owner if he crosses water wearing it.

Morse, Henry D. A Boston diamond merchant and cutter who is said to have first worked out by trial and error the angles and proportions for the ideal cut. See Chapter 3.

mounting. A trade term for that portion of a piece of jewelry in which a gem
or other object is to be set or has been set.

Mr. Diamond. A trademarked name for colorless synthetic corundum.

Multifacet Diamond. A trademarked name used to describe a brilliant cut upon
whose girdle there are at least 40 polished facets.

N

naat. A Dutch term for a thin, flat-twinned diamond crystal, or the junction
where the two crystals join; the knot.

naïf. A French word meaning natural but mispronounced by American diamond
workers "knife" and used to mean the unpolished and natural faces of a
diamond crystal—sometimes spelled nave or naïfe.

Napoleon Diamond. A 34-carat brilliant which the French Emperor bought to
wear on the hilt of his sword on his wedding day to Josephine and thereafter
wore for good luck. Was it lost at Waterloo? No one knows, but it was not
seen thereafter.

Nassak Diamond. Once it was 90 carats in weight and an eye of the Idol Siva,
deity of destruction and reproduction in India. It went to India as part of the
Deccan Booty in 1818, changed hands many times, and was eventually recut
to a 80.59-carat stone, an almost heart-shaped beauty. Harry Winston bought
it in Paris and cut it again, however, this time to a 43.38-carat emerald cut,
and sold it to a jeweler who sold it to a New York woman who wears it in
a ring.

natural grit. Grit made of real diamonds as opposed to synthetic grit made of
synthetic diamonds.

navet or navette. The term used in the colored-stone trade for what is called
in the diamond trade the marquise cut; it is boat shaped.

Nepal Diamond. A 79.41-carat diamond said to have come from Golconda
and a family treasure of the Maharajahs of Nepal until Harry Winston purchased it in the fifties and put a price tag of $1,000,000 on it.

Niarchos Diamond. See Chapter 4.

nick. A minor chip out of the surface of a diamond usually caused by a light
blow and more likely to occur along the girdle than elsewhere.

Nizam Diamond. A huge 300- to 400-carat diamond thought to be in the
Nizam of Hyderabad's treasury since the seventeenth century. Allegedly it
was broken during the Indian mutiny and is now 277 carats, egg shaped and
covered with irregular concave facets.

O

oblong cut. Same as emerald cut.

octahedron. One of the seven basic and the most common forms in the highest
symmetry class of the cubic or isometric system. It has eight equilateral,
triangular faces each of which intersects all three of the crystallographic axes
at an equal distance from the center. The highest symmetry class of the cubic
system is called the hexoctahedral. The diamond is an octahedron.

off-color diamond. In the American diamond trade this refers to any diamond that has a tinge of undesirable color, especially yellowish or brownish, easily apparent to the unaided eye.

old-European cut. A term applied to the earliest form of brilliant cutting; it is characterized by a very small table, a heavy crown, and great over-all depth. It is sometimes used interchangeably with old mine cut but the old-European cut is properly distinguished by having a circular girdle. It is a light-loser with little fire.

old mine cut. A term properly applied to early forms of brilliant cuts with squarish girdles, although often used for all lumpy brilliants.

old miner. Slang for a diamond cut old mine style.

opening a diamond. A trade term among diamond cutters for the polishing of a facet on a heavily coated or rough surface diamond in order to secure a "window" into the interior of the diamond.

Oppenheimer, Harry (1908–   ). Son of Sir Ernest and successor upon his father's death in 1957 to the chairmanship of De Beers Consolidated Mines, Ltd. See Chapter 2.

Oppenheimer, Sir Ernest (1880–1957). Long the chairman of De Beers and the Diamond Corporation, Ltd. See Chapter 2.

Oppenheimer Student Collection. The 1,500 carats of rough gem and industrial diamonds presented by Sir Ernest to the Gemological Institute of America in 1955 for educational purposes.

orange diamond. A diamond of distinct orange tint but also probably a diamond from the Orange River area in South-West Africa where most of these bright and sometimes flaming fancies are found. Rarely seen in America.

Orchid Diamond. A 30.50-carat African diamond with a pink-lavendar color, imported and cut by Lazare Kaplan in 1935 into a 9.93-carat emerald cut. Now privately owned.

O'Reilly Diamond. Now called the Eureka and owned by Peter Locan, an English diamond collector, this was the first diamond to be found in South Africa (1867). See Chapter 1.

Orloff Diamond. An historic diamond. See Chapter 4.

outside goods. Diamonds purchased by the Diamond Trading Co., Ltd. from companies outside the Producers Association—from Angola, Brazil, or Ghana, perhaps.

Oval Elegance. A trademarked 58-facet oval cut marketed by the firm of Lazare Kaplan and Sons, Inc., and claimed by them to make a diamond look larger and have more fire than other cuts: the above girdle facets are larger than is usual.

P

Pam Brilliant. A diamond of more than 100 carats which Queen Victoria was thinking of buying for her grandson the Duke of Clarence and heir to the British throne when his untimely death (1892) abruptly ended negotiations.

paragon. In sixteenth-century Europe this meant any diamond weighing more than 12 carats; today only a perfect or flawless diamond of more than 99 carats is properly given this title.

Pasha of Egypt Diamond. A notable East Indian stone, 40 carats, cut as an octagonal brilliant and considered by the Pasha of Egypt in 1848 as the most magnificent gem in the Egyptian treasury. Is it still in the United Arab Republic vaults? No one knows but it is known that ˙when Ismail, the first khedive of Egypt (1863–1879), was overthrown and exiled, he carried with him an immense treasure.

paste. A trade term used to mean any variety of glass gemstone imitation.

Patos Diamond. A 324-carat, brown diamond found in 1937 in the Patos mine in Minas Gerais, Brazil, and today lost to sight.

Paul I Diamond. A 10-carat pinkish diamond named for the son of Catherine the Great that once was thought to be red because of a red foil backing.

pavé or pavé setting. Pronounced "pah-vay," a French word meaning the style of setting stones as closely as possible so that the least amount of metal shows.

pavilion. Same as base; the portion of a faceted gem below the girdle.

Peacock Throne. A famous gem-encrusted throne in Delhi built during the early seventeenth century for Shah Jehan. See Chapter 4.

pear-shaped diamond. A variation of the brilliant cut with 58 facets but a pear-shaped girdle. If the narrow end is long and pointed, it may also be called a pendeloque, or pendant cut.

perfect. The Federal Trade Commission considers it an unfair business practice to use the word perfect or any other synonym such as flawless for any diamond not meeting standards for true perfection; that is, any diamond to be called perfect must be examined by a trained observer under a corrected eye loupe of not less than ten power and found to have NO imperfections or blemishes. The FTC also bans the word for the use of a poorly made or cut diamond, or one of inferior color. Because, however, the word is misused anyhow, the American Gem Society prohibits its use by Registered Jewelers.

perfect cut. Since perfectly cut stones are extremely rare, the American Gem Society bans the use of this term for the same reason it bans the word perfect.

Peruzzi, Vincent. A seventeenth-century cutter credited with the first brilliant cut. His cut, still employed in Europe, is often called the Peruzzi cut. See Chapter 3.

phenomenal diamond. A general term for any diamond that displays unusual optical effects, one which fluoresces or changes color when moved from daylight to fluorescent light. Also called a premier diamond.

philosopher's stone. An imagined, long searched for, never discovered stone which was believed by medieval alchemists to have the power to change rock or flint into gold or diamond.

phosphorescence. The property of continuing to emit visible light in darkness after exposure to radiation. Some diamonds (like many squid) do it, but they are unusual diamonds.

photoluminescence. The property of some diamonds and other gems to become luminescent when exposed to the action of visible or ultraviolet-light rays only. They are said to be fluorescent if luminescent during exposure, and photophorescent if luminescent or glowing afterwards.

Pigott Diamond. See Chapter 4.

pink diamond. A light-red diamond, more reddish than peach colored, less rosy than rose colored, and less purple than heliotrope. A fancy. The Williamson Diamond now owned by Queen Elizabeth II is the most famous pink diamond of modern times. The Chantilly Pink or Condé Pink is historic.

pipe. This is the common name for the cooled-down, column-like mass of rock in the neck of a volcano; if the rock is kimberlite the pipe may then be expected to contain diamonds.

pique. A French word meaning pricked still used by some diamond men to refer to small imperfections in diamonds.

pit. A large nick in a diamond, but not so big as to be called a cavity.

Pliny the Elder. A Roman naturalist (23 B.C.–79A.D.) who described the diamond. See Chapter 1.

pocket peddler. A man with his diamond goods in his pocket, who has no office or store.

Pohl Diamond. A fine quality 28-carat diamond found by Jacobus Jonker, who also found the Jonker, in 1935, cut by Lazare Kaplan into two fine stones, one of which went to an opera singer; the other, to Harry Winston.

point. In weighing diamonds, .01 of a carat. A .25-carat diamond, for instance, is said to weigh 25 points, or be a 25 pointer.

point cut. The earliest form of diamond cutting in which the natural faces of the diamond were simply polished, probably by hand. See Chapter 3.

Polar Star Diamond. A famous 40-carat Indian diamond of fine color and purity believed once to have belonged to Napoleon's older brother, Joseph Bonaparte. Later owned by the royal house of Youssopoff in Russia between 1820 and 1920 and now owned by Lady Deterding, Russian-born wife of the late British oilman. She wears it in a ring, but it detaches to form a pendant. It is almost an inch square.

polish. The polish of the diamond is the smooth lustrous surface which appears after all blemishes or wheel marks have been buffed away.

polished girdle. A girdle that has been lapped to either a lustrous curved surface or faceted.

polisher. The man who puts and polishes the facets on a diamond.

polishing. Lapping, blocking, or brillianteering; the reducing of a rough surface to a smooth flatness or curvature. See Chapter 3.

polishing directions. As with wood, the diamond responds to being polished in the direction of its grain.

polishing mark. A groove or scratch left on the diamond's surface by the act of polishing, a defect in finish.

pool. A sorting method of the Diamond Trading Co. which is no longer in use.

Pope Paul III Diamond. Charles V, ruler of the Holy Roman Empire, presented this stone to Pope Paul III when the latter entered Rome in 1536; in his autobiography Benvenuto Cellini tells of setting it.

Porter-Rhodes Diamond. A 153.50-carat diamond found in 1880 on the Kimberley claim of Mr. Porter-Rhodes and considered to be the finest African diamond found up to that time. Briefly owned by the third wife of the Duke of Westminster, the American-born Loela Ponsonby.

portrait stone. A flat style of cutting that permits the viewer to look through the stone to the object under it.

Portugal. An important producer of diamonds because of its ownership of Angola in Africa; once even more important because it held Brazil and controlled the mines there. Because of the explorations of Vasco da Gama, Portugal got into the diamond business earlier than any other European country and in the early sixteenth century its kings were known as "the richest sovereigns in Europe" because of their diamond trading via Goa. Defeats in Africa, uprisings and finally total rebellion in Brazil brought them to their present intermediate status, but their treasury is still stable and well-filled with diamonds.

Portuguese Diamond. A 127-carat emerald-cut diamond once owned by the Portuguese royal family but publicized by its purchaser, the much-married Peggy Hopkins Joyce, and its recent owner, Harry Winston, New York diamond merchant. Now in the Smithsonian Institution.

premier diamond. A diamond that changes color from blue to yellow depending on whether the light is daylight or incandescent light.

Premier mine. The South African open pit mine discovered in 1902 by Sir Thomas Cullinan which was the source of the largest diamond ever known, the 3,106-carat Cullinan. Today it is a shaft mine producer of more than 1,000,000 carats of diamond annually, most of them industrials. See Chapter 2.

Presidente Vargas Diamond or Vargas Diamond. See Chapter 4.

Princie Diamond. A 34.64-carat pink cushion-cut diamond once the treasure of the Nizam of Hyderabad but sold at auction by Sotheby's of London for $128,000 in 1960 to Van Cleef and Arpels, Paris jewelry firm. The jewelers held a party for it in Paris and christened it the Princie in honor of the Maharanee of Baroda's then fourteen-year-old son who was nicknamed "Princie."

proportions. A word used by diamond men to include the major factors that determine cutting quality: the relationships between the circumference of the girdle to the table, the facet angles, and even the details of finish, or polishing.

proportions, good. Precisely, this can be said of a diamond whose finished proportions are closest to the proportions determined mathematically to be the most revealing of beauty or reflection and fire.

Punch Jones Diamond. See Chapter 4.

Q

quality. The quality of a gem diamond can be rated only when the following factors have been analyzed by trained specialists: carat weight, proportions and cutting, clarity grade, color grade and shape, or style of cutting.

Queen Elizabeth Pink. The Williamson Diamond. See Chapter 4.

Queen Frederica Diamond. A wafer-thin diamond weighing less than 2 carats and measuring only 7 by 10 mm. engraved with the portrait of Queen Frederica, wife of the first King of the Netherlands. It is owned by the New York jewelers Max Fine and Sons, Inc.

Queen of Belgium Diamond. A 50-carat cushion-shaped diamond once owned by the Belgian royal family but recut to 40 carats and sold in New York.

Queen of Holland Diamond. A 136.50-carat intensely blue diamond cut in Amsterdam in 1904 and displayed there by the owners, F. Friedman, jewelers. On display at the Paris Exposition of 1924, it was then sold to an Indian maharajah for $1,000,000, but its present whereabouts are not known.

R

radium-treated diamond. A diamond whose color has been changed, usually to greenish, by being exposed to the radioactive rays of radium salts. A method used only experimentally because the diamond remains radioactive thereafter and may cause injury to its wearer.

Rainbow Diamond. A trade name for synthetic rutile frowned on by diamond men who prefer Rainbow Gem.

Rajah Diamond. One of two large diamonds which belonged to the late Bostonian Mrs. Jack Gardner, the other being the Light of India Diamond.

Red Cross Diamond. A 205-carat canary-yellow, square-shaped brilliant with a series of inclusions or imperfections which appear in the shape of a Maltese cross visible through the table facet. Found in the De Beers Company mines, the Diamond Syndicate of London presented the stone to the British Red Cross in 1918 but what they did with it no one seems to know.

red diamond. The rarest of all fancy-colored diamonds are red ones, and so any red-brown or rose-colored diamond is often called a red diamond. No really ruby-colored diamonds have ever been reported.

refraction. The bending of light rays. See Chapter 3.

refractive index. A measure of the amount a light ray is bent as it enters or leaves a gemstone. See Chapter 3.

Régale of France Diamond. A legendary stone brought by St. Louis (King Louis IX of France) to Thomas à Becket's shrine in England. It was said to be the size of a bird's egg but St. Louis, disguised as a poor pilgrim, turned it in for a small leaden figure of St. Thomas. What happened to the diamond then is anyone's guess—if indeed it was a diamond.

Regent Diamond. Once known as the Pitt Diamond. See Chapter 4.

Registered Jeweler. A title awarded by the American Gem Society to qualified retail jewelers. Qualifications include the passing of examinations based on prescribed coursework and thus the title testifies to gemological knowledge.

Rhine diamond. A misleading name for colorless beryl.

rhinestone. The name now given to colorless lead-glass brilliant-cut or single-cut imitation diamond. Once rhinestone was only applied to colorless quartz crystals from the Rhine River valley in Germany; when highly dispersive glass became available, it was substituted for the quartz.

Rhodes, Cecil (1853–1902). English colonial statesman and diamond pioneer, founder of the Rhodes Scholarships to Oxford University. See Chapter 2.

river. As used among diamond men, this word means the finest color grade in diamonds; an extraordinarily transparent stone may be called "an extra river stone."

river to light-yellow system. A color-grading system widely used to determine
the most commonly found colors in diamonds. River is top; yellow, lowest.

rose. If a diamond is rose cut, it may be called a rose; if it is rosy in color, it
may also be called a rose.

rose cut. An early style of cutting. It is usually rose shaped, that is, it has a flat
base, and a domelike top with a variety of triangular facets resembling petals
which come to a small point at the center like a rosebud. Also called a rosette.
See Chapter 3.

Russian Table Portrait Diamond. Said to be the largest portrait diamond in the
world, this diamond is now in the Kremlin with other Russian Crown Jewels.
It is 4 cm. long, almost 3 cm. wide, and weighs 25 carats.

S

St. Cloud. A suburb of Paris which is a diamond cutting center. Pronounced
"san clue."

Sancy Diamonds. See Chapter 4.

sawing. That phase of the diamond-fashioning process in which a crystal is
separated. See Chapter 3.

scintillation. The flashing or twinkling of light which in diamonds comes from
the facets. Comparative scintillation of two diamonds can be measured by the
number of facets on the stone and the quality of their polish. See Chapter 3.

scratches. On a diamond these are the same as anywhere else but only another
diamond can make them on a diamond.

Searcy Diamond. Originally a pretty stone picked up by a ten-year-old girl in
1926 while chopping cotton in a field near Searcy, Arkansas. No one would
listen to her dream that it was a diamond until she married a farmer who
took it to a jeweler who was impressed enough to send it to the Geology Department of the University of Arkansas. They in turn sent it to Tiffany's. In
1946 Tiffany's bought it from her for $8,500 and it is on display there today:
an uncut 27.20 carat of a fine yellow, or cape color.

setting. Generally speaking, the same as the mounting, but more specifically
only that portion of the mounting which actually holds the gem.

Shah Diamond. One of the few engraved diamonds. See Chapter 4.

Shah of Persia Diamond. A 99.50-carat yellow, cushion-shaped diamond once
in the Persian Treasury but brought to this country during World War I by
a Russian military expert, who said he'd been given it. Now elaborately set
in a pendant brooch it is surrounded by scores of smaller brilliants and rose-
cut diamonds and is in the Harry Winston collection of famous jewels.

shallow stone. A diamond with a too-blunt pavilion; it has a glassy appearance
called dealers "fisheye."

Shepherd Diamond. A flawless yellow stone weighing 18.30 carats and cut in
the cushion-brilliant style. It can be seen in the Smithsonian Institution, Washington, D.C.

Shipley, Robert M. (1887–   ). Founder of the Gemological Institute of
America in 1931 and the American Gem Society in 1934. Author of first
gemological courses and several books.

Sierra Leone. An important diamond producing country in Africa of both industrials and gems, some of which are quite large. First discoveries were made in 1930. See Chapter 1.

Sierra Leone Diamond. A 76-carat gem found in 1956 and cut into a pear shape. Owned by Harry Winston, New York.

sights. When parcels of diamonds are offered periodically by the Diamond Trading Company, Ltd., and Industrial Distributors, Ltd., to invited buyers, both the event in general and the lot selected for each individual company are known as sights.

simulated stone. Any substance that imitates a gemstone in appearance.

single cut. A simple form of cutting with a circular girdle, a table, 8 bezel facets, 8 pavilion facets, and sometimes a culet. It is used mostly for small melee and is also called Mazarin cut.

slightly imperfect. If flaws in a diamond are not visible to the unaided eye when the diamond is face up, the stone is known as slightly imperfect.

South-West Africa. An important diamond producer since 1908 when it was a German colony. Annual production, noted for large diamonds of fine quality, is about 900,000 carats.

specific gravity. The ratio of the density of any substance to that of water at 4° C. The S. G. of the diamond is 3.52, which is very heavy.

spread stone. A frequently used term in the diamond trade for a stone that has been cut with a table larger than 60 per cent of the girdle, and a thin crown.

square cut. An equal-sided, sharp-cornered form of step cutting.

square-emerald cut. A form of step-cutting with a square girdle outline but modified by corner facets.

Star of Este Diamond. An 26.16-carat fine quality Indian diamond once a treasure of the house of Este in Lombardy and inherited by Archduke Ferdinand of Austria-Este, whose assassination precipitated World War I. It is believed to now be owned by the exiled king of Egypt, Farouk.

Star of South Africa. See Chapter 4.

Star of the South. See Chapter 4.

step out. One of the two basic classifications of cutting; step cut or brilliant cut. In step cuts, all facets are four sided and in stairsteps, or rows, both above and below the girdle. The number of steps or rows may vary but the usual number is three on the crown and three on the pavilion. All steps are parallel to the girdle but outlines may vary. A rectangular step cut with cut corners may be described as a cushion step cut or, more popularly, an emerald cut.

Stewart or Spaulding Diamond. See Chapter 4.

Straits stones. Poor quality diamonds from Borneo, cut there by primitive methods.

Strass diamond. An old name for rock crystal or glass.

Strong-ite. A trademarked name for colorless synthetic corundum.

strontium titanite. A manufactured transparent gem material possessing a high degree of brilliancy and dispersion and little or no body color; it resembles the diamond. Like diamond, it is singly refractive with a high specific gravity

(5.13) but a hardness only of 5 to 6, much less than diamond. It was first produced by the Titanium Division of the National Lead Company in 1955, under the name of Starilian, now Fabulite.

swindled stone. A spread stone.

Swiss cut. A form of brilliant cutting with 16 facets and a table on the crown and 16 facets and a culet on the pavilion, or perhaps with 24 facets on the crown, plus the table, and only 16 and culet on the base.

Switzer, George. Curator of minerals, Smithsonian Institution, Washington, D.C.

symmetry. This is judged in a diamond on the basis of the degree to which the shaping and placements of facets and other portions of a finished stone yield mirror images of their opposite features. Typical lopsided results are irregular girdles, an off-center table and extra facets.

synthetic diamond. The first authenticated case of diamond synthesis was announced in 1955 by General Electric. For centuries men had tried to "make" diamonds; for decades scientists had claimed success with high pressure and high heat. General Electric's diamonds were tiny—only one-sixteenth of an inch in length—but produced by subjecting a carbonaceous compound such as sugar to a measured pressure of 800,000 pounds per square inch. Today in temperatures above 5,000° F. and under pressures of 1,500,000 pounds per square inch and using a molten metal catalyst, General Electric can turn carbon into diamond in a matter of minutes. Cube-shape crystals predominate at the lowest temperatures; more complex at the higher. Color varies from black to white, through green and yellow, but quality to date is all industrial. Some two tons a year are now being "grown" this way; other companies in Sweden and the Netherlands, the United States Army and De Beers itself are in production.

synthetic grit. The grit made of synthetic diamonds.

synthetic rutile. A manufactured transparent gem material produced commercially since 1948 by Linde Air Products Co. and the National Lead Co. It is noted for its high degree of dispersion (.330) which is much greater than a diamond's .044. It is doubly refractive but not nearly as hard as diamond. The chemical formula is TiO_2 and it comes in pale yellow, brownish red, bluish green and has many trade names: Miridis, Kenya Gem, Titania, Titangem, Tivu Gem, Diamothyst, Johannes Gem—and a few more.

synthetic sapphire. Colorless synthetic corundum or synthetic sapphire is often used, like synthetic rutile and strontium titanite, as a diamond imitation. It is highly dispersive (1.7), and harder than any other imitations (9, the hardness of sapphire).

synthetic spinel. This man-made material is used to imitate diamond and is so successful that even pawnbrokers are sometimes fooled. It is very refractive (1.7), with a specific gravity only slightly greater than diamond (3.6) and a hardness almost equal to that of synthetic sapphire (8 on the Mohs scale).

T

table. The large facet that caps the crown of a diamond or other gemstone. In the standard round brilliant it is octagonal in shape and bounded by 8 star facets. In an emerald cut it is an oblong.

table cut. Probably the earliest symmetrical form of fashioning diamonds in which opposite points of the octahedron were ground down to squares to form a large table opposite a large culet. The remaining 8 facets were then simply polished.

table down. When a stone is placed with the table on the surface of something it is said to be table down; this is the position it is put in for color grading.

table size. The size of a table in a faceted diamond, used in proportion analysis of cutting quality. In a round brilliant, measurements are taken from any two opposite corners. In shapes such as the pear or marquise, measure from corner to corner across the width.

Tanganyika. An important diamond-producing country since 1959 when the late John T. Williamson began working a pipe at Mwadui. Annual production is about 300,000 carats with about 80 per cent gem quality. See Chapter 2.

Tasmanian diamond. A misnomer for colorless topaz.

Tavernier, Jean Baptiste (1605–1689). A famous French gem dealer, traveler and memoir writer who made six journeys to the Orient and saw both royal treasures and slave-worked diamond mines. Without his book *Les Six Voyages de Jean Baptiste Tavernier* we would have no history of old diamonds. It has been translated as *Travels to India of Jean Baptiste Tavernier* and is available in the New York Public Library. See Chapter 4.

Tavernier A. Diamond. A 51-carat ovel-shaped brilliant sold to Louis XIV by Tavernier and subsequently stolen from the French Garde Meuble, or Royal Treasury. Never known to be recovered, its description comes so close to that of the Empress Eugenie Diamond that it is believed both are the same jewel.

Tavernier Blue Diamond. Generally believed to have been the blue diamond from which the Hope was cut. See Chapter 4.

Theresa Diamond. A 21.25-carat stone found near Kohlsville, in Washington County, Wisconsin, in 1886, and cut in New York into a handful of small stones weighing in total only 9.27 carats, the largest of which was 1.48 carats. The original stone was a curiosity because the top was yellowish, at the middle was a thin line about where its girdle might be, and below it was colorless.

thermal expansion of diamond. A miniscule expansion occurs in the dimensions of a diamond with any increase in heat.

thick crown. A term used to describe a crown which is thicker than the 16.2 per cent of the girdle's diameter said to be the ideal cutting proportion. Since most stones today have spread tables, thick crowns are a rarity.

Tiffany Diamond. See Chapter 4.

Tiros Diamonds. A group of four huge diamonds (from 173 carats to 345 carats each) found in the Tiros district of Minas Gerais in Brazil in 1938, the present whereabouts of which are unknown.

Tiru Gem, Titangem, Titania, Titanium Rutile, Titanstone. All trade names for synthetic rutile.

Tolkowsky, Marcel. The early twentieth-century mathematician who worked out and published the proper proportions for maximum brilliancy consistent with a high degree of fire, or dispersion from a round brilliant. See Chapter 3.

topaz. A gemstone sometimes used and misused in its colorless form as a substitute for diamond. It has a refractive index of 1.62, a specific gravity of 3.53 and a hardness of 8.

top cape. A top cape has a yellowish cast to the unaided eye; a term from the river to light-yellow system of color grading.

top crystal. A diamond in this color grade has only a slight yellow tinge. From the river to light-yellow system.

toughness. The ease with which a break can be produced in any substance. Diamond is brittle in that it powders rather than flattens under repeated blows. But compared to most gemstones it is exceptionally tough, and quite resistant to pressure except when struck fiercely along a cleavage direction. Jade is a tough gem.

Trade Practice Rules. The United States Federal Trade Commission rules for fair trade practices, promulgated at the request of specified industries and agreed to by representatives. The first Trade Practice Rules for the diamond and jewelry trade were made in 1938 and were revised in 1957.

transichromatic. Possessing the ability to change color temporarily. Some diamonds change color when brought into daylight after being kept in darkness for a long time—say in a vault—and then change back to the original color after a few hours. Others change color under X-ray.

Transvaal Diamond. A champagne-colored, pear-shaped stone of 67.89 carats that has been featured in several motion pictures and national exhibitions and is now owned by Baumgold Bros., New York.

treated diamond. A diamond that has been coated or otherwise treated to improve its appearance, including those diamonds bombarded for color changes.

Turkey I and II Diamonds. Two large diamonds, of 147 and 85 carats respectively, reported in the Turkish regalia in 1882.

twentieth-century cut. A rarely used style of brilliant cutting with 80 facets like the standard brilliant but inside the table facet there are 8 star facets.

twin crystal. Any physical unit comprising two or more crystal units of the same species that differ from each other by orientation of placement. Sometimes called *macles* in diamonds.

twinning lines. Visible lines on or within a fashioned diamond caused by twinning. Also called knot lines.

type I diamond. Of the two kinds of diamonds distinguished on the basis of properties, the most common is type I—including probably 999 out of 1,000 diamonds.

type II diamond. The one diamond in a thousand which has unusual physical or optical properties. It can be laminated, transparent, or colorless even when tested for most ultraviolet spectrum colors and they do not fluoresce easily. Further subdivided in type IIa, which does not phosphoresce under most short-wave light and will not conduct electricity and type IIb, which will phosphoresce under short-wave, emitting a strong blue, and will carry an electric current. Naturally blue diamonds are usually type IIb diamonds, the best known of which is, of course, the Hope Diamond. A few diamonds which have been mixtures of type IIa and type IIb have come from the Premier Mine in South Africa.

U

ultraviolet. That portion of the spectrum just shorter than visible light in wave length and important to diamonds because of its use in color changing. See bombarded diamonds or cyclotron.

Uncle Sam Diamond. See Chapter 4.

United States. Diamonds have been discovered in the United States in the eastern Appalachians, Alabama, the Carolinas, Georgia, West Virginia and Virginia, and Tennessee. The glacial drift of Wisconsin, Michigan, Indiana, and Ohio has yielded a few stones. Finds have been reported in Arizona, Idaho, Montana, and Oregon and in the gold washings in California. But the only prolific pipes (and they are insignificant on a world scale) have been in Arkansas, near Murfreesboro. See Chapter 1.

Union of Soviet Socialist Republics. Industrial diamonds were discovered in eastern Siberia in the mid-fifties. Gem diamonds have been found in the Ural Mountains in European Russia since 1829, but there have been no known large finds. Annual production figures are not known. See Chapter 1.

V

VSI. Abbreviation for very slightly imperfect. *VVSI.* Very, very slightly imperfect.

Van Aalten, William. A traveling diamond-cutter approved by the AGS who gives demonstrations of cutting on request. He is the seventh generation of his family—originally Portuguese Jews who fled to the Netherlands following the Inquisition—to work with diamonds; his grandfather cut diamonds during the Siege of Paris in 1870 while a great uncle went to Africa to prospect. He has worked in the United States for twenty-five years.

Vanderbilt Diamond. A 16.50-carat pear-shaped diamond made famous in the twenties when Reginald Vanderbilt bought it from Tiffany's for $75,000 to put in the diamond engagement ring he was giving Gloria Morgan. In the depression they were divorced and he sold the stone to a mid-western diamond dealer.

Van Niekerk, Shalk. See Chapter 1.

Venezuela. A diamond producing country of about 100,000 carats annually, most of which are industrials.

very slightly imperfect. A fine jeweler will use this term to mean that he can see flaws in a diamond under his special loupe that you can't. Very, very slightly flawless means it is difficult for even a trained eye with a ten power loupe to find the flaws—but they are there.

von Fersman, Alexander E. (d. 1945). A Russian mineralogist and geologist who was known as an authority on the Russian Diamond Fund, or collection of diamonds.

W-Y-Z

water. A term principally used in England or in English literature for the color and transparency of diamonds and other gems. "It is of the finest water," or "It is a ruby of the second water."

Williamson, John T. (1907–1958). Canadian geologist and discoverer (through academic deduction) of the Tanganyika pipe mine which bore his name until his death. His mines are now owned by De Beers and the Tanganyika government. See Chapter 1.

Williamson Diamond. A 54-carat pink cut by Briefel and Lemer of London to 23.60 carats and given by John T. Williamson to Queen Elizabeth II of England. See Chapter 4.

window cut. A cut that is square at the bottom and arched at the top like an old-fashioned window.

Winston, Harry (1896–   ). New York diamond merchant who started as a pocket peddler working largely on credit and rose through ability and stamina to be the greatest diamond merchant in New York, and one of the greatest in the world.

Winston Diamond. A flawless 154.50-carat colorless diamond found in the Jagersfontein mine in South Africa in 1952, cut to a 62.05 carat pear measuring an inch by an inch and one half and sold by Harry Winston to a private collector for $600,000.

yellow diamond. A yellow diamond which may be canary or champagne.

Zale, Morris. A Texan who owns 350 jewelry stores across the United States, 35 of which are fine jewelry stores with old family names. His total business, retail and wholesale, is thought to be $80,000,000.

zircon. Because of its high degree of brilliancy and fire colorless zircon has often been used as a diamond substitute. It has a specific gravity of 4.7, a refractive index of 1.9 and a hardness of 7.5 on Mohs scale of hardness.

Bibliography

CHAPTER 1

A small book published by the Field Museum of Natural History in Chicago in 1915 (Anthropological Series, no. 184) entitled *The Diamond, a Study in Chinese and Hellenistic Folk Lore* by Berthold Laufer provided me with the Alexander the Great legend, the Buddhist references, and indeed most of the Oriental comments (although not the opinions) since few diamond authorities have been either history or anthropological buffs and start Indian diamond history in the seventeenth century with Tavernier. Pliny the Elder can be read in part in a well-edited edition, *A Roman Book on Precious Stones* by Sydney Ball, Gemological Institute of America (Los Angeles, 1950). This Mr. Ball is not to be confused with Valentine Ball who furnished the modern translation of *Travels in India* by Jean Baptiste Tavernier (Oxford University Press, London: 1925). A basic book about South African Mining is Emily Hahn's *Diamond* (Doubleday and Company, Inc., New York: 1956) portions of which ran first in *The New Yorker*. *The Story of Diamonds* by A. C. Austin and Marion Mercer, also published by the Gemological Institute of America, Los Angeles (1939) is my source for the Brazilian history. English newspapers carried the stories of the Russian Diamond finds.

CHAPTER 2

The official biography of De Beers is *The Story of De Beers,* by Hedley Chivers (Cassell and Company, Ltd., London: 1939) and it is more lively, especially concerning the early years than might be imagined; current facts were obtained through the De Beers' American advertising agency, N. W. Ayer and Son. Other sources were necessary to get a well-rounded picture: William Plomer's *Cecil Rhodes* (D. Appleton and Co., New York: 1933) is good and so is John Gunther's *Inside Africa* (Harper & Bros., New York: 1955); Emily Hahn's book *Diamond* gives a good portrait of the late Sir Ernest Oppenheimer; Gordon Gaskill's profile of Harry Oppenheimer "South Africa's King of Diamonds" (*Reader's Digest*, May, 1964) was authoritative. *The New York Times* reported on undersea dredging activities in its May 9, 1963, columns. The story of diamond distribution was put together largely from primary sources—brokers and jewelers who were kind enough to explain how their business works. Selwyn Feinstein in the *Wall Street Journal* (August 19, 1964) discussed the current economics of the diamond market.

CHAPTER 3

Albrecht Dürer's diary is most easily read by English readers in W. M. Conway's *Literary Remains of A. Dürer* (London, 1889) usually only found in libraries on art, Dürer being best known as an etcher. The *Encyclopædia Britannica* is invaluable in tracing such men as Euclid, and provides a good bibliography for those interested in further reading about Jacques Coeur. I used A. B. Kerr's *Jacques Coeur, Merchant Prince of the Middle Ages* (Charles Scribner's Sons, New York: 1927) as my chief source, adding details from the scholarly work of Jean Baptiste M. Capefigue on Agnès Sorel, *A King's Mistress,* translated in Edinburgh from the French in 1887 by Edmund Golosmid. (Capefigue depended in turn on Pierre Brantome, the medieval social historian.) For cutting stories, I used *Precious Stones and Gems* by Edwin W. Streeter (G. Bell and Sons, London: 1880). Benvenuto Cellini, the Florentine goldsmith, wrote some interesting comments on diamond cutting in his treatise on gems and in his *Memoirs.* A. Mennickendam, a British cutter, is interesting although his history is not dependable; his book is *The Magic of Diamonds* (Hammond, London: 1955).

Laufer, Tavernier, Hahn and Austin, all mentioned in the bibliography of Chapter 1, were also helpful here, but the most helpful of all was G. Robert Crowningshield of the Gemological Institute of America, an authority on the well-cut diamond.

CHAPTER 4

The historic diamonds have been the favorite tramping grounds for writers about diamonds for at least a century and what is truth and what fiction is now impossible to determine. Edwin W. Streeter's book *The Great Diamonds of the World* (G. Bell and Sons, London: 1882) was long considered definitive. He turned to Tavernier for most of his Indian facts, using the Paris, 1679 edition of *Les Six Voyages de Jean Baptiste Tavernier.* Robert M. Shipley, a founder of the Gemological Institute of America, brought the subject up to date with *Famous Diamonds of the World* published in 1939 by the Institute and differed with Streeter on the Koh-i-Noor, following Professor Valentine Ball (see Chapter 1 bibliography). E. F. Twining's massive eight-hundred-page tome, *A History of the Crown Jewels of Europe* (B. T. Botsford, London: 1961), brings together a mass of information from all countries on gems, and clarifies many legends with original documents.

N. W. Ayer and Son's well-known diamond historian Dorothy Dignam culled all these plus modern newspapers for her company brochure *Historic Diamonds,* recently revised by Kathleen Horan. The standard history of India is the five volume study put out by Cambridge University, England, 1922.

Stefan Zweig's biography *Marie Antoinette* (The Viking Press, New York:

1933) begins where earlier biographies leave off and is delightful reading. The quotations from Thomas Carlyle come from Volume III of his *Critical and Miscellaneous Essays*.

Miss C. V. Wedgwood's remarks were made to me during her visit to Bryn Mawr College, Bryn Mawr, Pennsylvania; she is an authority on seventeenth-century English history.

The recent diamonds of note have been well-reported in the newspapers. The Smithsonian Institution's curator of minerals, George Switzer, was helpful on American diamonds. I also made personal visits to the great diamonds in American, French, English, and Turkish museums.

CHAPTER 5

The early history of American jewelry wearing can be found in Esther Singleton's *Social Life in New York under the Georges* (Bobbs-Merrill Co., New York: 1942) and *Maiden Lane*, a small history published by the Maiden Lane Historical Society in 1931.

Bess Furman's book *White House Profile* (Bobbs-Merrill Co., New York: 1951) and news stories provided information on the First Ladies. Mrs. Jacqueline Kennedy, I interviewed personally at some length for the *Ladies' Home Journal*, March, 1960, issue.

Diamond stories of the gilded age are told in Cleveland Amory's entertaining books: *Who Killed Society?* (1960) and *The Last Resorts* (1952); both are published by Harper and Bros., New York. Special material about Queen Alexandra was found in *The Gold and Glitter* by Consuelo Vanderbilt Balsan (Harper and Bros., New York: 1952). Twentieth-century jewelry fashions have been researched by Inez Robb and others; the Duchess of Windsor's jewels were well-publicized and I were there for the United Press Association when her husband became Governor General of the Bahamas. Princess Grace of Monaco, I have also interviewed; the *Philadelphia Evening and Sunday Bulletin,* among others, has covered her jewels. *Jeweler's Circular-Keystone,* a trade magazine published by the Chilton Company, Philadelphia, published the engagement ring marketing surveys.

CHAPTER 6

The opening poem by Robert Herrick, a goldsmith's son, is one of many lyrics written to Julia—a girl whom literary historians today are inclined to think never existed.

The primitive myths about circles and love knots are to be found in Sir James G. Frazer's great anthropological work *The Golden Bough* (Macmillan and Company, New York: 1951). Caesar's *Commentaries,* not as hard to read in English as in Latin, gives a good account of the early Celts and Britons. Ring stories of the Romans are in any social history of that empire; they are also brought together in a Victorian volume of considerable charm, George Frederick Kunz's *Rings for the Finger* (J. B. Lippincott Co., Philadelphia: 1917). S. H. Ball's translation of Pliny Secundus' *A Roman Book on Precious Stones* adds further detail; it was Mr. Ball who in his delightful comments on Roman writers also led me to the verses from Juvenal and the unhappy story of Berenice as told in the Satires. Professor S. Tolansky, a British gemologist, has researched the medieval use of diamonds as amulets.

Undoubtedly the Persians and Arabians had more diamonds than the Romans. We hear of Alexander the Great in the third century B.C. wearing diamonds; while India, then a satellite to Persia, paid its annual taxes in ten tons of gold dust, the Persian potentates undoubtedly garnered a few diamonds. But apparently they were kept as wealth or symbolism, rarely as ornament, and when worn, were arm bracelets. Chapter 1 and Chapter 3 go into Oriental diamond history more fully, particularly that of the Moguls.

In his *The Waning of the Middle Ages* J. Huitzingg discusses the way of life in Europe in the thirteenth and fourteenth centuries. Any biography of Henry VIII or Elizabeth I reports on the Tudor Jewels: Twining's book (See Chapter 4 Bibliography) is excellent on Crown purchases. The British Museum Catalogue gives the best succinct account of the posey rings. Marie Antoinette's two personal rings were unknown to many of her historians; Stephen Zweig's *Marie Antoinette* is the authoritative biography, documented by letters, of the role Axel de Fersen played in the Queen's life. Cooper Union's booklet on *Nineteenth Century Jewelry* (1955) and Marianne Ostier's *Jewels and the Woman* (Horizon Press, New York: 1958) bring us into the present, which the jewelry trade magazine, *Jeweler's Circular-Keystone,* rounds out with the Pearl Harbor engagement ring survey and other details. Mrs. Kennedy told her own ring story to Theodore White (*Life Magazine,* December 5, 1963).

CHAPTER 7

Most of the material for this chapter came from people rather than books. I am particularly indebted to Mr. Robert Blauner of Baumgold Bros. in New York, to the officials of the Diamond Dealers' Club, to Tiffany's, to Jill Ciraldo and Mr. Winston himself of Harry Winston, Inc., to Elaine Cooper of F. J. Cooper and Sons, Philadelphia, to Asscher's staff in Amsterdam, Ferstenberg's in Antwerp, the Topkapi's in Istanbul and to several jewelers who prefer to remain anonymous. The etiquette quotations came from *Social Etiquette in New York* (1881) and Emily Post's *Etiquette,* 9th edition (Funk and Wagnalls, New York: 1951).

The anecdotes were gathered by me throught various conversations or newspaper clippings. *The New York Times* quotations on investments were gathered by Caroline Bird for "Real Diamonds vs. Real Blue Chips" (*Times Sunday Magazine,* April 14, 1962). "Diamonds for the Masses" by John McDonald (*Fortune Magazine,* December, 1964) was also useful.

CHAPTER 8

Definitions for the glossary were basically culled from *The Diamond Dictionary* (1960) published by the Gemological Institute of America, 11940 San Vicente Boulevard, Los Angeles 49, California. Additions were made by the author using sources previously cited.

Acknowledgments

*T*here are many people without whom this book never could have been written. I am grateful to them all, the diamond experts with their special knowledge, the workers who helped me understand their skills and traditions, and the friends and family who lent a hand and cheered me on. All share whatever credit is due for accuracy, but none share the blame for any error—that belongs to me and my romantic, elusive subject, the diamond itself.

My particular thanks to Donald C. Thompson of N. W. Ayer and Son, Inc., and G. Robert Crowningshield of the Gemological Institute of America for their guidance. Thanks also to the N. W. Ayer and Son staff, Kathleen Horan, Mildred Kosick, Loys Malmgren, Gladys Hannaford, and the veteran Dorothy Dignam.

The many jewelers and diamond brokers whom I interviewed are for the most part mentioned by name in the text and listed in the index. Writers are mentioned in the bibliography.

Thanks go too to Dorothy G. Lister and Michelle Pynchon Osborn for their readings of the manuscript in progress, and to Dorothy S. Baker, Beverly Albertson, and Theresa J. Dickinson for their help with manuscript preparation and research.

Picture Credits

(figures indicate page numbers)

Asscher Diamond Works. 48, 49

N. W. Ayer and Son, Inc. 6, 20, 21, 37, 38, 39, 47, 53, 64, 67, 68, 69, 98, 103, 115, 138 (*top*), 151, 168, 172, 185, 186, 187, 188

The Bailey, Banks and Biddle Company. 122, 133

British Information Services. 146 (*bottom*)

The Cleveland Museum of Art. 155

Controller of Her Britannic Majesty's Stationery Office. 81 (*bottom*), 111, 112, 113

Crater of Diamonds. 117 (*top*)

De Beers Consolidated Mines, Ltd. 27, 28 (*top*), 32

Roy Doty and *The New York Times*. 195

Elgin-Columbia Diamond Division. 180

Gembooks: from "Handbook of Gems and Gemology." 56

Metropolitan Museum of Art. 105, 128, 129, 146 (*top*), 157

Metropolitan Opera Company (*Bert Morgan, photographer*). 136 (*left*)

MK Diamond Products. 72 (*bottom*)

National Broadcasting Company. 136 (*top*)

Peikin. 117 (*bottom*)

O. Philip Roedel, photographer. 172 (*top*)

Jack Steinberg, photographer. 126

Taft Museum. 87 (*top*)

D. B. Taraporevala Sons & Company Pvt. Ltd. (*Bombay*): reproduced from "Indian Jewellery, Ornaments & Decorative Designs' by Jamila Brij Bhshan. 7

Tiffany & Company. 40 (*center*), 123

A La Vieille Russie. 84, 138 (*bottom*)

The Wall Street Journal. 28 (*bottom*)

Harry Winston, Inc. 166, 190

Wide World Photos. Inc. 144

Index

Italic numbers denote illustrations.